The Options area of the screen presents four choices. Use them:

- ▶ **Internetwork Designer:** Determine which internetworking device/WAN link service you should use.

- ▶ **Configuration Tool:** Configure a multiprotocol (IPX/SPX, TCP/IP, AppleTalk) router.

- ▶ **Carrier Information:** Look up worldwide WAN carriers and review a WAN installation checklist.

- ▶ **Glossary:** Point-and-click to look up over 400 internetworking terms and acronyms.

Use the selections at the bottom of the screen as follows:

- ▶ **Exit:** Exit the program

- ▶ **Options:** Return to the Options screen

- ▶ **Help:** Get help on the program

- ▶ **Glossary:** Look up a term

- ▶ **Back:** Return to previous page

- ▶ **Next:** Go to next page

Note: If the program appears distorted, select standard VGA or Super VGA from the Windows Display Options (Windows Setup icon).

Expert Advice from the Network Experts

At Novell Press, we know that your network is vital to your business, and good, solid advice about your network is priceless. That's why Novell, in partnership with SYBEX Inc., prides itself on publishing the best networking books in the business.

Each book combines Novell's technical expertise with SYBEX's editorial and trade publishing experience, resulting in networking books of unparalleled accuracy, reliability, and readability. All Novell Press books are written by acknowledged experts in their field who have a special insight into the challenges and advantages of today's most popular networking products. Many Novell Press authors are past and current members of networking product development teams. For this reason, Novell Press fills the unique needs of networking professionals as no other publisher can.

Our books will help you work with the many versions of NetWare, use UnixWare, integrate UnixWare and NetWare, solve and avoid network problems, and much more. You can even study to become a Certified NetWare Administrator (CNA) or a Certified NetWare Engineer (CNE) with the help of Novell Press.

When you need advice about your network, you need an expert. Look for the network experts from Novell Press.

For a complete catalog of Novell Press and SYBEX books contact:

SYBEX Inc.
2021 Challenger Drive, Alameda, CA 94501
Tel: (510) 523-8233/(800) 227-2346 Telex: 336311
Fax: (510) 523-2373

NOVELL'S GUIDE TO

MULTIPROTOCOL
INTERNETWORKING

• • • • •

NOVELL'S® GUIDE TO
MULTIPROTOCOL
INTERNETWORKING

LAURA A. CHAPPELL

ROGER L. SPICER

Novell Press, San Jose

Publisher: Peter Jerram
Editor-in-Chief: Dr. R.S. Langer
Series Editor: David Kolodney
Acquisitions Editor: Dianne King
Program Manager: Rosalie Kearsley
Developmental Editor: David Kolodney
Editor: Dusty Bernard
Project Editor: Michelle Nance
Technical Editors: Radhika Padmanabhan, Ed Chapman
Novell Technical Advisor: Kelley Lindberg
Book Designer: Helen Bruno
Production Artist: Charlotte Carter
Screen Graphics: John Corrigan
Desktop Publishing Specialist: Ann Dunn
Proofreader/Production Assistant: Lisa Haden
Indexer: Ted Laux
Cover Designer: Archer Design
Logo Design : Jennifer Gill
Cover Photographer: Michael Kenna

Library of Congress Card Number: 93-85350
ISBN: 0-7821-1291-9

Manufactured in the United States of America
10 9 8 7 6 5 4 3 2 1

Warranty and Disclaimer

WARRANTY

SYBEX warrants the enclosed disk to be free of physical defects for a period of ninety (90) days after purchase. If you discover a defect in the disk during this warranty period, you can obtain a replacement disk at no charge by sending the defective disk, postage prepaid, with proof of purchase to:

> SYBEX Inc.
> Customer Service Department
> 2021 Challenger Drive
> Alameda, CA 94501
> (800)227-2346
> Fax: (510) 523-2373

After the 90-day period, you can obtain a replacement disk by sending us the defective disk, proof of purchase, and a check or money order for $10, payable to SYBEX.

For problems other than defective disks, fax a description of the problem to

> ImagiTech
> (408) 729-1580

DISCLAIMER

SYBEX and Novell Press make no warranty or representation, either express or implied, with respect to this software, its quality performance, merchantability, or fitness for a particular purpose. In no event will SYBEX, Novell, their distributors, or dealers be liable for direct, indirect, special, incidental, or consequential damages arising out of the use or inability to use the software even if advised of the possibility of such damage.

The exclusion of implied warranties is not permitted by some states. Therefore, the above exclusion may not apply to you. This warranty provides you with specific legal rights; there may be other rights that you may have that vary from state to state.

COPY PROTECTION

None of the programs on the disk is copy-protected. However, in all cases, reselling these programs without authorization is expressly forbidden.

This book is dedicated to Ray Spicer and Robert Chappell.

Acknowledgments

The authors wish to thank Novell's Network Management and Internetworking Products Division for their support on this book—especially Jan Johnson, Navin Jain, Tim Hayes for the idea, and Radhika Padmanabhan and Ed Chapman for their comprehensive technical reviews.

Special thanks to Dan Hakes for his many contributions, including humor, technical ability, and Sam Adams–induced advice on the WAN portion of this book.

We also thank the following companies and individuals for their assistance with the case studies included in this book: Ray Szpiech, Michigan National Bank; Larry Shiable, Trellis Communications; Mr. Joseph Hock, Arabella Hotel Group; Dorothe Faxel, Audiovisuelles Marketing und Computersysteme GmbH; and Gordon Jones, Bach Nguyen, Gill Rembert, and Mark Richardson, Novell, Inc.

The assistance and patience of the many folks from Novell Press and SYBEX are appreciated as well: Rose Kearsley, Michelle Nance, David Kolodney, Dr. R.S. Langer, Dusty Bernard, and Dianne King.

Of course, without the patience of our friends and families this book could not have been written. We thought about you many times over the evenings and weekends spent huddled over books, articles, specifications, and keyboards.

CONTENTS AT A *Glance*

TABLE OF Contents

P A R T   I I   *Interconnecting Wide Area Internetworks*   121

6   Fundamentals of Wide Area Internetworks   123

7   Implementing Point-to-Point WANs   137

*I*ntroduction

Configuring and installing an internetwork for the first time can be an intimidating task. Suddenly, you must be concerned with router capabilities, telecommunication devices, and optimization of the link to provide acceptable performance. Most books available today describe the internetworking options but do not follow through to define the constraints and concerns of running multiple protocols on the LAN or WAN.

This book was written to provide an introduction to the LAN and WAN environment while focusing on multiprotocol issues such as compatibility, performance, configuration, and optimization.

Who Should Read This Book

We designed this book to take a network installer or technician through the basics of internetworking LANs (local and remote) and introduce the issues at hand when configuring a multiprotocol internetwork. Generally, people are specialized in one or two protocols and one or two link types; this book covers three protocols (IPX/SPX, TCP/IP, and AppleTalk), as well as a wide range of link types (X.25, 56-/64Kbit/s, T1, Fractional T1, T3, frame relay, and so on).

If you are the network administrator and have decided to connect your LANs, this book provides you with the foundation necessary to hire the appropriate consulting team and articulate your company's needs.

What You'll Learn

By reading this book, you'll acquire a basic understanding of internetworking components, such as bridges, routers, multiplexors, and DSU/CSUs. You'll also learn the pros and cons of using one type of WAN link over another. The Internetworking Configuration program included on disk with this book defines internetworking terms and provides examples of internetwork configurations.

This book is not a "how-to" on installing and configuring a specific router product; however, we've included several examples of how Novell's Multi-Protocol Router is set up to perform specific tasks, such as SAP restriction.

How This Book Is Organized

This book consists of three parts that cover local internetworking, wide area internetworking, and internetwork management, as well as a set of appendices.

Part I, "Interconnecting Local Networks," focuses on internetworking LANs using bridges and routers. Chapter 1, "Fundamentals of Local Area Internetworks," defines repeaters, bridges, routers, and source routing.

Chapter 2, "Implementing Bridged Internetworks," provides examples of situations in which a bridge is the solution to internetworking.

Chapter 3, "Implementing Routed Internetworks," includes several examples of routing options and routing considerations such as load balancing, hop-count limitations, and a backbone architecture.

Chapter 4, "Implementing Multiprotocol Local Networks," covers the routing protocols used by Novell's IPX/SPX protocol, TCP/IP, and AppleTalk. This chapter is filled with hints on how to optimize your internetwork based on the inherent behavior of the protocols in use.

Chapter 5, "Internetworking Blueprints: Local Area Internetworks" examines three case studies of companies that have installed an internetwork. These case studies include a multibuilding fiber backbone, a fault-tolerant internetwork, and a network that requires a special configuration because of extreme amounts of interference.

Part II, "Interconnecting Wide Area Internetworks," focuses on wide area internetworking. Chapter 6, "Fundamentals of Wide Area Internetworks," introduces point-to-point and multipoint internetworks. This chapter includes basic information on various link types, such as X.25, 56-/64-Kbit/s, T1, Fractional T1, and frame relay.

Chapter 7, "Implementing Point-to-Point WANs," addresses the design issues and configuration options for 56-/64-Kbit/s, T1, and Fractional T1 links. Link speeds, cost factors, and connecting devices such as multiplexors and CSU/DSUs are described here.

Chapter 8, "Implementing Packet-Switched WANs," focuses on X.25 and frame-relay networks as well as the cost factors, configurations, and interconnecting devices used.

Chapter 9, "Implementing Multiprotocol Wide Area Internetworks," supplements Chapter 4, which focuses on protocol issues. Chapter 9 deals specifically with protocol configuration and performance over a telecommunication link.

Chapter 10, "Internetworking Blueprints: Wide Area Internetworks" examines three case studies of companies that have installed wide area internetworks. These case studies include an international ISDN network, a multiplatform WAN, and a data, voice, and video WAN.

Part III, "Managing the Internetwork," focuses on internetwork management protocols and options. Chapter 11, "Overview of Internetwork Management Options," includes details regarding the Simple Network Management Protocol (SNMP) and describes Novell's NetWare Management System (NMS) as a sample internetwork management system.

Appendix A, "Vendor Directory and WAN Installation Checklist," provides contact information for service providers and internetworking product vendors and a WAN installation checklist.

Appendix B, "Glossary," provides definitions of internetworking terms.

Appendix C, "Installing and Using the Internetworking Configuration Program," supplies information and configuration details for the Internetworking Configuration program that is included on disk with this book. This is a Microsoft Windows-based application that provides an interactive guide for bridge or router selection, wide area link selection, and a router configuration simulation. Also included in the application are an internetworking glossary, wide area service provider listing, and a WAN installation checklist. The minimum requirements are Windows 3.X, 4Mb memory, 3Mb hard drive space, 16-color VGA, and a mouse.

You will find *Novell's Guide to Multiprotocol Internetworking* a valuable reference and information-on-demand book. It is an excellent study guide for Certified Netware Instructors (CNIs), Certified Network Engineers (CNEs), or CNEs-in-progress. Where detailed product information is required, refer to the vendor's documentation.

Interconnecting Local Networks

Before you begin configuring and installing internetworks, you need a solid understanding of the various internetworking terms and devices. Part I of this book examines local area internetworking options and defines common terms used when discussing the hundreds of interconnectivity options. It provides a foundation of information to help you understand the chapters that follow.

Chapter 1, "Fundamentals of Local Area Internetworks," introduces you to the functionality of various local area internetworking devices, such as repeaters, bridges, and routers. If you are familiar with these items, you can skip to Chapter 2.

Chapter 2, "Implementing Bridged Internetworks," examines configuration options when installing bridges on a local area network. This chapter details transparent and source-route bridges, as well as the Spanning Tree protocol.

Chapter 3, "Implementing Routed Internetworks," defines routing options, considerations, and load-balancing techniques using routers on the network.

Chapter 4, "Implementing Multiprotocol and Local Networks," focuses on addressing and other issues relating to NetWare IPX/SPX, AppleTalk and TCP/IP internetworking. Chapter 4 provides examples of multiprotocol internetworks and describes addressing techniques and common internetworking errors.

Chapter 5, "Internetworking Blueprints: Local Area Internetworks," is split into three design scenarios. The first examines a company that connected separate, independent departmental LANs. The second section presents a company that installed a large internetwork that was installed in an area that experienced extreme interference. The third section discusses the benefits and results achieved from connecting multiple buildings into a campus internetwork using fiber optic technology and a backbone topology.

CHAPTER 1

Fundamentals of Local Area Internetworks

As companies grow in number of employees and in complexity, the desire to share information and valuable resources drives the need for connecting systems. In this chapter, we examine devices and configurations commonly used to create a local area internetwork. We also compare and contrast the functionality and placement of repeaters, bridges, and routers.

First, let's define and view the configuration of a basic internetwork.

What Is an Internetwork?

An *internetwork* consists of one or more linked *networks*. These networks can use Novell's Internetwork Packet Exchange/Sequenced Packet Exchange (IPX/SPX), AppleTalk, Transmission Control protocol/Internet protocol (TCP/IP), Open System Interconnection (OSI), or other network protocols. They can be Ethernet, Token Ring, ARCnet, Fiber Distributed Data Interface (FDDI), or other media access types, as shown in Figure 1.1.

FIGURE I.I

Internetworks can connect many different network types.

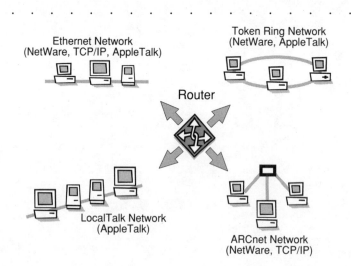

The key to implementing any type of internetwork is an understanding of the benefits, limitations, and configuration options available. In the following section, we examine the configuration options and limitations of many internetworking devices. First, however, we list the various benefits of internetworking.

Why Internetwork?

Companies link their local or remote networks primarily to

- ▸ Share files

- ▸ Share network resources (printers, modems, and so on)

- ▸ Access a centralized database

- ▸ Use electronic mail

For example, in a company that has two separate department networks (Marketing and Corporate), these networks can be connected to allow members of the Marketing department to use resources available on the Corporate network and vice versa, as shown in Figure 1.2. This is a cost-effective method for sharing resources among all users in the company.

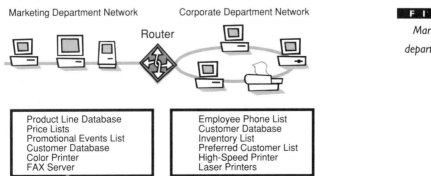

Marketing Department Network   Corporate Department Network

Router

Product Line Database	Employee Phone List
Price Lists	Customer Database
Promotional Events List	Inventory List
Customer Database	Preferred Customer List
Color Printer	High-Speed Printer
FAX Server	Laser Printers

FIGURE 1.2

Marketing/Corporate department internetwork

Internetworks have also become a necessity as businesses decentralize their computer systems and begin to expand the number of offices and communication protocols. For example, many SNA networks have given way to corporate SNA networks accessed by clients on a NetWare LAN. Many businesses understand that the key to their business success is reliable, efficient, and cost-effective communication throughout their organization.

Internetworking Devices

There are literally hundreds of methods for interconnecting network segments and networks using repeaters, hubs, bridges, and routers. Each of these devices has unique characteristics that should be considered when designing and implementing an internetwork. The remainder of this chapter focuses on their basic characteristics and uses.

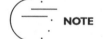 **NOTE** **Additional configuration information can be found in Chapters 2, 3, and 4.**

Figure 1.3 shows a local internetwork and the devices defined in this section.

USING REPEATERS

A *repeater* connects two or more cable segments to extend the length of the network and increase the number of devices on the cabling system. For example, a repeater could be used to extend a 150-meter thin Ethernet segment another 50 meters.

 NOTE **The 802.3 specifications limit thinnet Ethernet network segments to 185 meters in length. Repeaters can be used to extend the cabling system.**

The name "repeater" is appropriate since repeaters simply repeat bits from one physical segment to another. All information is passed on to each connected segment. If you are concerned with connecting two heavily used

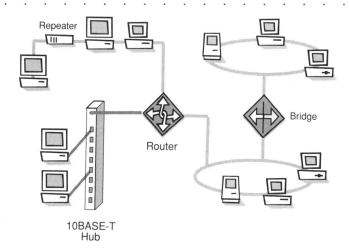

FIGURE 1.3

Internetwork connecting
Ethernet and Token Ring
networks

network segments, don't use a repeater; they cannot filter out information.

Repeaters are unaware of the networking protocol (TCP/IP, NetWare, AppleTalk, and so on) in use and are most often selected based on the media access type, such as thick or thin Ethernet cable. When a packet is transmitted from a client on one side of a repeater to a server on the same segment, the packet is repeated onto the other segment the repeater is connected to, regardless of whether the destination device resides on that segment. For example, in Figure 1.4, Client A is communicating with the server that resides on the same local segment. Each packet, however, is repeated on Client B's segment by the repeater.

If Client B's segment supported many heavy network users, the repeater would not be the best device for connecting these segments because of its inability to filter out unnecessary traffic from the attached segments. A bridge or router would be a better selection.

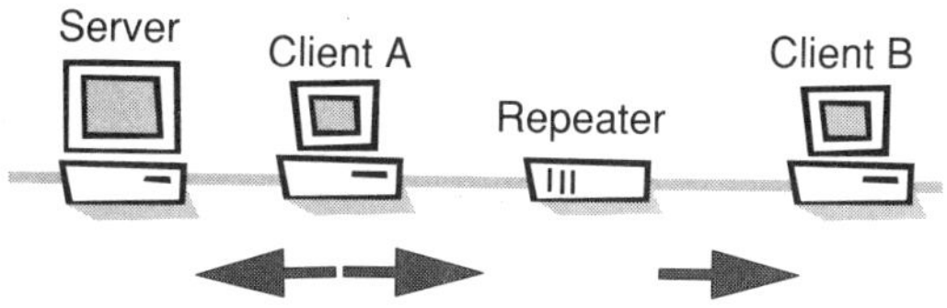

Server Client A   Client B

Repeater

FIGURE 1.4

Repeaters simply repeat all
packets onto each attached
segment.

Using Hubs and Hub Cards

By definition, hubs and hub cards are not internetworking devices. But because of their close association with internetworking devices (routers and bridges are sometimes built in to hubs, and hub cards are sometimes placed in routers or bridges), it is important to cover some of the main aspects of hub functionality.

Hubs are intermediary devices that stations connect to directly. The two most common types of hubs are Ethernet hubs, sometimes referred to as concentrators, and ARCnet hubs.

Ethernet hubs are used with 10Base-T networks, as shown in Figure 1.5. Each station is on its own network segment, with the hub acting as a repeater to send any transmission to all other ports. One advantage that many hubs provide is built-in management and troubleshooting capabilities.

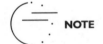 **NOTE**

Token Ring networks use an intermediary device called a multi-station access unit (MSAU). Token Ring hub cards have recently become available.

FIGURE 1.5

*Clients connect directly to
the hub.*

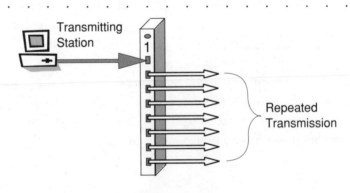

Transmitting
Station

Repeated
Transmission

10BASE-T Hub
with Management Agent

ARCnet hubs are either connected directly to workstations or connected to other hubs. There are two types of ARCnet hubs: active hubs and passive hubs. *Active hubs* are similar to Ethernet repeaters because they regenerate and reform signals, and passive hubs are similar to a signal splitter—no regeneration of the signal occurs.

Hub cards have recently become more common on networks. A *hub card* is an interface card that is placed in a file server or router. Stations are connected directly to the hub card's ports, as shown in Figure 1.6. Hub cards are available for Ethernet, Token Ring, and ARCnet networks. Hub cards generally have built-in management and troubleshooting capabilities. For example, Novell's Hub Services Manager can be used to query hub cards and detect port status, performance problems, or degradation.

Although repeaters and hubs play an important role in networking and are generally quite easy to implement, this book focuses on more complex internetworking devices, such as bridges and routers for local and wide area internetworks.

 NOTE

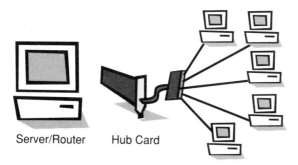

Server/Router   Hub Card

FIGURE 1.6

Stations connect directly to hub card ports.

Using Bridges

Bridges connect two or more cable segments, as shown in Figure 1.7, and help avoid cabling bottlenecks by filtering out traffic that is not destined for an attached segment. For example, in Figure 1.7 Client A is communicating with the server on its local segment. Since the bridge is aware of which segment the server is on, it does not copy the packet onto any other attached segments.

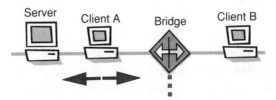

Bridges are unaware of the networking protocol (TCP/IP, NetWare IPX/SPX, AppleTalk, and so on) in use. Bridges are selected based on the media access method, such as Ethernet or Token Ring.

There are two primary types of bridges used—transparent bridges and source-route bridges—as described in the following sections.

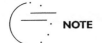 **NOTE**

Chapter 2 provides additional information on transparent and source-route bridges.

TRANSPARENT BRIDGES

Transparent bridges (also referred to as learning bridges) maintain a database of the stations on the network segments of each bridge port and forward or filter packets based on this information. This database is created as the bridge listens to traffic on each segment and notes the source address of all packets transmitted.

For example, in Figure 1.8 the bridge database indicates that Stations A, B, and C are on Segment 2. If Station B sends a packet addressed to Station C, the bridge does not forward it to Segment 1. By default, however, if a transparent bridge views a packet addressed to a station it does not recognize, it forwards the packet. Transparent bridges "learn" addresses based on packets viewed on the attached networks.

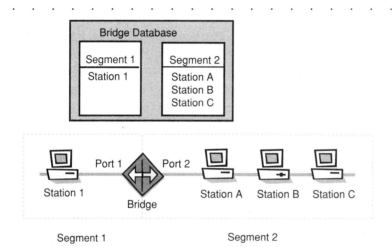

FIGURE 1.8

Transparent bridges "learn" addresses based on packets viewed on the attached networks.

SOURCE-ROUTE BRIDGES

Source-route bridges do not maintain a database of the stations on each connected segment; they forward packets based on the routing information contained in the packet. This routing information is placed in the packet by the source station. Source-route bridges are commonly used on Token Ring networks.

Before a station can communicate with another station on a source route network, it must "discover" the route to the destination station. The station transmits a route discovery packet that is copied and propagated throughout the entire network. Route information is placed in the discovery packet by each source-route bridge that copies it and places it on the next segment. Upon reaching the destination, the packet contains a "map" of each segment and bridge it had to cross on its way. The destination station returns the packet, allowing it to travel the same path back to the originator. The originator copies the route information from the returning packet and uses the information for subsequent communications.

Once a station has discovered a route to the destination station, it places that routing information in all data packets transmitted to that station. For example, in Figure 1.9, when Station A addresses a packet to Station B, it places Station B's hardware address as well as the route information in the packet.

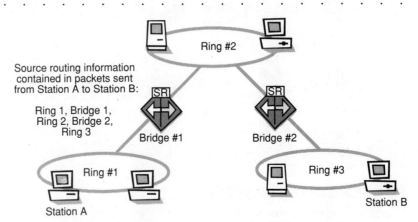

FIGURE 1.9

Bridges place source-route information in all data packets.

Bridges are generally slower than repeaters or hubs because they examine each packet in order to determine whether the packet should be forwarded (transparent bridge) or where the packet should be forwarded (source-route bridge).

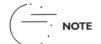 **NOTE**

For bridge configuration information and options, refer to Chapter 2.

USING ROUTERS

As shown in Figure 1.10, repeaters and bridges connect separate cabling segments, whereas routers connect separate local or remote networks. In this example, each network has been assigned a unique network address, AA-AA-AA-AA or BB-BB-BB-BB.

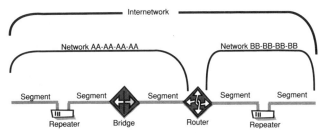

On an internetwork, packets that are not destined for the local network are addressed to the appropriate router. The router examines the packet to determine the direction in which to forward it. The router places the appropriate address on the packet and forwards it, as shown in Figure 1.11.

To:	Router ABC	To:	Station B
From:	Station A	From:	Router ABC
For:	Station B	For:	Station B
	Network B		Network B

Network A ⟹ Router ABC ⟹ Network B

Routers are *protocol dependent*. This means that a router must support a protocol, such as IP, NetWare IPX, AppleTalk DDP, or OSI IS-IS, in order to route those packets. Every router in the path must support the network-layer protocol (such as IPX) the source station uses. A router must also support the media access method (Ethernet, Token Ring, ARCnet, FDDI, and so on) for every network it is attached to.

Routers have these primary advantages over bridges:

▸ Routers offer a better path between end stations. Routers maintain a listing of known networks and the next destination to forward packets to. If a bridge does not recognize the destination address in a packet, it forwards the packet to all attached network segments.

▸ Routers offer greater protection against certain broadcast storms. Bridges do not offer any sort of "firewall" protection against service advertising or route discovery broadcast storms, which can disable the network.

▸ Routers segment traffic more efficiently. As mentioned above, if a bridge is uncertain as to the destination address, it forwards the packet to all attached segments. Routers, on the other hand, must know the next location for the packet in order to forward it.

Bridges, however, have several unique advantages over routers, including the following:

▸ Bridges are multiprotocol by design. Since bridges do not examine the network-layer information in the packet, they can forward packets regardless of the protocol in use. This is especially desirable when using a protocol that does not contain any routing information, such as DEC LAT (local area transport).

▸ Bridges are generally faster than routers. Although the performance difference between bridges and routers is becoming less noticeable as router technology advances, bridges still generally maintain a higher *forward/filter rate* than routers.

Routers can be classified as either "platform dependent" or "PC based." Throughout this book, we focus on a PC-based routing solution. The next sections briefly describe platform-dependent and PC-based router characteristics.

Platform-Dependent Routers

Platform-dependent routers use proprietary hardware. Although common in today's internetworking environment, these platform-dependent routers require the purchase of additional hardware, often at a prohibitive price.

PC-Based Routers

PC-based routers, as shown throughout this book, offer a unique solution to cost-efficient, flexible, and manageable routing needs. A basic PC-based router consists of the following components:

- ▸ 386/486-based PC with adequate memory and disk space
- ▸ Network interface cards
- ▸ Router software

Although newer than platform-dependent routers, PC-based routing solutions offer flexibility and a familiar platform (such as NetWare v3.1x runtime) to many network integrators.

When a single router must connect several networks that support multiple protocols and heavy internetwork traffic, the higher-speed proprietary bus of some platform-dependent routers may show better performance.

This chapter has examined and compared the most common internetworking devices used in the local area network environment: repeaters, hubs and hub cards, bridges, and routers. By understanding the basic functionality and benefits of each device, you can determine which device meets your internetworking needs.

Chapter 2 examines the options for bridging networks with transparent, source-route, and transparent source-route bridges and discusses the Spanning Tree protocol.

Chapters 2, 3, and 4 detail configuration options using bridges and routers. **NOTE**

Implementing
Bridged Internetworks

This chapter focuses on how bridges can be used to connect separate network segments and increase network efficiency. It examines bridging options (transparent and source routing), defines the benefits of installing a bridge, and provides several configuration options.

 NOTE   **You can find an overview of bridge functionality in Chapter 1.**

Why Bridge?

All LANs have a performance limit that is reached as they expand in size and complexity. Bridges solve some common bottlenecks and limitations that reduce network efficiency. These bottlenecks and limitations include

- ► Network segment size
- ► Amount of traffic

Let's first examine each of these limitations and define bridging options for overcoming each.

NETWORK SEGMENT SIZE

Specifications and network functionality define the maximum length of cables for each network. For example, on an Ethernet 10Base2 (thinnet) network, the maximum segment length is 185 meters. Although a repeater could be used to connect the segments and expand the network, a bridge increases network performance by keeping much of the traffic on local segments. Figure 2.1 depicts an Ethernet 10Base2 network that has been expanded using a bridge instead of a repeater.

Token Ring networks also have a ring size limitation. Figure 2.2 shows a Token Ring network that supports three file servers and 75 stations.

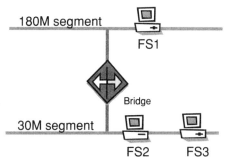

180M segment

FS1

Bridge

30M segment

FS2   FS3

FIGURE 2.1

*You can use bridges
effectively to extend the
distance between stations.*

Single Ring Network
75 Stations; 3 File Servers

Ring 1

FS1   FS3

FS2

FIGURE 2.2

*Single ring supporting three
file servers and 75
workstations*

In order to allow for growth and remain within the maximum ring size and maximum number of nodes, the ring shown in Figure 2.2 can be split into two bridged rings, as shown in Figure 2.3.

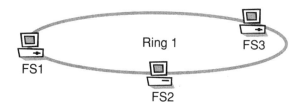

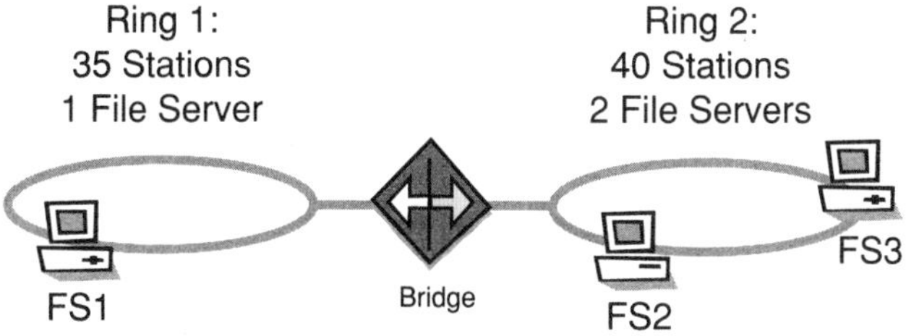

Ring 1:
35 Stations
1 File Server

Ring 2:
40 Stations
2 File Servers

FS1   Bridge   FS2   FS3

FIGURE 2.3

*Splitting a single ring allows
for growth.*

AMOUNT OF TRAFFIC

All LANs have a limited amount of bandwidth available that must be shared by all stations. Following is a list of bandwidth limitations of common LAN types:

LAN TYPE	BANDWIDTH
Ethernet/802.3	10 megabits/sec.
Token Ring/4	4 megabits/sec.
Token Ring/16	16 megabits/sec.
FDDI	100 megabits/sec.

As utilization of bandwidth increases on a LAN, performance decreases. For example, Figure 2.4 shows the utilization trend graph of a network that supports 70 stations on a single segment. Based on this trend graph (created by LANalyzer for Windows), this single Ethernet segment supports utilization bursts up to 70 percent. The timestamp is shown across the bottom of

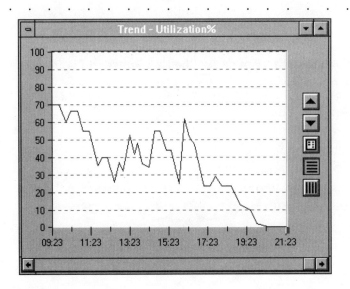

F I G U R E 2.4

High utilization on a single segment with 70 stations causes a decrease in performance.

the graph. The percentage of bandwidth used is listed down the left side of the graph.

Installing a bridge and splitting the network into two separate network segments reduces peak utilization on each segment to 38 percent, as shown in Figure 2.5.

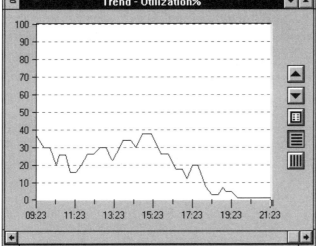

FIGURE 2.5

After the network is segmented, peak utilization is at 38 percent.

Chapter 3 provides more information on segmenting the network using a router.

NOTE

Besides overcoming various network limitations, bridges enhance the network by providing connectivity for protocols that do not provide any routing information such as DEC LAT. (Hence these protocols cannot be routed.) Since bridges are unaware of the upper-layer protocol, they can forward all protocols. Bridges are, however, aware of the frame types in use and must support each frame type they are requested to forward.

In the next section we examine transparent, source-route, and source-route transparent (SRT) bridges, as well as the configuration options for each. We also take a look at the Spanning Tree protocol and its practical applications in bridged internetworks.

Using Transparent Bridges

Transparent bridges are the most common bridge type used in the networking environment. They are often classified as "learning bridges" since they constantly monitor packets on each port to learn the location of stations.

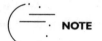 **NOTE** **Chapter I covers the basic operation of transparent bridges.**

One of the reasons transparent bridges are selected over source-route bridges is their relative simplicity. Small internetworks consisting of only one or two bridges do not require the added functions and associated overhead of more complex bridges.

Transparent bridges offer an easy method for connecting network segments and do not rely on additional software on user workstations (unlike source-route bridges). Figure 2.6 depicts a network connected with transparent bridges.

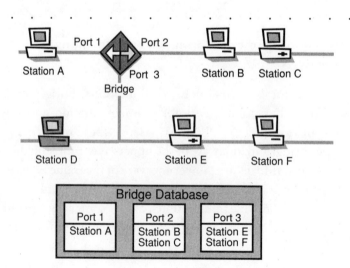

In Figure 2.6 the bridge has not learned of Station D because Station D has not transmitted any packets. Because of this, if another station transmits a packet addressed to Station D, the packet is forwarded to all segments the bridge is connected to. However, once Station D transmits, the bridge notes the segment it is located on and maintains this information in the bridge database.

Before installing transparent bridges on your network, review the section entitled "The Dreaded Bridging Loop" later in this chapter.

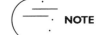

In many Token Ring environments, especially ones that include an IBM host, another type of bridge is commonly used—a source-route bridge. When you are working on a Token Ring network that is already using source routing, you must use this bridge type to ensure connectivity between rings. Next we examine the various options for installing and configuring source-route bridges.

Using Source-Route Bridges

Source-route bridges require additional software on each communicating station. This section expands on the basic functionality of source-route bridges presented in Chapter 1. It also examines configuration options and considerations for source-route bridges.

Unlike transparent bridges, source-route bridges refer to routing information contained in packets to determine where to forward packets; they do not maintain a database of known stations on each port. In source-routing environments, stations place routing information in each packet that is destined for another station on the network. This routing information is obtained and stored by each station. To obtain this routing information, stations perform *route discovery.*

The entire source-routing technology is not as complex as many people believe. It is very similar to the way we address letters. For example, if you wanted to send a letter to the Novell Corporate office in Provo, Utah, you would first need to obtain the address and write it on the front of the envelope. To obtain the address, you could call the office and ask for it. This is similar to route discovery.

There are two types of route discovery packets that a station can be configured to use: all-route broadcasts or single-route broadcasts. These packets are handled differently by source-route bridges configured as all-route or single-route bridges. Single-route bridges forward single routes and all-route broadcasts. All-route bridges forward all-route broadcasts only, as shown in Figure 2.7.

F I G U R E 2.7

All-route versus single-route
discovery packets and
bridges

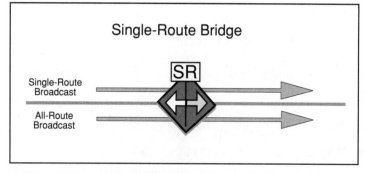

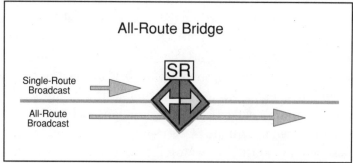

Let's examine how all-route discovery broadcasts work in a source-route network.

THE ALL-ROUTE DISCOVERY PROCESS AND ALL-ROUTES BRIDGE

Token Ring stations can be configured to use either all routes or single routes when broadcasting route discovery packets. All-route discovery packets are forwarded by both all-route and single-route bridges, as shown in Figure 2.7. This section focuses on all-route bridges and all-route discovery packets.

When a station wants to communicate with another station but does not yet have any routing information, it must discover the route to the destination station using route discovery broadcast packets. In Figure 2.8, Station A transmits an All-Route discovery packet addressed to Station B.

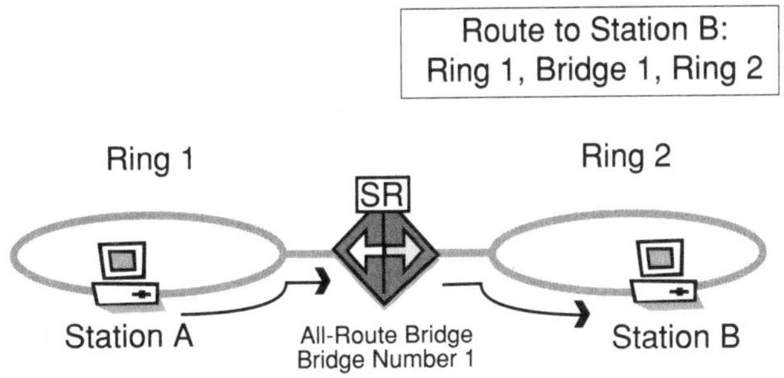

Route to Station B:
Ring 1, Bridge 1, Ring 2

Ring 1   Ring 2

Station A   All-Route Bridge
Bridge Number 1   Station B

FIGURE 2.8
Source-route bridges place
route information in the
packet when it is forwarded.

When source-route bridges are configured, they are assigned a bridge number, and each port that connects the bridge to a ring is assigned a ring number. When a source-route bridge forwards the discovery packet, it places the ring number and bridge number information in the packet. When Station B receives the frame addressed to it, it simply transmits a reply, indicating that the route information should be read in reverse order by all source-routing bridges.

Understanding this process is a necessity in source-route environments that use multiple source-route bridges and rings. Let's examine this process on a larger Token Ring network that uses all-route broadcasts and all-route bridges.

Figure 2.9 shows a Token Ring network that consists of five rings and five source-route bridges. In this example, Station A transmits an all-route discovery broadcast on its local ring. Bridges 1 and 2 both forward the frames to the next ring. The all-route discovery frames are propagated throughout the network. Two copies of the all-route discovery frame cross Ring 3 (one from Bridge 2 and one from Bridge 3) and are passed on to Ring 5.

▶ . . . . ◀

FIGURE 2.9

*All-route discovery on a
five-ring source-route
network*

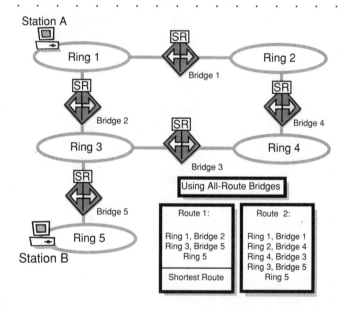

As the all-route discovery frames cross the all-route bridges, route information is inserted in the frame by each source-route bridge as it forwards the frame. Station B responds to each all-route discovery frame by simply returning the frames along the same path, only in reverse order. Station A uses route information contained in the first reply from Station B and can now send frames directly to the station using the fastest route (Route 1) based on route information it receives. This procedure is repeated for each additional station that Station A wants to communicate with. This information is maintained in Station A's route table.

As you can imagine, all-route discovery traffic can be overwhelming on a large Token Ring network. For this purpose, stations can be configured to transmit single-route discovery frames and bridges can be configured as "All Route" or "Single Route."

THE SINGLE-ROUTE DISCOVERY PROCESS AND SINGLE-ROUTE BRIDGES

As we've already seen, discovering a route using all-route broadcasts and all-route bridges floods the network with packets, possibly causing multiple copies of the same packet to cross the same ring on the network. When you configure stations to transmit single-route broadcast frames and place single-route bridges in strategic locations on the network, discovery frames must traverse a specific route on the network.

Single-route systems are used for two reasons: first, to reduce the duplication of frames across rings and reduce the "flooding" effect of route discovery and, second, to force communications across a specific route on the network in order to load-balance or prioritize a route.

Figure 2.10 depicts the same network used earlier, but this time all bridges except one have been configured as single-route bridges. Station A is configured to use single-route discovery frames.

In Figure 2.10 single-route discovery frames are transmitted from Station A onto the local ring. Bridge 1 and Bridge 2 copy and forward the frame onto their attached rings, Ring 2 and Ring 3, respectively. No response is received from the route discovery frame forwarded to Ring 2 because Bridge 4 does not forward the single-route discovery frame since it is configured as an all-route bridge.

Upon receipt of the single-route discovery frame from Ring 3, Bridge 5 and Bridge 3 forward the frame to their attached rings, Ring 5 and Ring 4, respectively. No response is received from the route discovery frame forwarded to Ring 4. The only response to the frame is from Station B, located on Ring 5. Compared to the previous example, only one route discovery frame is received by the destination station. Only one response is transmitted back to Station A. On a large internetwork, single-route bridges

Using a properly configured single-route scheme ensures a single path between stations.

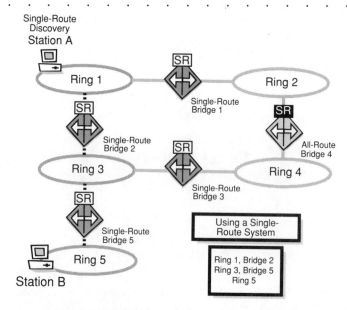

provide an efficient method for reducing the amount of route discovery traffic propagating through the network.

Although setting up single-route systems ensures that only one path exists between stations, it does not ensure that it is always the shortest path. For example, in Figure 2.11 Station C is sending a single-route discovery frame to Station D. The frame must cross a longer path because Bridge 4 is configured as an all-route bridge and cannot forward the single-route frame.

 NOTE

Novell's ROUTE.COM and ROUTE.NLM have three parameters, "def", "gbr", and "mbr", that determine whether data, general broadcasts, or multicast broadcasts, respectively, are sent as all-routes broadcasts or single-route broadcasts.

One issue users should consider when configuring and installing bridges on a Token Ring source-route network is the seven-bridge limitation that a source route packet can cross. Some implementations, such as Novell's MultiProtocol Router/source-route bridge, can support a greater number of

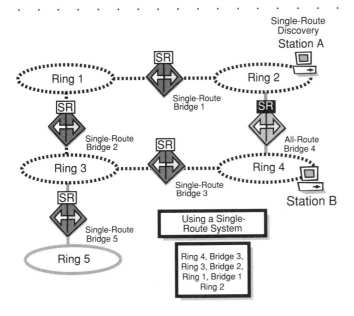

FIGURE 2.11

A single-route scheme does
not always ensure the
shortest path between
stations.

"hops" across bridges; most Token Ring card and driver vendors, however, do not currently support more than seven bridges and eight rings.

As more bridges are being installed and configured on a network, one more consideration should be addressed: bridging loops. The next section examines the cause and result of installing a network that contains bridging loops.

The Dreaded Bridging Loop

Bridging loops can disable a network by flooding it with packets that loop continuously through the system. First, let's examine how a bridging loop occurs. Figure 2.12 depicts a simple two-segment Ethernet network that uses three transparent bridges.

F I G U R E 2.12

Bridging loops are caused
by parallel bridges.

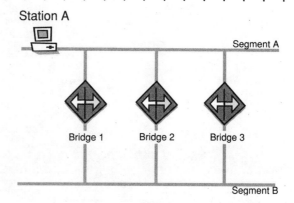

In Figure 2.12 the Ethernet networks are connected by three parallel transparent bridges. The bridges were placed parallel to one another because the technician was trying to configure a fault-tolerant system. Let's see what effect bridge loops have on this network as the bridges are enabled and attempt to build their bridge tables.

Station A transmits. (It does not matter who they are addressing the packet to in this example.) Each bridge receives the packet and notes that Station A is on Segment A. Each bridge copies and forwards the packet to Segment B. One of the bridges will, by the rules of network access, transmit first onto Segment B. For this example, assume that Bridge 1 is the first to transmit onto Segment B, as shown in Figure 2.13.

The packet appears on Segment B as if Station A originated it from that segment and actually resides on Segment B. Next, Bridges 2 and 3 receive the packet and note that Station A is actually on Segment B. Bridges 2 and 3 forward the packet to Segment A, as shown in Figure 2.14.

Next, assume that Bridge 2 is the first to transmit onto Segment A. Bridges 1 and 3 see the packet and now believe Station A is on Segment A. Bridges 1 and 3 copy the packet and queue it up to transmit onto Segment B, as shown in Figure 2.15. As you can see, not only do packets loop through the network, they also multiply.

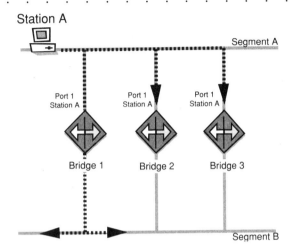

FIGURE 2.13

Bridge 1 is the first to transmit onto Segment B.

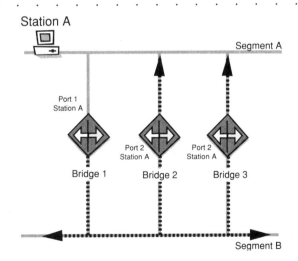

FIGURE 2.14

Bridges 2 and 3 now believe Station A resides on Segment B.

The packet continues to loop through Segment A and Segment B.

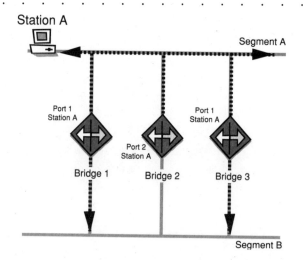

The physical configuration defined in Figures 2.13 through 2.15 is not necessarily incorrect. Parallel bridges can provide redundancy and fault tolerance if they are configured to ensure that only one data path exists at any given time. One way to ensure a single data path is to use the Spanning Tree protocol, allowing bridges to automatically set themselves up in a loop-free "tree" configuration. The next section describes how the Spanning Tree protocol can be used to configure efficient, loop-free paths.

NOTE   **Routing loops can also occur on a network, but the effect is less devastating since packets are addressed to a specific router and the routing hop count ensures that packets do not circulate endlessly on the network.**

Implementing the Spanning Tree Protocol

The Spanning Tree protocol was designed to enable bridges to dynamically discover a loop-free data path, thereby avoiding the problems caused by bridging loops.

NOTE

The IEEE (Institute for Electrical and Electronic Engineers) 802.1D standard defines the basic functionality required by compliant bridges, as well as operations of the Spanning Tree protocol. 802.1D is one of the series of standards known as the IEEE 802 specifications. Ethernet (802.3) and Token Ring (802.5) specifications are also part of the 802 specification series.

Using the Spanning Tree protocol, bridges transmit a special message—a configuration BPDU (bridge protocol data unit)—to each other in order to calculate a single "spanning tree" configuration. The information contained in these configuration messages enables the bridges to

- ▸ Select a single root bridge

- ▸ Determine the shortest distance to the root bridge

- ▸ Elect a bridge on each segment that will forward packets toward the root bridge

- ▸ Determine bridge ports that should be placed in a blocking or forwarding state

Figure 2.16 depicts a Token Ring network with five rings and five bridges that has been configured using the Spanning Tree protocol. In this example, Bridge A is the root bridge and Bridges B and D have ports that are in a blocking state (dashed line). Ports that are in a blocking state do not forward packets.

The root bridge is the top of the tree, with the network segments branching out from it. All bridges configure themselves in relation to the root bridge. Configuration BPDU packets are transmitted throughout the network until all bridges know their placement in the spanning tree. If a bridge learns that there is a parallel bridge that has a shorter path to the root bridge, the bridge places one of its ports in a blocking state, allowing the closer bridge to be the designated bridge for communications sent to the root bridge.

FIGURE 2.16

*Token Ring network with
five rings and five bridges,
configured using the
Spanning Tree protocol*

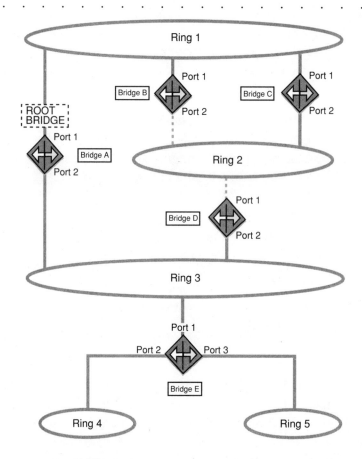

When you set a bridge or bridge port to configure automatically, you rely on the Spanning Tree algorithm to select a single data path and use information obtained from Configuration BPDU packets to reconfigure automatically when any bridge failure occurs. Generally, all bridges should be automatically configured (using the Spanning Tree algorithm) except the root bridge.

SELECTING THE ROOT BRIDGE

By default the root bridge transmits Configuration BPDUs at 2-second intervals to ensure that it is up to date on the network configuration. Because the root bridge should be located centrally in respect to the entire network, the selection of the root bridge should not be left to chance. You can manually select the root bridge by assigning a low bridge ID number. The bridge with the lowest bridge ID number becomes the root bridge.

In the case of Novell's MultiProtocol Router product (which can be configured as a bridge and uses the Spanning Tree protocol), it is best to avoid using the NetWare server as a root bridge. The reason for this is simple: overhead. The NetWare server should not be loaded up with unnecessary responsibilities (such as root bridge updates).

Figure 2.17 depicts a Spanning Tree view of the network shown in Figure 2.16, with the logical connections displayed. As you will note, all LAN segments and bridges are placed in relation to the root bridge.

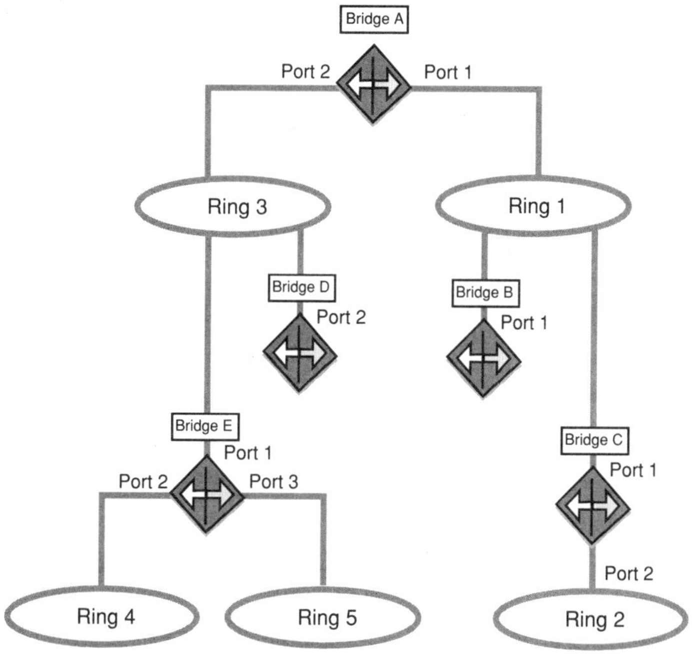

FIGURE 2.17

Logical view of a spanning tree

NOTE

For detailed information on the Spanning Tree protocol, refer to the IEEE 802.1D specifications, "Media Access Control (MAC) Bridges."

AUTOMATIC RECONFIGURATION OF THE SPANNING TREE

One of the greatest advantages of configuring bridges using the Spanning Tree protocol is its dynamic reconfiguration ability. Because the bridges communicate topology information among themselves on a regular interval using Configuration BPDUs, if a bridge fails this information is rapidly disseminated through the entire network. This dissemination of new configuration information is called *convergence*. Figure 2.18 shows the newly reconfigured network after a bridge failure. No manual intervention was required to switch to an alternate data path. Port 2 of Bridge B is no longer in a blocking state; it now forwards packets to Ring 2.

A third type of bridge combines the features and functions of source-route and transparent bridges. This bridge type is appropriately called *source-route transparent* (SRT).

Using Source-Route Transparent (SRT) Bridges

Source route-transparent (SRT) bridges can be used in environments that have some but not all clients using source routing. SRT bridges first look at the contents of the packet to determine if it has a source-route field. If there is a source-route field, the SRT bridge uses the information in this field to appropriately forward or discard the packet. If no source-route field is present, the SRT bridge acts as a transparent bridge and forwards the packet based on addresses it maintains in its bridge information database.

 NOTE

A routing indicator bit denotes if source routing is used in the packet. This bit is set to 1 if source routing is used and left at 0 if no source routing is used.

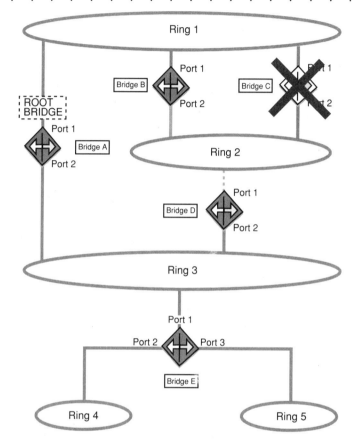

One of the primary advantages of SRT bridges is that they support a greater variety of bridging traffic. This added functionality, however, may degrade bridge performance since the bridge must examine each packet to identify the presence of source-route information regardless of whether packets are using source routing. SRT bridges must also maintain a bridge database for every client on the attached network segments. (For additional information on the functionality of source-route and transparent bridges, refer to the preceding sections in this chapter.)

Bridge Enhancements

Some bridges offer additional features to enhance performance. The next sections briefly describe two bridge features that can affect internetwork performance: filtering and "on-the-fly" forwarding.

FILTERING

Filtering is set up by the installation technician or system administrator and enables a bridge to block traffic based on user-defined criteria. The filtering criteria available are dependent on the bridge's abilities and features. Common filtering criteria are hardware address and protocol. The NetWare MultiProtocol Router, for example, allows filtering based on their hardware address, bridge interface, protocol, or ring number.

For example, to filter out all traffic going onto the backbone from a device that communicates only on the local network segment, a hardware address filter is enabled. If, however, you want to block all IPX traffic from the backbone because your backbone is configured for only IP traffic, configure a protocol filter that blocks all IPX traffic from the backbone. Filtering is an effective method for reducing traffic on heavily used networks.

ON-THE-FLY FORWARDING

Fast-packet-switching bridges generally employ a unique handling method, on-the-fly forwarding, for packets that are being forwarded through bridges. This method of forwarding increases the bridge forward rate by allowing the bridge to begin forwarding the packet on one port while it is still being received on another port.

Forwarding is performed on the fly when the bridge looks at the destination address (the first 6 bytes) and begins to forward the packet immediately. Instead of buffering the entire packet to determine the destination address and then forward the packet, these bridges build a packet destination address field and begin forwarding the frame as it is being received.

Although bridges that forward on the fly improve throughput tremendously, they are often relatively expensive.

Upon completion of this chapter, you should be aware of the many reasons for implementing a bridge on a network. You should also know the basic functionality and configuration options for transparent, source-route, and source-route transparent (SRT) bridges on a local network, as well as the purpose of the Spanning Tree protocol.

For information relating to bridging on a WAN, refer to Chapter 7.

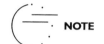 **NOTE**

The next chapter describes the benefits, configuration options, and features of routers on a LAN.

Implementing Routed Internetworks

This chapter focuses on the purposes and methods available for connecting separate local area networks using a router. Beginning with an overview of the benefits that routers provide, the chapter examines options for connecting similar and dissimilar networks, such as Token Ring, Ethernet, ARCnet, LocalTalk, and FDDI, with routers.

This chapter also explains how routers learn of available routes using either vector-based or link-state routing methods. First, let's answer a common question: Why route?

Why Route?

Bridges are used to connect network segments on a single network. Routing is used to connect networks that use the same or different network types and protocols. Routers provide these advantages for internetworking:

- ▸ Dissimilar network type support
- ▸ Redundant transmission paths possible
- ▸ Fragmentation and flow control
- ▸ Logical addressing used
- ▸ Manageable internetworking

First, let's examine each of these benefits and their impact on internetwork performance.

MULTIPLE NETWORK TYPES

Routers can be used to connect various network types, such as Ethernet, Token Ring, ARCnet, LocalTalk, and FDDI. (Bridges are generally used to connect similar network types, such as Ethernet-to-Ethernet or Token Ring-to-Token Ring.) Figure 3.1 depicts an internetwork for a company that has four unique network types: Ethernet, ARCnet, LocalTalk, and Token Ring. A multiprotocol router (such as Novell's MultiProtocol Router)

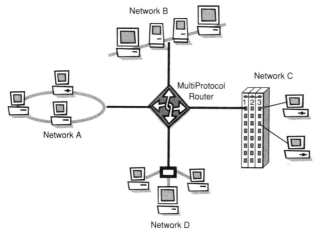

FIGURE 3.1

*Routers connect different
network types.*

connects these networks, allowing departments to share resources and data.

MULTIPLE TRANSMISSION PATHS

As defined in Chapter 2, bridges work best when there is only a single transmission path between end stations. Routers, on the other hand, offer a method for allowing multiple paths. This adds internetwork redundancy and fault tolerance.

For example, in Figure 3.2, a NetWare internetwork has been configured using parallel routers. If one router fails, a path between the networks still exists.

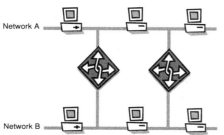

FIGURE 3.2

*Multiple transmission paths
provide redundancy and
fault tolerance.*

FRAGMENTATION AND FLOW CONTROL

Some lower layer protocols have a limited packet size that can be supported. For example, Defense Data Network (DDN) limits message sizes to 8063 bytes. Fragmentation enables a router to split up transmissions into separate packets at one end of a transmission and reassemble them at the other end. The routing protocol in use, such as Internet protocol (IP), must support fragmentation and reassembly as well.

Flow-control mechanisms available in some routing protocols enable routers to exchange information regarding route availability and congestion. As shown in Figure 3.3, if a router is congested (Router 3), it can report this information to other routers on the link, enabling them to use an alternate route.

FIGURE 3.3

Routers exchange flow-control information.

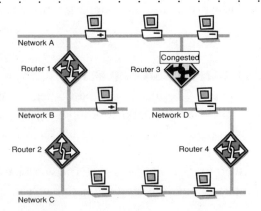

In the example shown in Figure 3.3, Router 3 is congested and broadcasts this condition to the other routers attached to the same segments as Router 3 (Router 1 and Router 4). The other routers can now use alternate routes to reach the destination network. This ensures that very little delay is encountered when routers become overloaded.

LOGICAL ADDRESSING

Logical addresses are used when routing information across the network. Data-link addressing, such as Token Ring or Ethernet hardware addresses, is adequate for delivery on the local network or on a bridged network. However, on an internetwork where information may travel across various network types and communication links, end-to-end media-independent addressing is required. The network layer protocols, such as IPX and IP, supply the end-to-end addressing used by routers to deliver information across complex networks. For more information, refer to the next section in this chapter, "Router Functionality."

The following is an example of data-link addressing and end-to-end (internetwork) addressing. On a single Token Ring LAN, stations address packets using the Token Ring card's 6-byte hardware address. To address stations located on another network, a Token Ring station uses a logical address (sometimes called a software address or protocol address).

As shown in Figure 3.4, routers use the logical address (network address) to make routing decisions. Station 1 sends a packet to the router with a logical address for FS1. The router, Router 1, reads the network address and forwards the frame to Network B. Details of this process are given later in this chapter.

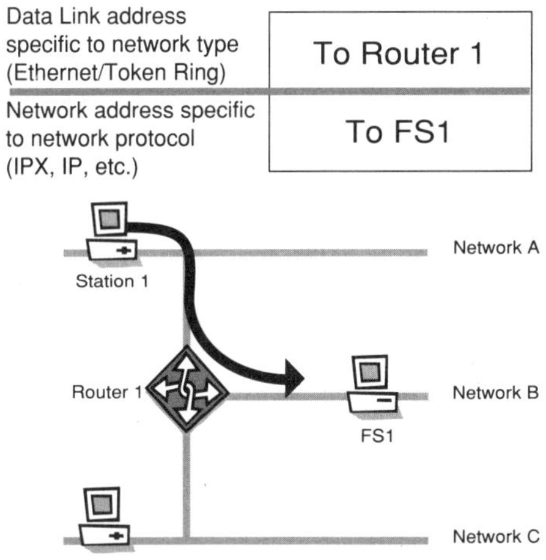

Data Link address specific to network type (Ethernet/Token Ring)

To Router 1

Network address specific to network protocol (IPX, IP, etc.)

To FS1

Station 1

Network A

Router 1

FS1

Network B

Network C

FIGURE 3.4

Routers forward packets based on the logical network address defined in the packet.

MANAGEABLE INTERNETWORKING

Some routers, such as Novell's MultiProtocol Router, include management abilities enabling administrators to monitor and troubleshoot routers from a centralized management console. Refer to Part III, "Managing and Troubleshooting an Internetwork," for more details on management options and capabilities.

Before going further into router options, let's follow a packet as it crosses an internetwork that contains both routers and bridges.

Router Functionality

This section begins with an overview of how routers transmit packets through an internetwork. Understanding the basic addressing and routing schemes helps clarify the routing process and provides a solid foundation for internetwork troubleshooting.

All packets travel through an internetwork based on the same general packet characteristics. Figure 3.5 depicts the basic fields found in all internetwork packets, regardless of the protocol in use.

FIGURE 3.5

Packets transmitted through an internetwork contain hardware and software addresses.

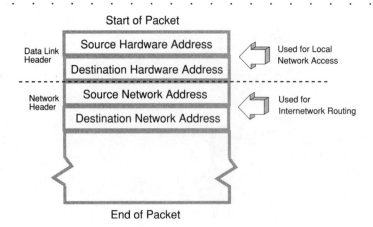

For more information on IPX/SPX, TCP/IP, and AppleTalk network addressing, refer to Chapter 4.

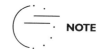 **NOTE**

The destination hardware address is used only to transmit a packet on the local network. Stations can place only the address of a local station, server, or router in this field. To reach a station that is located on another network, the source station uses the network address of the destination station. Network addresses are unique for each network protocol type (such as IPX, IP, and DDP).

When a station transmits a packet across the network, it addresses the packet to the appropriate router's hardware address. The actual destination station's software address is placed inside the packet.

When the router receives the packet, it strips off the data-link header (containing the source and destination hardware address, it is sometimes called the packet or MAC header) and examines the network header to determine where to route the packet. The router places a new header on the packet (using its own address for the source hardware address) and forwards the packet to the next router. If, however, the router is attached to the destination network, the packet is directed to the destination station on that network.

To understand this process thoroughly, let's follow a packet as it travels through an internetwork that connects Ethernet and source-routing Token Ring networks using both bridges and routers. The internetwork, shown in Figure 3.6, also supports multiple protocols and a fiber backbone.

Let's follow a packet that is sent from Station 1 to FS1.

STEP 1: CROSSING NETWORK CC-CC-CC-CC

Station 1 is a NetWare workstation using source routing. When Station 1 first accessed the network (with NETX.COM), it received a response from Router 3. The source-route information contained in Router 3's response was stored in Station 1's source-route table.

Refer to Chapter 2 for additional information on all-route and single-route bridges.

 NOTE

F I G U R E 3.6

*Multiprotocol internetwork
using bridges and routers*

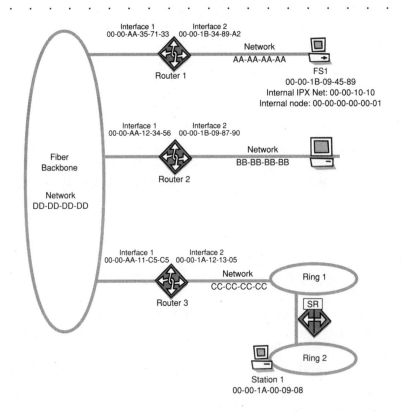

When Station 1 sends a SAP (Service Advertising protocol) or RIP (Routing Information protocol) request to locate remote network services (such as FS1), Router 3 forwards a reply to Station 1 with the internetwork address of FS1 and its own hardware address.

To communicate with FS1, Station 1 transmits a packet to Router 3 using the source-route information it obtained earlier. FS1's internetwork address is placed in the network (IPX) header. The source-route bridge examines the packet and forwards it to Ring 1.

On an IPX network, file servers are assigned an internal IPX network address and have a default node address of 00-00-00-00-00-01. This address is the final destination for file read and write requests and is used as the destination network address.

NOTE

At this stage, the packet would contain the addressing information shown in Figure 3.7.

Start of Packet

Data Link Header	Source Hardware Address: (Station 1)	00-00-1A-00-09-08
	Destination Hardware Address: (Router 3)	00-00-1A-12-13-05
Network Header	Source Internetwork Address: (Station 1)	CC-CC-CC-CC 00-00-1A-00-09-08
	Destination Internetwork Address: (FS1)	00-00-10-10 00-00-00-00-00-01

End of Packet

Note: On IPX networks packets addressed to a NetWare 3.x/4.x file server
        process are actually sent to the Internal IPX address of the server.

Packet addressing from
Station 1

STEP 2: CROSSING THE FIBER BACKBONE

When Router 3 receives the packet, it strips off the data link header and examines the network header information inside (Destination Network AA-AA-AA-AA). The router examines its routing information tables to determine where to transmit the packet. The router places a new packet header in front of the network header and transmits the packet to Router 1 on Network DD-DD-DD-DD, the fiber ring. Figure 3.8 depicts the packet at this point.

FIGURE 3.8

*Packet addressing when
sent by Router 3*

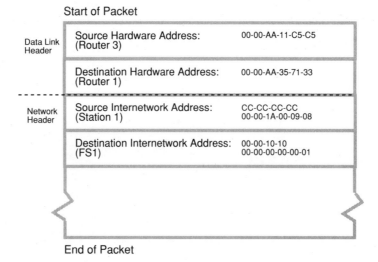

Start of Packet

Data Link Header	Source Hardware Address: (Router 3)	00-00-AA-11-C5-C5
	Destination Hardware Address: (Router 1)	00-00-AA-35-71-33
Network Header	Source Internetwork Address: (Station 1)	CC-CC-CC-CC 00-00-1A-00-09-08
	Destination Internetwork Address: (FS1)	00-00-10-10 00-00-00-00-00-01

End of Packet

STEP 3: CROSSING NETWORK AA-AA-AA-AA

When Router 1 receives the packet, it strips off the FDDI data link header, examines the network routing information inside, places a new Ethernet header on the packet, and forwards it to Network AA-AA-AA-AA. Figure 3.9 depicts the packet-addressing information at this time.

The last "hop" is internal to FS1. All NetWare servers maintain an internal virtual network. Once the transmission is received from Router 1, the packet is sent to the file services (virtual node address 00-00-00-00-00-01) on the internal network (IPX internal network number 00-00-10-10).

One question that may arise from examining this packet routing is, "How do the routers know where to send the packet next?" There are two algorithms used to create and maintain routing information tables: distance vector and link state. The next sections explain how each of these methods for building and maintaining routing information tables works.

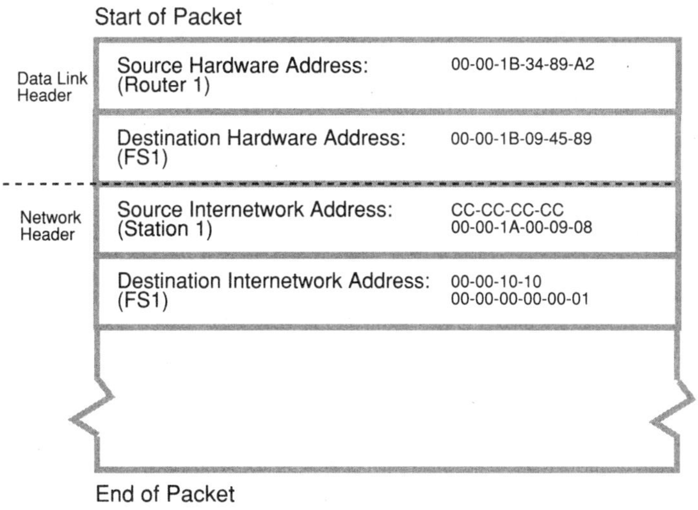

Start of Packet

Data Link Header	Source Hardware Address: (Router 1)	00-00-1B-34-89-A2
	Destination Hardware Address: (FS1)	00-00-1B-09-45-89
Network Header	Source Internetwork Address: (Station 1)	CC-CC-CC-CC 00-00-1A-00-09-08
	Destination Internetwork Address: (FS1)	00-00-10-10 00-00-00-00-00-01

End of Packet

FIGURE 3.9

*Packet addressing when
sent by Router 1*

Distance Vector Routing

Distance vector routing is the oldest and most common routing algorithm. Distance vector routers build their routing information tables based on information received from other routers—second-hand information. The routers pass on this information to other routers on each of their attached segments. For example, Figure 3.10 shows an internetwork that has four networks and three distance vector-based routers.

In Figure 3.10, Router 1 knows it is connected to Network A and Network B. Router 1 broadcasts routing information to each attached network indicating that these networks are one hop away from each other. A *hop* is equivalent to the number of routers that must be crossed to access a network. For example, Router 1 indicates that if a packet from Network B that is destined for Network A is transmitted to it, the packet will cross one router (one hop) to reach the network.

Router 2, on Network B, updates its routing information table to reflect that Network A is two hops away through Router 1. Router 2 also transmits information about networks that it can provide a route to.

► . . . . ◄

F I G U R E   3.10

Distance vector-based routers broadcast information about known routes.

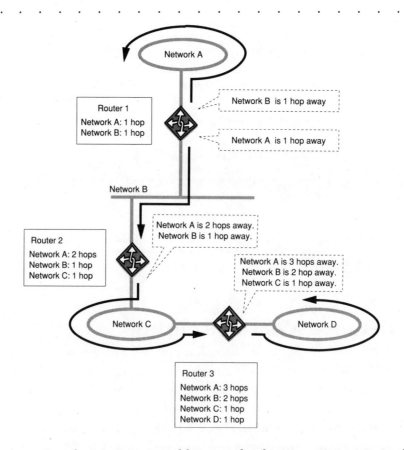

Router 3 updates its routing tables accordingly. Router 3 is connected to Network D and, therefore, transmits routing information about Network D, as shown in Figure 3.11. This information is propagated throughout the network.

Routing information is generally exchanged when routers are brought up, on a periodic basis, and when routes change. Be aware, however, that the frequency of routing information exchange is protocol specific. For example, the TCP/IP protocol dictates that periodic routing information is broadcast every 30 seconds. IPX/SPX, however, broadcasts routing information every 60 seconds, and DDP (AppleTalk) updates every 10 seconds.

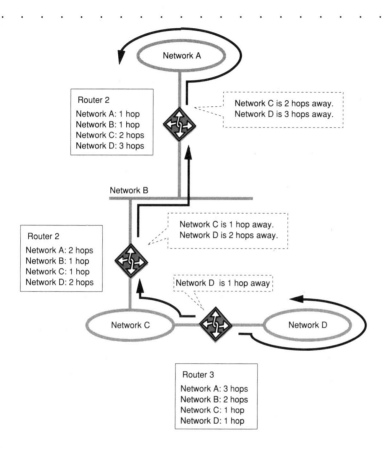

FIGURE 3.11

*Router 3 transmits routing
information about
Network D.*

Let's examine what happens when a route becomes unavailable. In Figure 3.12, Router 3's connection to Network C has been eliminated. There are two ways in which another router can learn of this route configuration change: through a "route change" transmission or through route aging. Using a "route change" transmission, routers can propagate "route no longer available" messages throughout the network.

Upon receipt of new routing information, routers update their routing information tables and broadcast the new route information onto all attached networks. If, however, a router could not communicate at all (router was "downed"), a route-aging mechanism must come into play to remove

Routers update their routing tables and report routes that are no longer available.

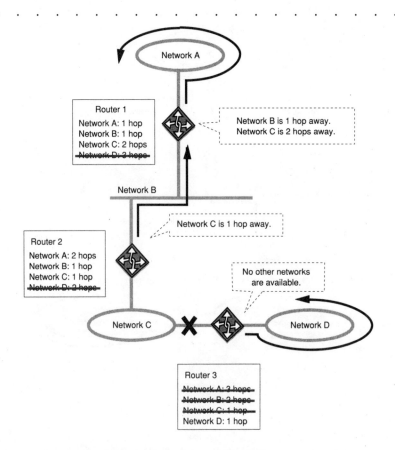

the route information from a router's tables. For example, if a router does not receive periodic routing information confirming the entries in the routing tables, the route entry is removed from the table. This route information aging time varies according to the routing protocols used.

The time required to update all routers on routing information changes is called convergence. One of the negative attributes of distance vector-based routing is slow convergence. Using distance vector-based routing methods, each router receives route-change information, updates its tables, calculates the hop counts to existing routes, and broadcasts new routing information.

One of the major disadvantages of distance vector-based routing solutions is the count-to-infinity problem. Let's examine the cause of this problem and define "infinity."

THE COUNT-TO-INFINITY PROBLEM

The count-to-infinity problem is one of the major disadvantages of distance vector-based routing. This condition is caused when a router (or link to a router) becomes unavailable. The convergence time is slow and, therefore, incorrect routing information can propagate through the system. Let's examine a network that is experiencing a count-to-infinity situation. Figure 3.13 depicts such a network.

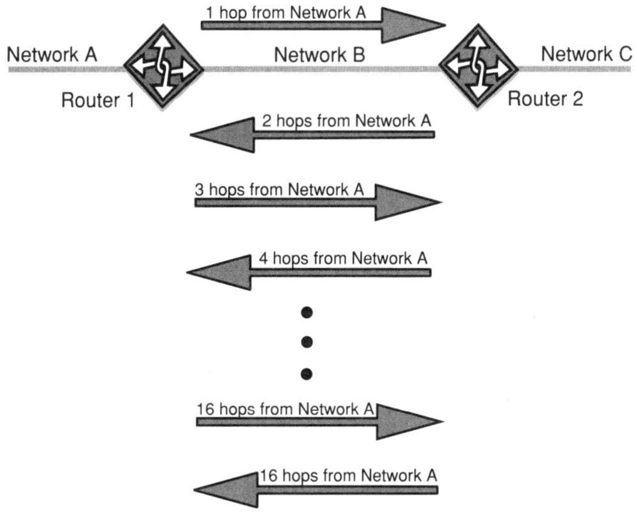

Network A   1 hop from Network A   Network B   Network C
Router 1   Router 2
             2 hops from Network A

3 hops from Network A

4 hops from Network A

•
•
•

16 hops from Network A

16 hops from Network A

FIGURE 3.13

The count-to-infinity problem is a major disadvantage of distance vector routing.

The term "count-to-infinity" should really be renamed "count-until-expiration" since a set-able parameter determines the maximum number that is reached.

 NOTE

In this example, Router 1's connection to Network A has been destroyed. Router 1 knows it cannot reach network A itself, but Router 2 advertises that Network A is two hops away. Router 1, therefore, assumes that it is now three hops from Network A and Router 2 is the way to access Network A. Router 2 still believes that Router 1, however, is the way to Network A, and it resets its routing information tables to reflect that Network A is now four hops away, using Router 1 as the best route. Once again, Router 2 broadcasts this information and Router 1 resets its tables again to reflect that it is now five hops away, using Router 2 as the best way to Network A.

The routers continue to reset their routing information tables and increase the hop count value until "infinity" is reached. "Infinity," however, is not truly infinity. In this case infinity is the maximum number of hop counts a routing protocol can accept before a routing information packet is discarded. For example, the NetWare routing system allows a maximum of 15 hops; if a packet indicates a network is 16 hops away, the network is assumed unreachable.

Routing protocols can take various steps to avoid the count-to-infinity problem. A common way is to not send routing information back in the direction it was received from. For example, if a NetWare router builds its route table entry based on information coming into Interface A, the router broadcasts the availability of the route out all interfaces except Interface A. One routing protocol called Split Horizon broadcasts a network as unreachable on the interface from which it learns about the network. Basically, the router says, "I learned about network xx from you so you can't get to network xx through me." In Figure 3.13, this would have prevented Router 2 from sending route information back onto network B (since this is where it received its route information). For our simple example, it would have prevented the count-to-infinity problem. When there are multiple routers to a destination, however, the count-to-infinity problem may still occur. Slowly converging distance vector-based routing protocols continuously plague large internetworks using this method for routing.

One of the solutions to this problem is available through link-state routing protocols. An analogy has been drawn between using distance vector-based routing tables and using street signs. For example, if you wanted to get to Oakland from San Jose, California, you would follow all the street signs pointing to Oakland. These street signs, however, may not indicate the most direct route. A map, on the other hand, provides an overview of all routes available, allowing you to select the most direct one yourself. Whereas distance vector-based routing is similar to using the street signs pointing the direction, link-state routing is similar to using a map.

Link-State Routing

As discussed above, distance vector-based routing protocols periodically broadcast route information (road signs) to each other, whether or not the information has changed. Link-state routing protocols, on the other hand, only exchange information about the specific routes (areas on the map) that have changed.

Link-state routing is considered smarter, faster, and more accurate than distance vector-based routing. Figure 3.14 lists distance vector-based and link-state routing protocols.

Protocol Suite	Distance Vector Protocol	Link-State Protocol
IPX/SPX	IPX RIP	NLSP
TCP/IP	IP RIP	OSPF
AppleTalk	RTMP	AURP
OSI	----	IS-IS

F I G U R E 3.14

Distance vector and link-state routing protocols

Routers using link-state routing protocols learn about their network environment by "meeting" their neighboring routers. This is done through a "hello" packet. This network information is then sent to each of the neighboring routers using a Link-State packet (LSP). The neighboring routers copy the contents of the packet and forward the LSP to each attached network—except the one the LSP was received on. This propagation of information is called *flooding*.

NOTE   **The format and type of "hello" packet is specific to the link-state protocol used.**

Routers using link-state routing protocols build a network "map" based on the LSP first-hand information. Figure 3.15 depicts a network that is using a link-state routing protocol.

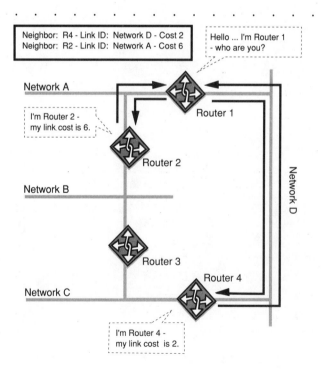

FIGURE 3.15

Link-state routers obtain first-hand routing information.

Router 1 transmits a "hello" packet to learn about its neighboring routers. Each neighbor replies with information regarding the link it is attached to and the route cost. The route cost is assigned automatically, manually, or through management protocols. Router 1 builds its routing database directly from the information received in response to the "hello" packets.

The next step in link-state routing is to transmit LSP packets throughout the network. Router 1 transmits an LSP packet to its neighbors; the LSP packet contains information about Router 1's neighbors and their associated costs. This packet is copied by each neighbor and the LSP is forwarded to each of their neighbors. Because the routers maintain the original LSP packet, whenever another router needs LSP information it requests a copy of the original from its neighbor. Since the LSP information is never altered by a router, it is considered to be first-hand information.

Routers create a map of the network based on all the LSPs seen. They do not recalculate their route database before forwarding route-change information, thereby reducing the time required for convergence and eliminating the count-to-infinity problem.

As shown in Figure 3.14, link-state routing protocols have been developed for each protocol suite listed. Link-state routing protocols are beginning to replace distance vector routing protocols.

Next let's examine how routers can be used to load balance a network that is experiencing very high utilization.

Using Routers to Load Balance a Network

It is possible to improve the performance of a single network by splitting it into two separate networks and placing a router between them. This section also addresses the location of the router and whether a server/router or external router solution is appropriate.

Let's examine a scenario where you would want to place a router on the network simply to increase performance. A 42-station Ethernet network is experiencing excessive traffic, causing performance to decline dramatically. The excessive traffic is due to the recent addition of stations on the network.

By using a network analyzer (LANalyzer for Windows), the company has graphed the traffic on the Ethernet cabling system, as shown in Figure 3.16. The bandwidth has increased to a point where performance is unsatisfactory (peak utilization is 65 percent).

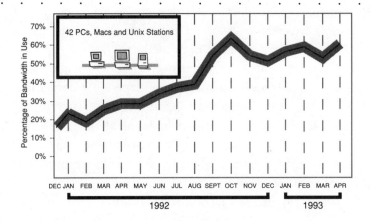

The graphed utilization indicates the amount of total cabling bandwidth in use. An overloaded cabling system is similar to the freeway during rush hour. As you well know, traffic slows down during rush hour because of heavy traffic and frequent accidents. To improve network performance of this network, we will segment the network. Figure 3.17 shows the current network configuration.

This network has 42 devices—PCs, Macintoshes, and UNIX workstations, all connected to a single set of 10Base-T hubs—on a single network. These 10Base-T hubs are located in a wiring closet on the ground floor of the building. Currently, this network has two NetWare file servers.

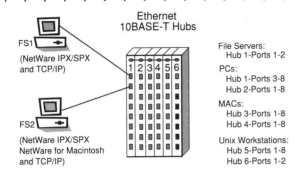

FIGURE 3.17

*Cabling configuration
before splitting the network*

TURNING THE SERVER INTO A ROUTER

Placing a second network interface card in one of the servers turns the server into a server/router (once mistakenly named an "internal bridge"), as shown in Figure 3.18.

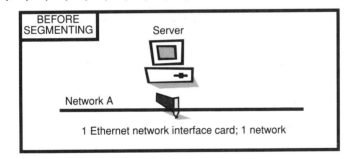

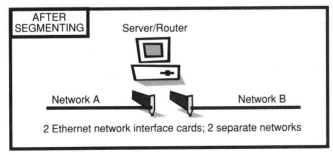

FIGURE 3.18

*Placing a second network
interface card in a
NetWare server turns it
into a server/router.*

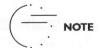 **NOTE**

Installing the Novell MultiProtocol Router on a NetWare server provides better performance and greater management and optimization capabilities than simply installing a second network interface card.

To ensure that the network is split properly and that an appropriate server is used as a router, some research into a network's existing configuration is required. We divided the network properly by answering the following questions:

▸ Can the desired server support the routing protocols?

▸ Which stations communicate most often with which servers?

▸ Can the desired server support the amount of routing traffic?

First, let's determine which server, if any, is the best candidate for becoming a server/router and where the network should be split.

Can the Desired Server Support the Routing Protocols?

Routers are "protocol dependent"—they must support a protocol in order to route packets. As shown in Figure 3.17, server FS1 supports NetWare IPX/SPX and TCP/IP protocols. Server FS1 does not support AppleTalk and, therefore, cannot route AppleTalk packets. This server is not a suitable router if Macintosh clients are to be placed on both networks.

Server FS2 supports NetWare IPX/SPX, TCP/IP, and AppleTalk protocols. This server can route all three network protocols and is a more appropriate candidate to become a server/router. Before determining whether the best option is to turn FS2 into a server/router and where the network should be split, we must answer the remaining two questions.

Which Stations Communicate Most Often with Which Servers?

Using Novell's LANalyzer for Windows to analyze the network traffic, we can determine the most active clients on the network. By capturing all traffic to FS2 and sorting the stations listed by kilobytes per second, we can determine the top ten users of FS2. We used this method to track the top ten users of both servers. These stations are listed in Figure 3.19.

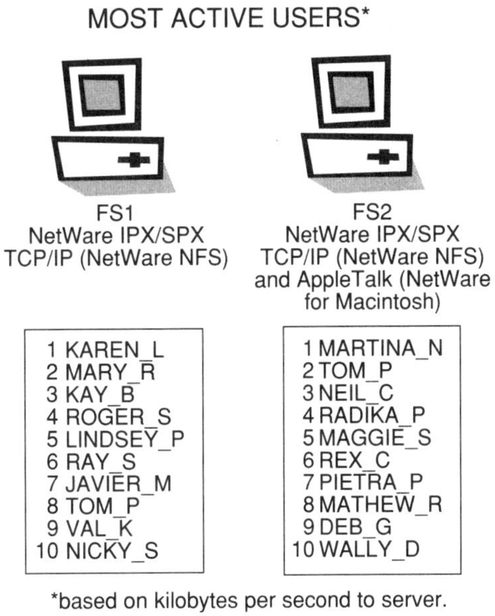

MOST ACTIVE USERS*

FIGURE 3.19

Determine the most active users for each server.

FS1
NetWare IPX/SPX
TCP/IP (NetWare NFS)

FS2
NetWare IPX/SPX
TCP/IP (NetWare NFS)
and AppleTalk (NetWare
for Macintosh)

1 KAREN_L	1 MARTINA_N
2 MARY_R	2 TOM_P
3 KAY_B	3 NEIL_C
4 ROGER_S	4 RADIKA_P
5 LINDSEY_P	5 MAGGIE_S
6 RAY_S	6 REX_C
7 JAVIER_M	7 PIETRA_P
8 TOM_P	8 MATHEW_R
9 VAL_K	9 DEB_G
10 NICKY_S	10 WALLY_D

*based on kilobytes per second to server.

This information is used to split the network. When splitting the network, be certain the most active users are placed on the same segment as their primary server. If one user is listed as one of the most active clients of both servers, you may consider placing that user on a network both servers are connected to. For example, the table shown in Figure 3.19 shows that TOM_P is one of the most active users on both networks.

Figure 3.20 is a conceptual diagram of how the network can be split into two separate networks. Notice that the 10Base-T hubs are now placed in two groups. Placing two network interface cards in FS2 and configuring it with two network addresses makes FS2 the server/router. The most active users are wired into the concentrator set that is connected directly to the server they most often use.

FIGURE 3.20

The network has been split in half using FS2 as the server/router.

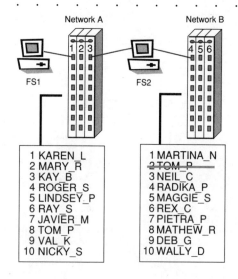

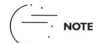

NOTE

For information on IPX, TCP/IP, and AppleTalk network addressing, refer to Chapter 4.

The final question to consider when splitting a network in half to increase performance is, "Can the server handle the job?" The next section defines how to determine if a server can handle all its present responsibilities and possibly also become the router for the internetwork.

Can the Desired Server Support the Routing Traffic?

NetWare servers can become overloaded because of heavy client requests with insufficient memory or CPU, a disk drive bottleneck, and so on. To be certain your server can handle the additional duties of routing packets, you must determine if the server is keeping up sufficiently with current requests.

When a NetWare server cannot handle a client's request because it is too busy, it responds to the client with a Request Being Processed packet. This is a special NetWare Core protocol (NCP) packet designed to provide congestion control for a NetWare server. If a server is constantly transmitting these congestion-control packets, the server would not be a good candidate for becoming a router. This type of packet can be tracked with a network analyzer, such as LANalyzer for Windows.

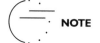

Refer to Novell's *Official Guide to NetWare LAN Analysis* for more details on Request Being Processed packets. NOTE

Another indication of an overloaded server is a high utilization percentage shown by NetWare's MONITOR utility. This value is a measure of how heavily utilized the server CPU is. If the utilization consistently ranges above 80 percent, the server is not a good candidate for providing routing services.

WHAT IF NO SERVER CAN BECOME A SERVER/ROUTER?

If your network does not have a server that is suitable for use as a router when splitting the network, an external/dedicated router must be used. Installing an external router relieves a file server from the duties of routing. In this situation, we installed Novell's MultiProtocol Router software on a 386 PC containing two Ethernet cards, as shown in Figure 3.21.

There are several advantages to installing a PC-based (software only) router system such as Novell's MultiProtocol Router. As mentioned earlier,

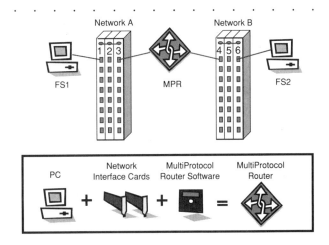

F I G U R E 3.21

Routing responsibilities are placed on an external MultiProtocol Router.

routing responsibilities are removed from the server, ensuring that the server does not handle additional, unnecessary load. As you may already know, PC-based routing solutions are generally less expensive than proprietary, hardware/software routing solutions. A third and final advantage of using a product such as the MultiProtocol Router is familiarity with the technology and interface. For example, many people are comfortable with NetWare v3.1x's installation and configuration methods. Since the MultiProtocol Router is based on run-time NetWare, many people are already familiar with the menu-based product installation and configuration.

This chapter has introduced routing concepts and configuration options. The final section provides some ideas for optimizing a routed internetwork, either during the planning stages or after installation.

Tips for Optimizing Routed Internetworks

There are numerous methods for optimizing a routed internetwork. The following sections cover two effective options:

- ▸ Network backbone
- ▸ Filtering/SAP restriction (NetWare-specific)

NETWORK BACKBONE

A backbone can be used to connect networks that span a campus, business park, or floors of a building. The key to installing an efficient backbone system is to follow several very simple rules. These backbone rules address the following issues:

- ▸ Backbone-attached devices
- ▸ Backbone network type
- ▸ Redundancy/fault tolerance

Backbone-Attached Devices

Only servers and routers should be connected to the backbone—not workstations. This is important because it isolates workstation traffic to the local segment, as shown in Figure 3.22. In this example, an FDDI backbone connects three networks that support approximately 60 workstations each.

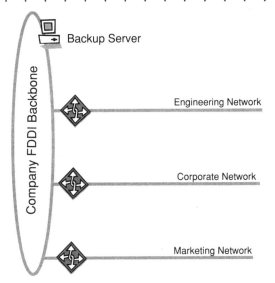

FIGURE 3.22

An FDDI backbone links
three Ethernet networks.

The backbone (FDDI) has only four devices attached to it—three routers and one backup server. Routers ensure that all traffic that is local to each network does not travel across the backbone. The backup server on the backbone is used to centrally back up all servers on the internetwork. The backup server has been placed on the backbone to reduce traffic on individual segments during backup times. For example, when a server on the Engineering network is backed up, the information is transmitted from the Engineering network onto the backbone to the backup server. If this backup server were located on an individual segment, backup would create heavy traffic on the Engineering network, the backbone, and the backup server's network, as shown in Figure 3.23.

Moving the backup server off the backbone causes excessive traffic on three segments.

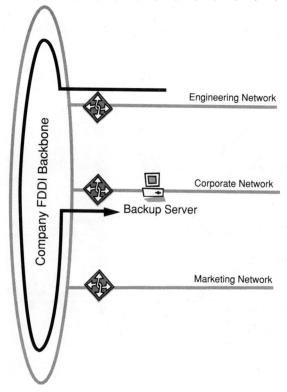

Network Types

For best results, use a network type that supports higher bandwidth than your individual networks for your backbone. For example, if your networks are all 4 megabit-per-second Token Ring networks, install at least a 16-megabit-per-second Token Ring backbone.

One of the most desirable backbone network types is FDDI because it provides a 100-megabit-per-second bandwidth and includes fault-tolerant features (discussed later in this chapter).

Figure 3.24 lists some options for backbone network types.

Individual Networks	Backbone Network
ARCnet	Ethernet or Token Ring
Ethernet	FDDI
Token Ring/4	Token Ring/16
Token Ring/16	FDDI
LocalTalk	Ethernet or Token Ring

FIGURE 3.24

Backbone options

Redundancy/Fault Tolerance

Because the backbone network is your high-speed freeway through the internetwork, some redundancy or fault tolerance should be built in. Some network types, such as Token Ring and FDDI, include redundancy and fault-tolerant features and are, therefore, well suited as backbone networks.

Token Ring networks include built-in, transparent management information and communication. If a workstation is suspected of causing errors on the ring, the Token Ring protocol includes special measures for automatically locating and removing the faulty station.

FDDI networks include dual counter-rotating rings. The secondary ring is a backup ring, in case of damage to the primary. If the primary ring fails, the FDDI network can automatically loop back using the second ring, as shown in Figure 3.25.

FDDI backbones can also be configured using a technique called *dual homing,* where critical devices (such as routers and servers) are redundantly linked to the backbone ring. A dual-homed device is attached to two concentrators that, in turn, are attached to the main ring. Figure 3.26 depicts dual homing a critical router.

If the primary concentrator fails, the critical router retains access to the ring through the secondary concentrator. Refer to Appendix A for more FDDI references.

In FDDI, the secondary ring
provides fault tolerance.

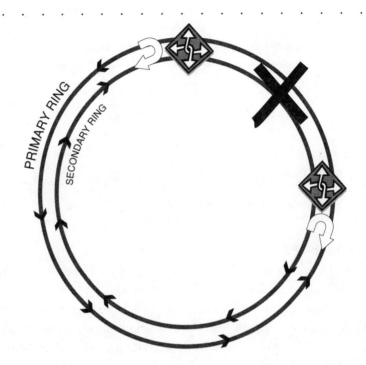

FILTERING

Routers automatically filter (discard) packets that should not be forwarded to another network because they are destined for the local LAN. There are, however, some routers that provide additional filtering capabilities to enhance internetwork performance. For example, Novell's MultiProtocol Router includes the ability to filter Service Advertising protocol (SAP) traffic. This filter is particularly useful on internetworks that have numerous NetWare servers.

NetWare servers transmit SAP packets every 60 seconds. By default, routers propagate SAP information throughout the network to ensure that each network server and router is aware of all services available on the network. On an internetwork that supports 250 servers, there are at least 250 SAP packets on the network every minute. This traffic increases utilization and may cause workstations to timeout because they cannot obtain access

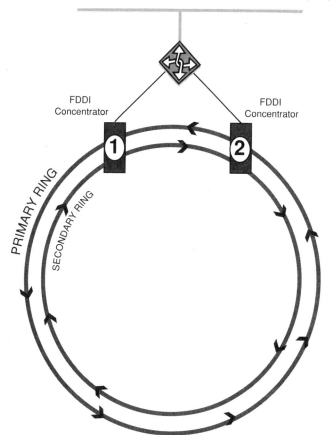

FIGURE 3.26

*Dual homing a critical
router*

to the cabling system—it's too busy. Imagine trying to merge into a lane of traffic that is backed up with cars for miles.

Figure 3.27 depicts a network that has been configured with Novell's MultiProtocol Router using the SAP restricter.

In Figure 3.27, the MultiProtocol Router has been configured to restrict all SAP broadcasts from FS1. Only devices on Network A can "see" FS1. File servers FS2, FS3, and FS4 are not aware of FS1 because they do not receive any SAP broadcasts indicating there is such a server.

There is another reason for using the MultiProtocol Router's SAP filter: security. When users cannot see a server, they cannot access a server.

FIGURE 3.27

The SAP filter ensures that
FS1's SAP broadcasts
remain on Network A only.

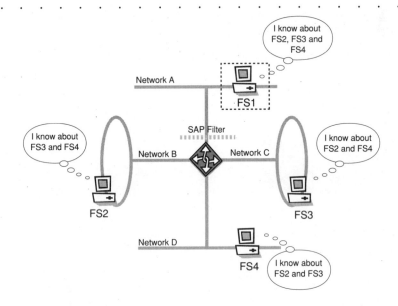

Filtering abilities are implementation specific and vary from vendor to vendor.

Routers are designed to internetwork medium to large networks and offer various benefits not available when using bridges. Having completed this chapter, you are aware of the benefits that routing provides the internetwork. You should also have a solid grasp on the way routers exchange routing information using distance vector and link-state algorithms.

The next chapter focuses on configuring and implementing routers on a multiprotocol internetwork.

CHAPTER 4

Implementing Multiprotocol Local Networks

There are a number of possible configurations for connecting networks. When you are deciding on the most appropriate method for linking LANs, however, it is important to consider the protocols in use. You must ensure that the routers you install are capable of forwarding the desired traffic. This chapter examines the key considerations when connecting networks that utilize different protocols such as IPX/SPX, TCP/IP, and AppleTalk.

Connecting Multiprotocol LANs Using a Bridge

Since bridges are protocol independent, they are unaware of protocols in use. When a packet is received by a bridge, the bridge examines the information in the data-link header and forwards the packet or discards it if the destination is located on the same side the packet was received from. Bridging is required to interconnect networks that use protocols that cannot be routed. For example, the DEC LAT (Local Area Transport) protocol does not have the ability to be routed. In order to connect multiple DECnet networks, a bridge is required.

 NOTE **For more information on bridging technologies, refer to Chapter 2.**

When you are configuring a network to utilize a bridge, the network addresses used must be the same on either side of the bridge since, logically, a bridged network is a single network. For example, Figure 4.1 shows a large internetwork that uses bridges to connect two Ethernet segments.

 NOTE **If you configure an IPX network to use unique addresses on each side of the bridge, an error is displayed on the NetWare server consoles: "Router Configuration Error — Router XXXXX claims that LAN x is XX-XX-XX-XX."**

When packets are transmitted from a station on one side of the bridge to a station on the other side of the bridge, they are traversing only one

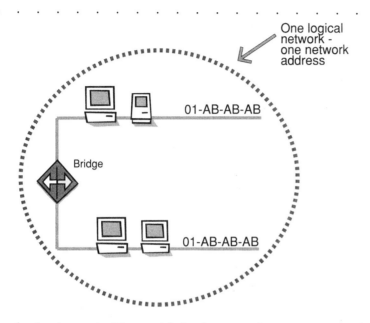

One logical
network -
one network
address

*A bridged network is
logically a single network.*

network. As shown in Figure 4.1, both network segments use the same
IPX network address, 01-AB-AB-AB.

> **Many people misconfigure IPX bridged networks, assigning a
> unique network address to the servers on each side of the bridge.
> This may, in part, be due to the misleading label of "bridge" once
> applied to NetWare routers. NetWare 2.1x included "external
> bridge" software that required a unique network address for each
> side of the "bridge." The "external bridge" software was actually
> router software; therefore unique network addresses were
> required.**

 NOTE

Figure 4.2 shows the same network supporting UNIX stations as well.
Note that the IP addresses assigned to the UNIX stations begin with the
same network address: 130.57. Each, however, has a unique host address:
10.1 or 10.2. Why did we assign the same network addresses on each side
of a bridge? The answer is simple: because the bridge forwards packets

F I G U R E 4.2

Network addresses for a
bridged TCP/IP and
IPX/SPX network

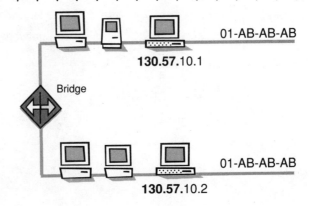

based on the MAC data-link layer address, not the network address. The bridge connects separate network segments, not separate networks.

Connecting Multiprotocol LANs Using a Router

Back in the 1980s, the native NetWare operating system (v2.x) supported NetWare's IPX/SPX protocol and AppleTalk; however, most NetWare LANs utilized only Novell's IPX/SPX protocol. When NetWare v3.11 was introduced, a new protocol was bundled with the operating system: TCP/IP. An increasing number of LANs are taking advantage of the added interoperability provided by using multiple protocols on a network.

As LANs are internetworked, special concerns arise regarding the addressing and optimization of the various protocols used on the internetwork. This chapter focuses on three types of internetworked protocol configurations:

▸ IPX/SPX internetworks

▸ TCP/IP internetworks

▸ AppleTalk internetworks

Since the IPX/SPX protocol is, by default, enabled on all NetWare LANs, let's examine this protocol first.

CONFIGURING NETWARE IPX/SPX INTERNETWORKS

NetWare uses IPX RIP (Routing Information protocol) to exchange information about route availability. By default, every 60 seconds NetWare IPX routers transmit a RIP packet that contains routing information. This information is used to update other IPX routers on the network. Upon receipt of a RIP packet, a router adds 1 to the hop count of each route advertised and broadcasts a RIP packet to the other networks it is connected to. IPX RIP is a vector-based routing protocol.

For more information on vector-based routing, refer to Chapter 3. **NOTE**

There are several basic guidelines to follow when configuring an IPX router. These guidelines apply to the addressing used on the IPX internetwork. First, let's examine the guidelines for assigning IPX network addresses.

IPX Network Addresses

The IPX network address identifies a single NetWare network. Routers use this address to determine whether or not to forward packets. If the packet should be forwarded, the router uses the network address information contained in a packet to determine the best route to the final destination. Since it is impractical for all traffic to be distributed throughout the entire internetwork, this process allows for isolation of local traffic and serves as an efficient means of forwarding traffic destined for other networks.

Contrary to popular belief, the "best" route is based on ticks ($1/18$ of a second), not hops (the number of routers that must be crossed to reach the destination). On local IPX internetworks, the tick count is always the hop count plus 1 (2 hops/3 ticks). On a WAN, however, the tick count is factored based on the type of link supported by the router. **NOTE**

When you are configuring an internetwork, each NetWare LAN must have a unique network address, as shown in Figure 4.3.

The network address is configured for each side of an IPX router based on the logical LAN board configured. For example, the NetWare Multi-Protocol Router uses a configuration program, INETCFG, to create the bind statements that attach the IPX protocol to the logical LAN board and assign the IPX network address. Figure 4.4 illustrates the assignment of the network address to a logical LAN board.

FIGURE 4.3

Each NetWare LAN must have a unique network address.

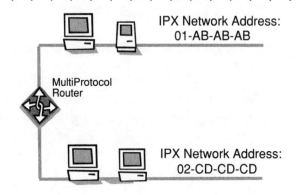

FIGURE 4.4

Unique network addresses are assigned when IPX is bound to the logical LAN board.

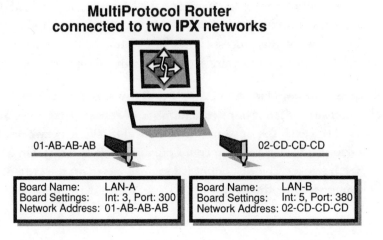

When configuring the NetWare MultiProtocol Router, do not assign the same IPX network address to multiple logical LAN boards.

 NOTE

Adding NetWare Servers to the Internetwork

Once the IPX router has been configured and installed on the network, special care must be taken when adding NetWare servers to the internetwork. All NetWare servers residing on a single network must have the same IPX network address assigned.

NetWare 4.x detects and automatically configures itself to use the IPX address already in use, if there is one.

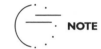 NOTE

For example, if at a later date another server is added to the configuration shown in Figure 4.4, the IPX address assigned when IPX is bound to the logical LAN board must match the network address previously assigned. Figure 4.5 shows another server added to the network 01-AB-AB-AB. The logical LAN board of the new server has been bound to IPX using the address 01-AB-AB-AB.

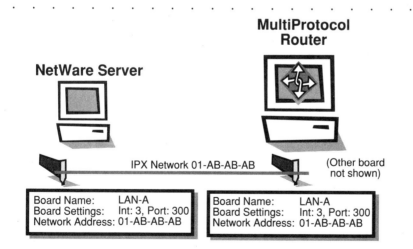

FIGURE 4.5
A server that is added to the internetwork must use the defined IPX network address.

The third and final network addressing issue deals with the internal IPX address that is used with all NetWare 3.x and 4.x servers.

Internal IPX Address Concerns

NetWare 3.x (and later) servers are configured with an internal IPX address that is similar to a network address for the processes "inside" the server. This address must be unique for each NetWare server throughout the entire internet.

NOTE

A common symptom of servers that have duplicate internal IPX addresses is that the servers cannot "see" each other although they are properly wired and, by all other indications, are functioning properly.

This internal IPX address must be unique to all other IPX network addresses used. For example, Figure 4.6 shows an internetwork consisting of two Ethernet networks and five NetWare servers connected by a NetWare MultiProtocol Router. The logical LAN boards of FS1, FS2, and FS3 have the IPX network address of 04-AA-AA-AA. The NetWare MultiProtocol Router's logical LAN board that is connected to that network must use the same network address. FS4 and FS5 have been configured with logical LAN boards that use the IPX network address 05-BB-BB-BB. The NetWare Multi-Protocol Router's logical LAN board that is connected to this network also uses the network address 05-BB-BB-BB. Each server has been assigned a unique internal IPX address.

The most common internetworking configuration mistake seen on Net-Ware IPX/SPX LANs is in network addressing. Verify that each network is assigned a unique 4-byte network address and the internal IPX address is unique as well. Many MIS directors maintain a "blueprint" of their inter-network, listing all network addresses and internal IPX addresses in use.

NOTE

For examples of network blueprints, refer to Chapters 5 and 10.

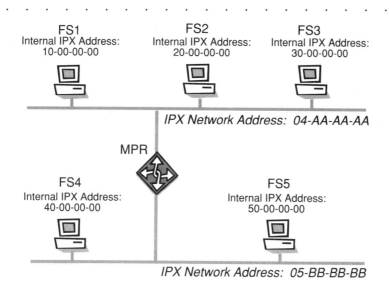

FIGURE 4.6

*All servers on the
internetwork must have a
unique internal IPX address.*

Restricting Excessive SAP Broadcasts

NetWare uses the Service Advertising protocol (SAP) to distribute information about available services throughout the internetwork. Every 60 seconds, NetWare servers transmit SAP information onto their locally attached network(s). SAP packets are transmitted by clients to find services as well. For example, a client that wants to connect to a file server issues a Get Nearest Server SAP.

This SAP traffic can cause communication problems on larger networks by flooding the network with SAP broadcasts. If an IPX client cannot communicate on the network because it is flooded with SAP packets, the client may timeout. Because of this SAP broadcast problem, it is often desirable to filter out specific SAP traffic on the network.

> **The SAP Restricter was developed for Novell's own network to reduce the number of SAP broadcasts on the corporate backbone. The excessive SAP broadcasts were causing IPX stations to timeout.**

NOTE

Figure 4.7 shows the effects of enabling the SAP Restricter on a NetWare MultiProtocol Router that connects two networks. The MultiProtocol Router has been configured to restrict SAP information about FS2 from being broadcast onto the other LAN. When Client A or Client B issues the SLIST or NLIST (NetWare 4.0) command, it cannot see server FS2. The SAP Restricter is used for large internetworks that support many NetWare servers. For example, Novell's internetwork of over 700 servers was an ideal candidate for using Novell's SAP Restricter.

FIGURE 4.7

The NetWare MultiProtocol Router can be configured using the SAP Restricter.

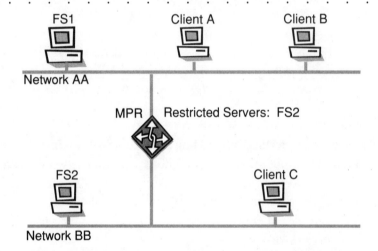

Services cannot be restricted from a client that has attached to the router that is using the SAP Restricter. In other words, when a client issues a Get Nearest Server SAP request (by executing the NETX command) and is attached to a NetWare MultiProtocol Router that has the SAP Restricter enabled, the client is able to view all services known to the MultiProtocol Router—even services that are restricted on that router. This is because the client queries the Server Information Table of the NetWare MultiProtocol Router. To ensure that the services are not visible to the end station, configure the client's NET.CFG file with another server listed as the preferred server.

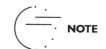

NOTE

The NetWare MultiProtocol Router includes the SAPCFG configuration utility that configures SAP restriction options.

Let's examine another configuration that could benefit from the use of the SAP Restricter: a large internetwork that is connected using a Token Ring backbone. Figure 4.8 shows a corporate internetwork that connects three departments: Engineering, Marketing, and Administration. There is a total of 65 file servers on this internetwork—45 in the Engineering group, 15 in Marketing, and 5 in Administration. The backbone has been experiencing some congestion because of the excessive SAP traffic being broadcast every 60 seconds by every server on the internetwork. This company has connected its separate networks using four NetWare Multi-Protocol Routers as the primary connections to the backbone. Forty of the Engineering servers are non-production servers and are used only for development purposes. You restrict the SAP information about these 40 servers from the backbone by placing a SAP Restricter on two of the Multi-Protocol Routers.

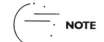

NOTE

For more information on the SAP packet structure and functionality, see _Novell's Guide to NetWare LAN Analysis_ (Sybex, 1992).

In this example, MPR1 and MPR2 have been configured with the SAP Restricter. These routers do not transmit information about the non-production servers on Engineering Network A or Network B to the backbone. The five production servers, however, are advertised on the backbone to ensure access from the Marketing and Administration networks.

Hop Count Limitations

One final concern when linking IPX-based LANs is the hop count limitation that is imposed by the current Novell RIP implementation. On an IPX network, a packet can cross a maximum of 15 routers before it is discarded. Routers check the hop count field in the IPX header of each packet they receive. If the hop count is less than 15 and the packet should be forwarded, the router increments the hop count by 1 and forwards the packet onto the

FIGURE 4.8

*The SAP Restricter is used
to reduce SAP traffic on the
corporate backbone.*

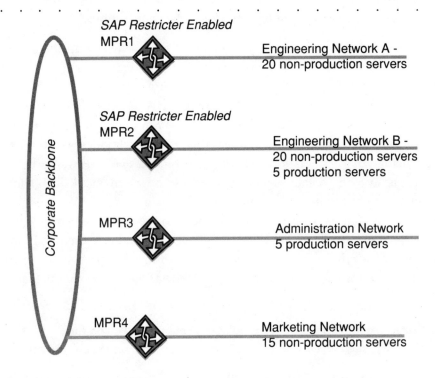

next network. Once the packet has been forwarded by 15 routers, the next router discards the packet.

This hop count limitation can be a bothersome restriction on large internetworks that do not use a backbone configuration. Packets have to cross numerous routers and networks to reach their final destination, as shown in Figure 4.9.

The network shown in Figure 4.9 has been configured without a backbone—Client A cannot connect to FS1 because it is 16 hops away. A network or service that is 16 hops away is considered unreachable. This configuration also causes unnecessary traffic to cross each network. For example, a client on the Token Ring network Ring 1 must cross eight Ethernet networks and three Token Ring networks to communicate with a server on Ring 5. Implementing a backbone configuration eliminates the hop count

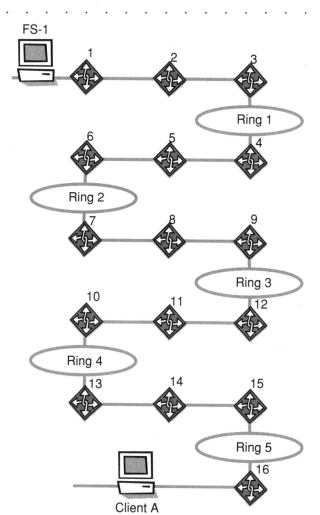

FIGURE 4.9

Network that does not use
a backbone configuration

issue and reduces traffic on each network. Figure 4.10 shows the same network reconfigured to use a single backbone with eight routers connected directly to the backbone.

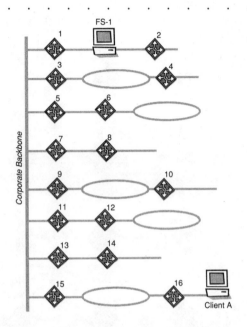

Now that a backbone has been installed, Client A is only three hops away
from FS1. The maximum number of hops between any two Token Ring networks is 4. The maximum number of hops between any two end stations is
4. If each router was connected directly to the backbone, the maximum
number of hops between the two end stations would be 2.

The hop count information can be used to optimize network communications and ensure minimum distances (in hops) between end stations.

This section has discussed the major issues involved when configuring
an IPX internetwork. Next let's examine configuration issues for TCP/IP
networks.

CONFIGURING TCP/IP INTERNETWORKS

For many "old-timers" using NetWare LANs, TCP/IP is a new and often
confusing protocol to configure. IPX network configurations, by com-
parison, may seem simplistic. The following sections discuss the basics of
setting up a TCP/IP internetwork that connects local LANs.

IP Network Addressing

Network addressing can be quite complex in the TCP/IP environment because of the flexibility offered by the IP addressing system. Unlike IPX network addresses, IP addresses are assigned to each station as well as the network routers and servers. Since a large number of technical support calls received by Novell deal with IP addressing, this section provides numerous examples of IP internetwork addressing schemes.

IP addresses are 4 bytes long and contain both a network address and a host ID (unique for each station on the network). On an IP network, each network is assigned a 4-byte IP address that is categorized as Class A, Class B, or Class C. First, let's examine the differences among these address types.

Class A addresses are used on networks that have a large number of IP hosts—up to 16,777,216 hosts on a single network. Class B addresses are used on medium-sized networks, and Class C addresses are used on smaller networks—up to 255 hosts on a single network. The size of the host ID section of the address indicates the number of hosts possible on the network. As shown in Figure 4.11, Class A addresses have a 1-byte field for the network address and 3 bytes for the host ID. Class B addresses have 2 bytes for the network address and 2 bytes for the host ID. Class C addresses have 3 bytes for the network address and 1 byte for the host ID.

IP addresses are represented in dotted decimal notation; that is, each byte is separated by a dot (131.9.1.2.). To identify the class of an address, look at the value of the first byte. The first byte of all Class A addresses begins with a number from 1 to 127. The first byte of all Class B addresses begins with a number from 128 to 191. The first byte of all Class C addresses begins with a number from 192 to 254. As in IPX addressing, all devices on a single network must use the same network address. Each device's host ID, however, must be unique, as shown in Figure 4.12.

If you are connecting to the Department of Defense Internet, you must apply to the Network Information Center (NIC) for an IP address. This IP address assigned to you must be used by any station connecting to the Internet.

NOTE

FIGURE 4.11

Class A, B, and C addresses have network addresses and host IDs of different lengths.

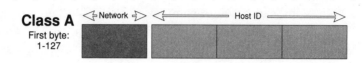

Class A
First byte:
1-127

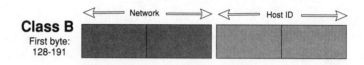

Class B
First byte:
128-191

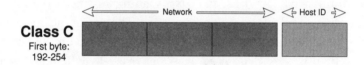

Class C
First byte:
192-254

FIGURE 4.12

Each device on a single network must use a unique host ID.

IP Network: 31.0.0.0 (Class A Address)

(Host ID: 0.0.1)   (Host ID: 0.0.2)   (Host ID: 0.0.3)
IP Address: 31.0.0.1   IP Address: 31.0.0.2   IP Address: 31.0.0.3

NetWare NFS   LAN Workplace   UNIX host
Server   Client

Assigning Addresses to the Router

When you are configuring a multiprotocol router, each interface must be assigned the correct network address when being bound to the IP protocol. The network portion of the address must match the address in use by the physically attached network. The host ID must be unique for that network. For example, Figure 4.13 shows the IP addresses assigned to a NetWare

MultiProtocol Router that connects two IP networks. Each logical board has a unique network address.

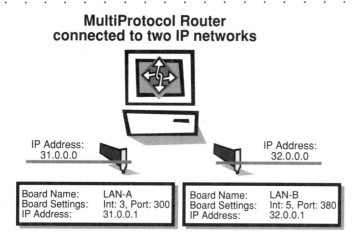

**MultiProtocol Router
connected to two IP networks**

IP Address:
31.0.0.0

IP Address:
32.0.0.0

Board Name:	LAN-A
Board Settings:	Int: 3, Port: 300
IP Address:	31.0.0.1

Board Name:	LAN-B
Board Settings:	Int: 5, Port: 380
IP Address:	32.0.0.1

FIGURE 4.13

The router must be configured to match the network address of the physically attached IP networks.

The host ID assigned to each logical LAN board must be unique on that network only. For example, Figure 4.14 shows the address of two devices— a NetWare MultiProtocol Router and a UNIX host—that are on the same network. They both use the same network address (31.0.0.0), but their host IDs are unique (0.0.1 and 0.0.2).

Using IP Subnet Masks

IP subnet masks are used to denote which portion of an IP address is the network address and which portion is the host ID. By default, the following network masks are assigned:

Class A address: 255.0.0.0

Class B address: 255.255.0.0

Class C address: 255.255.255.0

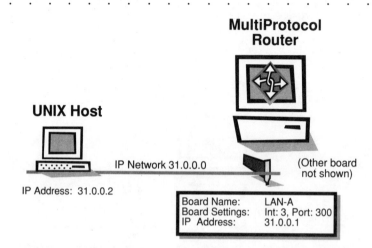

In binary, 255 is a byte that consists of all 1's (11111111). These binary
1's denote the portion of the address that is "masked off" as a network
address.

There are some networks that require special subnet masks. These are
generally networks that are accessing the DoD Internet. The Network Information Center (NIC) assigns a single address to be used by a company
when it is accessing the Internet. All hosts on that company network that
communicate on the Internet must use the same IP network address. This
could be done easily on a single network that accesses the Internet; however, on a large internetwork that must have unique network addresses on
each side of a router, it requires the use of a subnet mask. The subnetwork
mask allows the single network address assigned by the NIC to be divided
into "sub networks" assigned to the company's internetwork.

Figure 4.15 shows an internetwork that has three network segments. The
company has been assigned a Class B address, 130.57.0.0. 130.57 is the network address that all hosts must use to access the Internet. We must assign
a network addressing system that allows all networks to have a unique network address, yet each host on the network must use 130.57 as its network
address for accessing the Internet. We are going to "mask off" a portion of
the host ID to use as a subnetwork address.

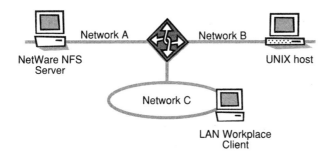

IP Network Number Assigned: 130.57.0.0
(Class B Address)

F I G U R E   4.15

*A large internetwork has
been assigned 130.57 as
the network address to use
for accessing the Internet.*

Each device is assigned an IP address with a subnet mask of
255.255.255.0. This indicates that the first 3 bytes of the IP address are the
network address and only the last byte of the IP address is the host ID. By
default, 137.57.0.0 is a Class B address with a subnet mask of 255.255.0.0—
only the first 2 bytes indicate the network address. When we assign the subnet mask of 255.255.255.0, the network portion of the IP address is now
137.57.x (where x is a unique number defined for each subnetwork). Figure 4.16 shows each device's IP address and subnet mask.

Each device has been assigned an address beginning with 130.57. The
third byte is used to define the subnet. Each device on a network segment
uses the same subnet number and subnet mask. Only the final byte defines
the host ID of the device. Keep in mind that the Internet will route to the
company based on a network address of 130.57.0.0. It is only within
the company internetwork that the third byte is recognized as part of a
network address. Keeping an accurate diagram of your network addressing
system can help easily define subnet masks and IP addresses used on the
internetwork.

In some cases, working with subnet masks can become more complex
because you may not want to use an entire byte for the subnet number. In
these cases you can use binary to assign a subnet mask. Let's assign subnet
numbers to the same network but use only 4 bits for the subnet number.
Figure 4.17 shows how the subnet number is defined for a Class B address

that uses only a 4-bit subnet portion. Notice that the first 4 bits of the third byte are masked off with binary 1's. The fifth through eighth bits are part of the host ID. The decimal value of this subnet mask is 255.255.240.0.

FIGURE 4.16

The network has been split into three subnets— 01, 02, and 03.

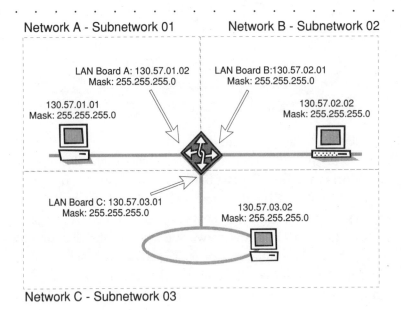

FIGURE 4.17

Assigning a 4-bit subnet portion for a Class B address

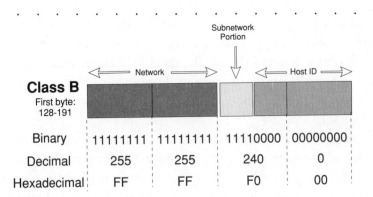

	Network		Subnetwork Portion	Host ID
Class B First byte: 128-191				
Binary	11111111	11111111	11110000	00000000
Decimal	255	255	240	0
Hexadecimal	FF	FF	F0	00

Next let's examine how each of the IP addresses is defined when using a binary subnet mask. First, we assign a subnet address using the first 4 bits of the third byte, as shown in Figure 4.18. We have assigned a subnet number of 8 (binary 1000). Next we can begin assigning host IDs for the devices on this subnet. We have created three valid IP addresses, each having a subnet address of 8. When we assign IP addresses to the stations, we determine the decimal value of the entire third byte, including the subnet mask portion.

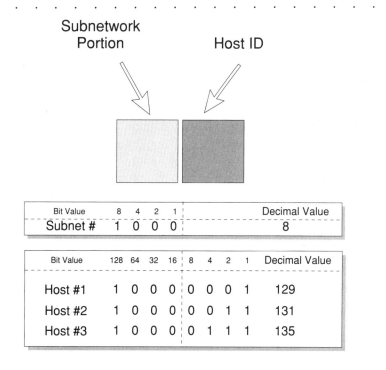

Calculating IP addresses for hosts using a binary subnet mask

Bit Value	8	4	2	1	Decimal Value
Subnet #	1	0	0	0	8

Bit Value	128	64	32	16	8	4	2	1	Decimal Value
Host #1	1	0	0	0	0	0	0	1	129
Host #2	1	0	0	0	0	0	1	1	131
Host #3	1	0	0	0	0	1	1	1	135

Figure 4.19 shows the IP addresses and subnet masks on a network that has been assigned the IP network address 130.57.0.0.

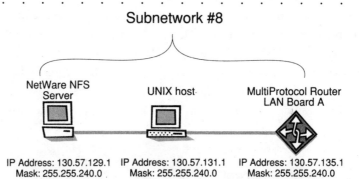

F I G U R E 4.19

Assigning IP addresses to
hosts using a binary
subnet mask

Subnetwork #8

NetWare NFS Server

UNIX host

MultiProtocol Router LAN Board A

IP Address: 130.57.129.1
Mask: 255.255.240.0

IP Address: 130.57.131.1
Mask: 255.255.240.0

IP Address: 130.57.135.1
Mask: 255.255.240.0

IP addresses are usually assigned in a configuration file on each host. Another option when assigning IP addresses on an internet is Proxy ARP (Address Resolution protocol). Next we examine the ARP protocol and Proxy ARP.

Using ARP and Proxy ARP

ARP (Address Resolution protocol) is used by IP hosts to locate a hardware address for another IP host. For example, Figure 4.20 shows a single network segment with two IP hosts.

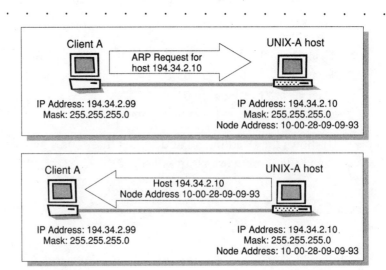

Client A

ARP Request for host 194.34.2.10

UNIX-A host

IP Address: 194.34.2.99
Mask: 255.255.255.0

IP Address: 194.34.2.10
Mask: 255.255.255.0
Node Address: 10-00-28-09-09-93

Client A

Host 194.34.2.10
Node Address 10-00-28-09-09-93

UNIX-A host

IP Address: 194.34.2.99
Mask: 255.255.255.0

IP Address: 194.34.2.10
Mask: 255.255.255.0
Node Address: 10-00-28-09-09-93

When a LAN workplace client (Client A) wants to establish a telnet session with a UNIX host (Host UNIX-A), the user types **TNVT220 UNIX-A**. The host name, UNIX-A, is defined in the client's host table. This name is associated with the device that has the IP address 194.34.2.10 (Class C address). To obtain the hardware address (Ethernet node address) of UNIX-A, Client A broadcasts an ARP request onto the network. Each host on the network examines the ARP request to determine if its address is in the request. UNIX-A responds with its hardware address. This hardware address is used to form a packet addressed to UNIX-A and is stored in Client A's ARP table for the next time it wants to transmit to UNIX-A.

Proxy ARP is used when configuring a *stub network*—one that is connected to another network but does not have its own network address, perhaps because of a restriction on the number of network addresses. When a router is installed to implement Proxy ARP, it responds to ARP requests on behalf of clients, indicating that the router itself is the intended node address. Although not a common configuration for TCP/IP networks, proxy ARP can be used when network address restrictions are in force.

Now that we've examined the issues of routing IPX and IP protocols, let's look at the AppleTalk protocol and the routing considerations when connecting separate AppleTalk networks.

CONNECTING APPLETALK INTERNETWORKS

A key characteristic of the AppleTalk protocol suite is its very dynamic nature. For example, nodes are dynamically assigned addresses, a node's default router may change constantly, and resources are being advertised and "discovered" more often than in other environments. This dynamic nature makes AppleTalk easier to use in the smaller workgroup environment; however, it may complicate its use in larger internetworks (or across WANs).

AppleTalk Communications

When a new AppleTalk station is placed on a network, a router on that network supplies the station's network number and zone name. (Addressing issues and zones are covered later in this chapter.) The AppleTalk station randomly selects a node ID and verifies that it is unique on the network. The network number, node ID, and zone information are stored in a special area of memory, called P-RAM (parameter RAM), of the station. Each time that station is rebooted, it requests verification of this information.

The startup process is only one of the duties of an AppleTalk router. AppleTalk routers have three primary functions:

▸ To supply startup information for AppleTalk nodes

▸ To supply routing services across the network

▸ To locate remote resources for AppleTalk nodes

The router that supplies startup information for a node may not remain the node's default router—called "A-ROUTER"—for long. AppleTalk routers transmit routing information every 10 seconds. Each time an Apple-Talk node sees a routing packet, it resets the value of A-ROUTER to the router that sent the last routing packet. If there are eight AppleTalk routers on a network, the nodes change the value of A-ROUTER eight times every 10 seconds. Although this traffic is limited to a single network, it has important implications for internetworking.

Keep the following in mind when internetworking AppleTalk LANs:

▸ Since AppleTalk nodes constantly change the value of A-ROUTER, routers with inconsistent configurations result in problems with the startup process, locating resources, and routing.

▸ AppleTalk makes extensive use of broadcast and multicast addresses. This has special implications for *bridged* networks. Bridges must pass all multicast, as well as broadcast, traffic. Bridges are less effective filtering devices for the AppleTalk protocol than for other protocols.

▸ Proper placement of AppleTalk routers creates a more efficient network and helps to ensure consistent and predictable routing. Figure 4.21 shows an AppleTalk network that uses a backbone configuration. Only routers should be connected to the backbone.

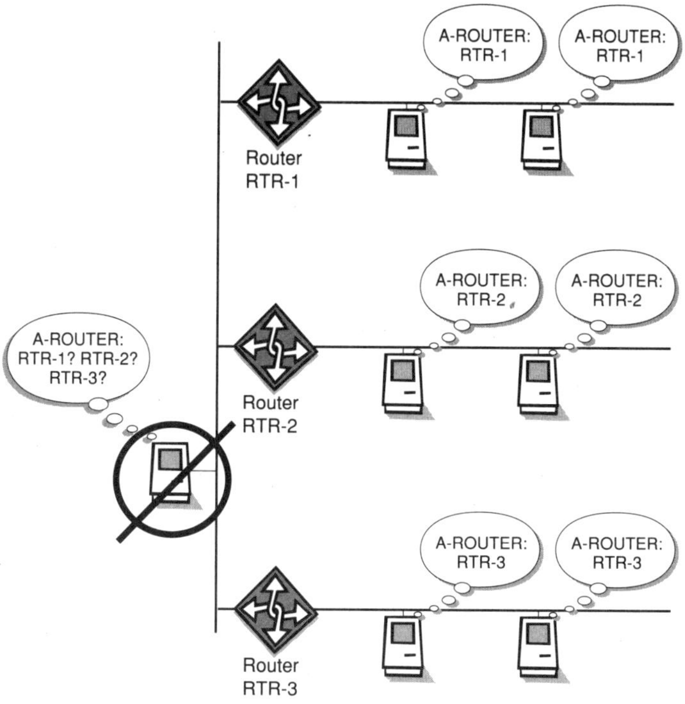

FIGURE 4.21

Limit routers and use a backbone topology.

Proper configuration of an AppleTalk network requires a thorough understanding of AppleTalk addressing. Next we examine the AppleTalk routing protocol, network numbers, network ranges, and zone names.

AppleTalk Network Numbers and Ranges

The AppleTalk network-layer protocol is called Datagram Delivery protocol (DDP). Like other network-layer protocols, DDP addressing includes a network portion and a node or host portion. The 16-bit network portion is called the network number and, like the network number of IPX and the network portion of an IP address, it is assigned by the network administrator (and therefore is subject to human error). One similarity to IPX is the use of an internal network for AppleTalk file and print services. The internal AppleTalk address is specified on the LOAD APPLETLK line on a NetWare server and is not used in a NetWare MultiProtocol Router that has not been configured to support AppleTalk file or print services.

NOTE

You have seen that IPX addresses are expressed as hexadecimal numbers and IP addresses are expressed in dotted decimal format. DDP uses decimal numbers for its network number designation. A 16-bit address space should yield 65,535 network numbers; however, numbers over 65,279 are reserved.

There are two aspects of AppleTalk addressing that are very different from other common network-layer protocols and often confuse network administrators. One issue is the assignment of a range of numbers specifying an AppleTalk network address. This addressing feature appeared in 1989 with the introduction of AppleTalk Phase 2.

Originally AppleTalk used only a single network number, but because the node portion of the network address (called the node ID) uses only 8 bits, the number of nodes on an AppleTalk network could not grow to more than 254. (0 and 255 are reserved.) This restriction is especially limiting considering that user node IDs must be in the range 1–127. Server nodes use IDs in the range 128–254. To allow for network growth, Apple introduced Phase 2. Phase 2 allows a range of numbers to designate a network address, and each network number within that range can support 253 nodes. (0, 255, and 254 are reserved in Phase 2.) You can allow for network growth by supplying one network in the range for every 20 to 30 nodes on the network. For example, if you have 100 Macintosh users on your network you might specify a range of five networks, such as 1001–1005. If significant growth is expected or new nodes often appear on the network (if PowerBooks often attach to the network) use a larger range. It is important when dealing with a network range to apply the same general rules that you would for a single network number. Figure 4.22 illustrates important addressing rules for AppleTalk networks. Always follow these three rules:

- ▸ All routers attached to a common network must use the same network range for that interface.

- ▸ All networks separated by routers must have unique network ranges, and ranges may not overlap.

- ▸ A bridged network must use the same network range on both sides of the bridge.

The second unique and sometimes confusing feature of AppleTalk addressing is the use of AppleTalk zones.

AppleTalk Zones

Zones are logical subdivisions of a network or internetwork. On large internetworks a user may need to select only a few resources from a large selection. For example, users in the Sales department may want to view and use only the Sales department servers, printers, and modems. Users access the Macintosh Chooser and select a zone name (such as Sales) and resource type (such as the file server icon) to see a list of all the Apple-Talk servers commonly used by Sales.

Zones are associated with networks when an AppleTalk router is configured. Figure 4.23 illustrates a network configured with multiple zones. Keep the following rules in mind when setting up zones on a network.

> ► A single zone may be assigned to more than one network. For example, Figure 4.23 depicts a network where the Sales group commonly uses resources on three different networks. You can have the same zone on all three of the networks.

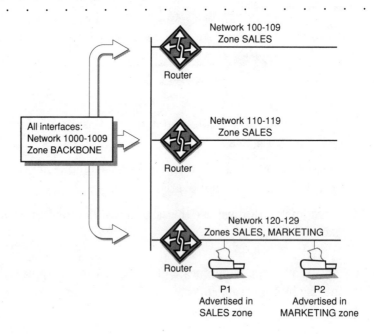

FIGURE 4.23

*AppleTalk zone
configuration*

▶ A single network may have more than one zone associated with it. For example, in Figure 4.23 one network supports two printers. One of the printers is commonly used by Sales and one is used by Marketing. One network printer is advertised in the Sales zone. The other printer is advertised in the Marketing zone.

▶ All routers on the internetwork must agree on the network range and zone name associations. For example, in Figure 4.23, all three router interfaces on the backbone are configured for the same network range and the same zone name information.

Administrators can configure AppleTalk printers to be advertised in a specific zone with the Namer utility (supplied with the printer), and NetWare queues can be advertised in zones specified in the ATPS (AppleTalk Print Services) configuration file. NetWare servers are advertised in the first zone of the internal AppleTalk network. The NetWare MultiProtocol Router allows selection of a default zone.

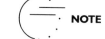 NOTE

Accessing Resources across an Internetwork

When a Macintosh user opens the Chooser, a request for a list of known zones is sent to the source of the last Routing Table Maintenance Protocol (RTMP) packet seen by the workstation. In AppleTalk jargon this is referred to as a ZIP (Zone Information Protocol) request sent to A-ROUTER. When the workstation selects a zone and resource, such as a file server in the Sales zone, a request is sent to A-ROUTER to obtain a list of all file servers that reside in the selected zone. A-ROUTER in turn sends a multicast NBP (Name Binding Protocol) request to all of the networks that share the selected zone. Each of the resources of the selected type in the target networks will return its name to the Macintosh workstation. Figure 4.24 shows how the Macintosh workstation sends requests to find resources and how information is returned to the workstation.

F I G U R E 4.24

*A Macintosh workstation
locates remote resources.*

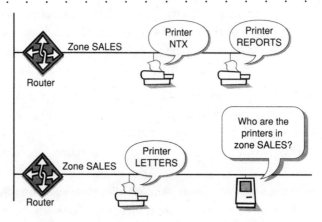

The more networks sharing the selected zone, the more requests are sent from A-ROUTER. For example, if zone Sales is on five networks, A-ROUTER will send requests to each of the five networks. Each resource of the selected type replies to the workstation. If an internetwork is configured with zones spanning many networks and each zone contains many resources, the traffic may increase dramatically because of the large number of replies. Figure 4.25 shows how traffic is increased if a selected zone spans many networks and many resources are on each network.

 NOTE

Requests and replies continue to be generated as long as a user leaves the Chooser open.

Use the following guidelines to minimize the amount of traffic generated by the lookup process:

▸ Assign zones only to networks where users will *commonly* access resources. For example, if the sales department commonly uses the file servers and printers on only three different networks but one individual prints a monthly report on a printer residing on a different network, the Sales zone should be configured on only the three commonly accessed networks. The single user can select the remote printer from a different zone in the Chooser in order to print the monthly report.

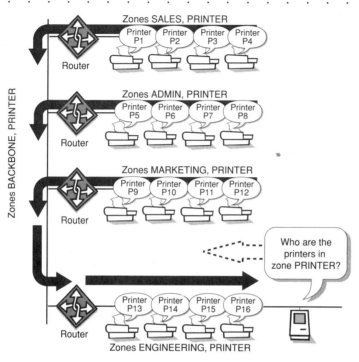

FIGURE 4.25

Locating a common resource in a zone that spans many networks

- Restrict the number of resources on a single network or zone. For example, on a large network, do *not* put a zone called Printers on all networks. Although this may be an easy way for users to see all printer names at once, it dramatically increases the amount of traffic on the network if users often change printers.

- Apple's operating system versions 7.0 and later are capable of peer-to-peer networking. This is accomplished by workstations advertising as an AFP (AppleTalk Filing Protocol) server. If you have 5 dedicated AppleTalk servers and 45 Macintosh workstations advertising resources in the same zone, selecting AppleTalk Servers through the Chooser results in a response from 50 servers. To reduce internetwork traffic you should restrict System 7.x sharing. As you upgrade to System 7.x, establish user guidelines for naming conventions and sharing resources.

Router-to-Router Communication

All protocol suites provide some way to exchange routing information. NetWare and TCP/IP use a protocol called RIP (Routing Information protocol). The AppleTalk equivalent to NetWare RIP, or TCP/IP RIP, is RTMP (Routing Table Maintenance protocol). RTMP packets are sent out every 10 seconds and serve two purposes. First, they provide the current default router (A-ROUTER) for AppleTalk clients, as previously discussed. Second, RTMP allows routers to exchange their routing tables. RTMP informs other routers about all of the networks a router has a valid route to. Every router sets a timer for each of the routes in its routing table. If the routes are not confirmed through RTMP packets before the timer expires, the router changes a route's status from "good" to "suspect" and, eventually, "bad" before removing the route from the routing table. This process is called *aging*. It is common for AppleTalk routes to go from "good" to "suspect" and back to "good" again as the routes are reconfirmed with the next RTMP packet. By default, AppleTalk routers send routing updates every 10 seconds and change the status of a route if it is not revalidated within 20 seconds. If a router's table is too large to send in one RTMP packet, it can be split into more than one packet.

AppleTalk clients also age router information. If a node doesn't see any RTMP packets within 50 seconds, it sets the value of A-ROUTER to 0. When the node detects another RTMP packet it will assign a new A-ROUTER value.

Seed and Non-Seed Router Interfaces   Most routers have network number and zone information configured by an administrator. Some routers, however, learn this information from the network. A router interface that has been configured with network and zone information by an administrator is called a *seed* router interface. An interface that learns its configuration information from the network is called a *non-seed* router in-terface. A NetWare router interface that has the network range of 0–0 is a non-seed interface. This interface intercepts RTMP packets to learn their configuration information. Since non-seed interfaces do not need to be changed when network reconfiguration occurs, this speeds the process of changing network configuration and shortens network downtime.

Keep the following rules in mind when implementing an AppleTalk internetwork with non-seed router interfaces:

▸ There must be at least one seed interface on each network, as shown in Figure 4.26.

▸ On NetWare routers, the internal AppleTalk network is always seeded.

▸ Apple recommends that even in a non-seeded environment, all AppleTalk routing should be shut down for 10 minutes after recon-figuring the network. (This includes all seed and non-seed routers.)

Hop Count Issues Hop counts in AppleTalk are used in much the same way as in NetWare. A source node sets the hop count field to 0 when it sends a packet. Each router increases the hop count by 1. A router should not forward a packet with a hop count of 15 to another router, but it does

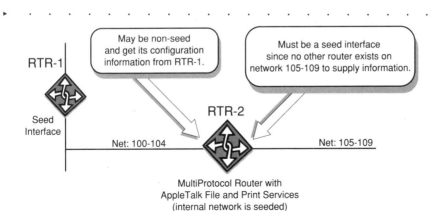

There must be at least one seed router on each AppleTalk network.

deliver it if the receiving node is on a network directly connected to the router. When a router sends an RTMP packet, it specifies the first and last network number in the network address range and the distance (in hops).

"Notifying a neighbor" is a way to speed updates to routers when routes become unavailable. When a route to a network is no longer available (the route status becomes "bad"), a router will notify its neighbor by specifying the network as unreachable. The notification is in the form of a hop count of 31.

Old routing table information is updated whenever newer information specifies a route to a network that is the same number of hops or fewer. Also, routing tables are updated if a router receives any information regarding a table entry with a route status of "suspect" or "bad."

AppleTalk Filtering   You should consider two main classes of filtering for AppleTalk networks if they are available. They are packet filtering and protocol filtering.

Packet filtering is the most flexible and granular filtering available and allows you to specify which packets to restrict based on their node addresses or network addresses. A disadvantage of packet filtering is that it is very CPU intensive since each packet must be examined and compared against the routing criteria.

The addition of any station may also require router configuration changes.

Protocol filtering forwards or restricts packets based on the protocols used. The filtering criteria may be very simple, specifying that any Apple-Talk packets should not be routed through the port connected to the backbone. This type of filtering is generally easy to configure and maintain, but the lack of flexibility to determine station-by-station routing services is a disadvantage. The filtering criteria can be more specific and complex if desired. For example, routers can be configured to exclude certain zones in their ZIP responses. When a Macintosh user opens the Chooser to access remote resources, filtered zones (and all of the devices in those zones) do not display.

The ideal router allows a combination of protocol and packet filtering. Such a router would allow restrictions based on protocol information and exceptions for specific stations.

Phase 1, Phase 2, and Transition Routing   The discussion in this section focuses on Phase 2 AppleTalk internetworks. Phase 1 lacks support for Ethernet 802.3 and Token Ring. Phase 1 also has severe restrictions on the number of nodes on a network and in the use of zones. Simply put, Phase 2 allows for larger networks and more networking options. If possible, use Phase 2 routers. If it is necessary to preserve Phase 1 devices on your network, transition routing provides a means to add Phase 2 networks and devices while maintaining a current investment in Phase 1 devices. This should be a transition to Phase 2, not a long-term network strategy. Some routers such as the NetWare MultiProtocol Router provide the flexibility to route both Phase 1 and Phase 2 packets. Since the router is software based it provides easy reconfiguration when Phase 1 devices are upgraded.

As you have seen, all protocols have their strengths and weaknesses. Ease of use and automated functions for end users can result in additional traffic and more complex configuration issues for network administrators. This chapter has focused on the internetworking issues on local internetworks. (Chapter 9 expands on this chapter, including protocol-specific information that affects performance in the WAN environment.)

The next chapter examines various network blueprints for LAN internetworks.

CHAPTER 5

Internetworking Blueprints:
Local Area Internetworks

This chapter focuses on three internetworks that use bridges and routers for connectivity. These design scenarios include a checklist of network components (Network-at-a-Glance), a brief description of the design scenario company and its network requirements, one or more key features of the network, and finally, one or more blueprints of the network configuration. The network blueprints include network addresses and link types wherever possible. (Network addresses have been changed to ensure privacy of network information for the design scenario participants.)

The three design scenarios in this chapter include the following key features:

▸ Fault-tolerant internetworking

▸ Isolating a network

▸ SNA connectivity

▸ Dealing with interference

▸ High-speed campus backbone

Design scenario participants were supplied with a Design scenario Questionnaire that required a simple overview of their network components, protocols and link types, needs assessment, and reason for internetworking. The participants were asked to submit a blueprint of their network layout—a necessity for large internetworks. Although the detail of the blueprints ranged from simplistic to extremely complex, all participants knew the overall views of their internetworks. These design scenarios illustrate the need for a network blueprint to keep abreast of network configuration changes, possible bottlenecks, and enhancements.

Design Scenario #1: Configuring a Fault-Tolerant Internetwork

This design scenario concentrates on an internetwork that uses redundancy to ensure minimal connectivity downtime. When configuring redundant links, be particularly careful when assigning network addresses. Make a blueprint that lists all assigned addresses.

Refer to Chapter 4 for more information on network addressing for IPX/SPX, TCP/IP, and AppleTalk networks.

 NOTE

NETWORK-AT-A-GLANCE

Listed below are the company name and the major hardware and software components that needed to be included in the internetwork.

Company:	Michigan National Bank
Number of servers:	66
Number of clients:	6502
Network type:	Token Ring
Number of segments:	78
Routers:	18 (39 proposed by year-end 1993) NetWare MultiProtocol Routers
Bridges:	1 IBM source-route bridge
Protocols:	IPX/SPX, TCP/IP, SNA
Applications:	Business-specific and standard desktop applications

NETWORK DESCRIPTION

Michigan National Bank internetworked their LANs in order to allow connectivity among the various departments and branches. This connectivity enabled the offices to share electronic mail and peripherals. The placement of their routers was carefully planned to allow for adequate load balancing between token rings.

The nature of the banking industry makes the need for fault-tolerant links imperative. For this reason, Michigan National Bank used the NetWare MultiProtocol Routers to provide redundant links between their primary backbone and secondary rings. This configuration was used in two of their main offices as well as at the corporate headquarters.

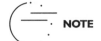 **NOTE** **Michigan National Bank's wide area link configurations are diagrammed in Chapter 10.**

Each office was designed with the same basic configuration in mind: one primary Token Ring backbone supporting IPX and IP traffic. Major network-wide services, such as NetWare Global Messaging and the CD-ROM servers, are connected directly to the backbone ring. A test network is separated from the backbone by a router enabling the network administrator to try out device and application configurations before placing them onto the production network.

KEY FEATURE: REDUNDANT LINKS

As shown on the blueprint diagram in Figure 5.1, this network consists of a primary backbone network that connects to eight secondary networks. MPR-1 and MPR-2 provide redundant links from the backbone (see IPX networks 20, 40, 60, and 70). If MPR-1 becomes unavailable, these networks can still access the backbone through MPR-2. The same redundant link configuration was used for the rings containing IPX networks 90, 11, 12, and 13.

KEY FEATURE: TEST NETWORK

Michigan National Bank participates in many Novell beta programs. Beta testers are required to have a nonproduction test network to load and test Novell's beta products. In this case, network TEST is where their first two NetWare 4.0 servers were installed and tested. In larger networks, a testing

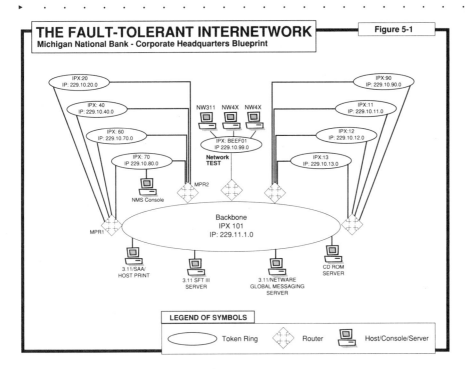

THE FAULT-TOLERANT INTERNETWORK
Michigan National Bank - Corporate Headquarters Blueprint

Figure 5-1

F I G U R E   5.1

Design scenario #1:
Michigan National
Bank-Corporate
Headquarters network
blueprint

ground helps spot configuration errors and possible network conflicts before putting a product on the company network.

Design Scenario #2: Campus Network

This design scenario focuses on how Novell has connected the buildings of its San Jose, California, campus. The network connects six buildings containing approximately 60 LANs, 100 NetWare servers, 4 VAX servers, and 800 workstations. A high-speed fiber optic backbone provides high-performance access to all networks across the campus.

NETWORK-AT-A-GLANCE

Listed below are the company name and the major hardware and software components that needed to be included in the internetwork.

Company:	Novell Inc.
Number of servers:	100 NetWare servers, 4 VAX servers
Number of clients:	800
Network type:	Ethernet, Token Ring, FDDI
Routers:	20
Protocols:	IPX/SPX, TCP/IP, AppleTalk, DECnet, OSI
Applications:	Standard desktop applications, desktop publishing, graphics, presentation packages, network management, custom applications for human resources

NETWORK DESCRIPTION

Novell's San Jose campus is responsible for developing products for network management, internetworking, UNIX connectivity, and messaging. There are also departments for human resources and technical publications, technical support, and education course development. It is necessary to provide connectivity among the engineering groups located in several buildings and connections to the technical support, technical publications, and education departments. Because of the development environment it is important to have a robust network that allows restriction of traffic to some areas while allowing access between the groups. The network is also very dynamic. The number of systems may vary greatly from day to day.

KEY FEATURE: FIBER-OPTIC BACKBONE

To guarantee high availability of the network over a wide range of bandwidth requirements, a high-speed fiber-optic backbone utilizing fault-tolerant FDDI cabling is used to link the campus networks. As shown in Figure 5.2, all of the buildings have an attachment to the FDDI backbone. Many of the buildings were originally wired with thin Ethernet cable, but this was later replaced with a Cabletron 10BaseT cabling system. The Cabletron hubs run Ethernet over fiber to the Novell MultiProtocol Router, which is attached to the FDDI backbone.

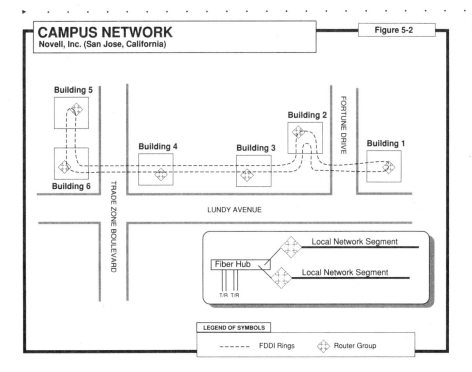

F I G U R E 5.2

Design scenario #2: Novell Inc. San Jose campus. Each building is attached to the FDDI backbone through the NetWare MultiProtocol Router.

Two important considerations in implementing the campus backbone were cable length and cable placement. Some of the fiber cable runs exceeded length specifications for a single link and required fiber-optic repeaters. Connecting all of the buildings required crossing some public streets. A significant amount of time may be required to get the necessary permits to pull cable across public streets.

Design Scenario #3: Interference-Protected LAN

This design scenario concentrates on a network that operates in a harsh environment—a Nimitz-class aircraft carrier. Large electric motors and a powerful search radar inhibit communication using twisted-pair wiring and, in some cases, even coaxial cable. The network has the following characteristics:

- ▶ The network is multi-story (seven stories).

- ▶ The LAN operates in a heavy industrial environment.

- ▶ This LAN is exposed to large amounts of electromagnetic interference.

- ▶ MilSpec standards are enforced.

NETWORK-AT-A-GLANCE

Listed below are the company name and the major hardware and software components that needed to be included in the internetwork.

Company:	U.S. Navy
Number of servers:	2
Number of clients:	250
Network type:	Ethernet, 10BaseF (Fiber)
Number of segments:	3 primary segments
Routers:	3
Bridges:	2 (to be replaced by routers)
Protocols:	IPX/SPX, OSI
Applications:	Word processing, spreadsheets, specialized database

NETWORK DESCRIPTION

This network was installed on the carrier to allow the supply system of the ship to be accessed from all departments onboard. The network backbone resides on the starboard (right) side of the ship only. Long Ethernet segments branch off from this backbone toward the port (left) side of the ship.

The coaxial cable used for the Ethernet network throughout most of the carrier was adequate to shield it against any EMI generated by the motors and machinery onboard ship but could not maintain signal integrity when exposed to the powerful search radar system. A fiber-optic segment was installed in the island where exposure to the search radar system prevents data communication on the network.

Since this network is used to track all supplies for the ship, it must be a reliable system. Interestingly enough, the biggest problem the network faces on a daily basis is the ship's personnel. The sailors have often tapped into the coaxial cable system hoping to improve their television reception. To ensure integrity of the backbone system, redundant links were implemented. For example, as shown in Figure 5.3, if network 50015001 becomes unavailable, the port-side computers can still access the server via networks 50015002 and 50015003.

KEY FEATURE: EMI RESISTANT

The network runs from three stories below the flight deck to the "island." The island is a tower that rises above the flight deck and houses a powerful search radar. Coaxial cable is usually sufficient for EMI shielding, but in extreme conditions fiber should be used. The MilSpec (Military Specification) Standard also dictates that fiber should be used for all new network installations.

KEY FEATURE: SERVER REDUNDANCY

To ensure minimum downtime, the server has been upgraded with SFT III. The high-speed back channel connecting the two duplexed servers ensures that all server resources are still available in the event of a hardare failure. The back channel provides additional redundancy in case of a link or server failure.

FIGURE 5.3

Design scenario #3:
Nimitz-class carrier—
interference-protected LAN

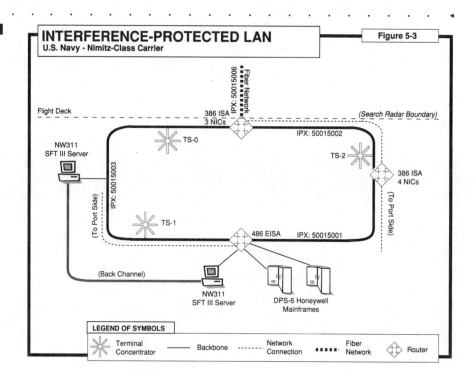

INTERFERENCE-PROTECTED LAN
U.S. Navy - Nimitz-Class Carrier

Figure 5-3

KEY FEATURE: COMMODITY-BASED COMPONENTS

A requirement of this network was the use of off-the-shelf components to ensure that the network could be quickly and easily repaired. All specialized equipment is in the process of being removed from the network. For example, the two proprietary bridges will be replaced with PC-based routers. This enables the ship's technicians to simply swap out a computer system if a router fails. The router is scaled to an EISA 486 platform to ensure maximum performance. As faster processors and bus speeds become commonly available, the router can be upgraded with off-the-shelf components, as well.

The preceding design scenarios illustrate how considerations of fault tolerance, distance/cable limitations, and environmental factors must be included in the design of local internetworks. As we move to the wide area internetwork, key factors include the number of sites to be internetworked, throughput requirements, and service provider offerings. These issues are covered in the next part of this book.

Interconnecting Wide Area Internetworks

Over the past decade, companies have begun to realize the value of intercommunication between branch offices and corporate headquarters. Most major companies that have multiple sites now rely heavily on their communication systems to transfer voice, data, and, often, video between these locations. The need for reliable, efficient, and cost-effective communication is increasing at a quick pace.

Part I of this book focused on the configurations and connectivity options for local LAN internetworks. Part II moves from local internetworks to wide area networks, or WANs. WANs are composed of geographically dispersed networks that are connected via services offered by communication carriers, such as AT&T and US Sprint.

Chapter 6, "Fundamentals of Wide Area Internetworks," provides an overview of point-to-point and switched WAN links, including 56Kbit/s, T1/E1, Fractional T1, X.25, and frame-relay services.

Chapter 7, "Implementing Point-to-Point WANs," discusses the design and configuration options for high-speed links using point-to-point services. This chapter includes several scenarios that depict WAN link needs analysis and costs.

Chapter 8, "Implementing Packet-Switched WANs," examines the design, configuration, and implementation options for packet-switched networks, such as X.25 and frame relay.

Chapter 9, "Implementing Multiprotocol Wide Area Internetworks," deals with the protocol issues specific to WAN communication. Issues involving IPX/SPX, TCP/IP, and AppleTalk are revealed and explained in depth.

Chapter 10, "Internetworking Blueprints: Wide Area Networks," depicts several actual WAN design scenarios. These case studies include a branch office solution, a national network, and an international network.

Part II provides tips and hints for needs analysis, cost evaluation and performance optimization as well.

CHAPTER 6

Fundamentals of
Wide Area Internetworks

Internetworks can connect networks that are geographically dispersed (remote networks). These networks, interconnected across great distances, are referred to as *wide area networks,* or *WANs.* WANs allow networks that are located in different buildings, cities, or states to share data and network resources. There are several options for connecting remote networks into WANs. These connectivity options are called WAN links. WAN link components and configuration options are discussed in this chapter and throughout Part II of this book.

Figure 6.1 shows a WAN internetwork that connects LANs located on the west coast and east coast of the United States.

The WAN shown in Figure 6.1 allows users in the east coast office to log in to the servers located on the west coast, access the databases, and even print at the west coast office if desired. WANs can also connect networks that are located in different countries. For example, a WAN can connect networks for a company that has a main office located in Germany with branch offices in the United States and Canada, as shown in Figure 6.2. This figure shows the three offices connected using a packet-switched network (described later in this chapter).

FIGURE 6.1

WAN internetworks can
connect two or more
networks that are
geographically dispersed.

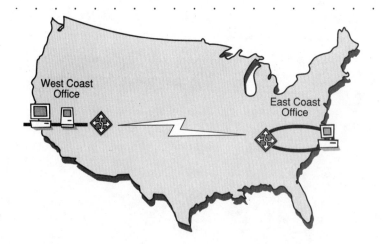

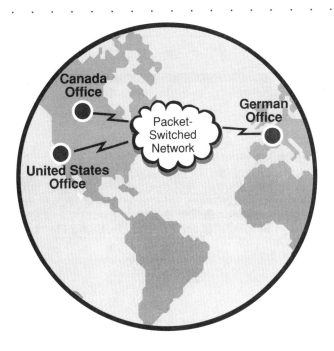

FIGURE 6.2

*Internetworks can also
connect networks that are
located in different
countries.*

There are many options available when connecting remote networks into WANs. This chapter examines the link speeds and the two types of WAN internetworks: point-to-point and multi-point WANs.

Link Types

First, it is important to understand that in most cases, WAN link speeds are not comparable to LAN speeds. If you are installing an X.25 internetwork, for example, do not expect to experience the same throughput as you get on your Token Ring LAN. Figure 6.3 depicts the maximum link speeds of various switched, non-switched, and LAN types.

Speed is a primary concern when selecting the WAN type. Let's examine each of these WAN types and define how each WAN type is used.

*In general, WAN link
speeds are much slower
than LAN speeds.*

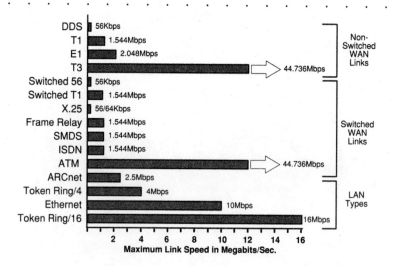

Point-to-Point WANs

As the name implies, a point-to-point internetwork directly connects two
or more separate LANs. "Point-to-point" refers to the topology (or layout)
of the internetwork. The link established between sites is direct, with a dedicated point-to-point line such as a T1 line (discussed later in this chapter).

One example of a point-to-point link is shown in Figure 6.1. In this example, one office is located on the west coast of the United States, another
on the east coast. WAN routers are connected to each network and configured to communicate directly with each other. Clients on each network
use their normal commands and operating systems to access the other
network.

Point-to-point networks can be expanded to include additional sites as
well. For example, in Figure 6.4 we added another site to the example
shown in Figure 6.1. In Figure 6.4, each office has two dedicated lines—one
to each of the other offices.

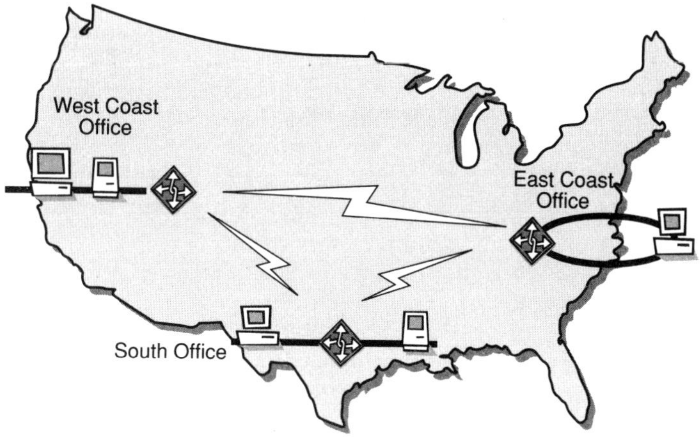

FIGURE 6.4
Point-to-point WAN
connecting three sites

Point-to-point WANs can use either dial-up or dedicated lines, each having unique advantages and disadvantages. This chapter examines the following options for point-to-point links:

- Analog dial-up lines
- Dedicated lines

The chapter also examines and compares the point-to-point link options provided by many (but not all) service providers. These link options include

- 56-/64-Kbits/s
- T1/E1
- 56
- T3/E3

ANALOG DIAL-UP LINES

Dial-up connections are initiated by the routers. When a user has data to transmit to another location, the router dials the desired location to establish the link. The link is terminated once the data has been successfully sent.

Dial-up point-to-point configurations are generally adequate when supporting batch applications, such as point-of-sale transactions and order entry (non–time sensitive). Dial-up is suitable when only occasional connections between offices are required. For example, Figure 6.5 depicts a video rental company that has six offices. Dial-up lines are acceptable in this situation because the video store offices connect to the headquarters office (Chicago, Illinois) only once or twice daily to check on orders processed.

Typical dial-up lines support from 1200bps to 9600bps speeds and are often used when there are few devices and users per network. Costs for dial-up lines are based upon use and can add up quickly. Poor-quality connections and unexpected disconnects are not uncommon.

F I G U R E   6.5

Dial-up lines are sufficient for batch applications and low-volume transactions.

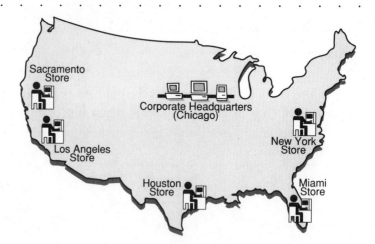

When selecting a modem, users are confronted with a bewildering array of numbers. Here is an explanation of the most common. The "V" series of the international standards specifies modem and signal characteristics. The minimum requirements of any modem should be V.22 and V.22bis. (Any number followed by "bis" or "ter" is the second or third related standard.) V.22 is for 1200bps modems. V.22bis is for 2400bps modems. Prices of modems compliant with the V.32 and V.32bis standards have recently dropped below the $300 mark. These modems allow data rates of 9600bps or 14,400bps. One other standard that is gaining in popularity is the MicroCom Networking protocol (MNP). Different classes of MNP offer error detection and error correction. Class 5 MNP is becoming very popular on higher speed modems because it adds data compression (sending the same amount of data with fewer bits) and effectively doubles the throughput of your dial-up link.

NOTE

DEDICATED LINES

Often referred to as "leased lines" or "private lines," dedicated lines offer greater performance when higher volume data transfers and time-sensitive transactions are required. Dedicated lines can be used in conjunction with multiplexors to enhance communication efficiency as well. Dedicated lines are available from various carriers, including AT&T, US Sprint, and WilTel. Dedicated lines guarantee error-free transmission lines, fixed cost, and low latency. No connection setup is required with dedicated lines.

Figure 6.6 depicts a computer distribution company that has three warehouses. Each warehouse must communicate with the others to check on inventory throughout the day. To accomplish this, each warehouse has installed two dedicated lines in order to connect with each of the other offices. When users at one location want to query the inventory of another location, they simply log in to the desired remote server.

Many types of dedicated services are available and are selected based on the throughput and speed desired. Dedicated lines are billed at a flat monthly rate and often require additional equipment (such as a CSU/DSU) to connect to the leased line.

FIGURE 6.6

Dedicated lines can support
time-sensitive transactions.

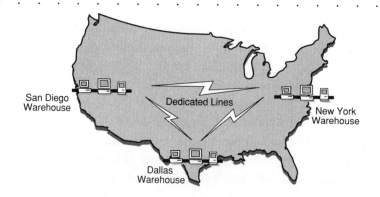

NOTE

**A DSU/CSU (digital service unit/channel service unit) is the device
that sits between your network and your wide area carrier's network. The DSU portion formats data to be transmitted across the
common carrier's digital circuits. The CSU portion processes the
signal and provides loopback testing for digital transmissions to
the network. The design of the CSU must be certified by the FCC
to ensure it can do its job of protecting the public carrier's transmission systems.**

SERVICE TYPES

Various point-to-point WAN services are offered by AT&T, US Sprint,
WilTel, and others. These services include 56-/64-Kbit/s, T1/E1, Fractional
T1, and T3. A brief overview of these services follows. Additional information on these configurations is included in Part III, "Managing and Troubleshooting an Internetwork."

56-/64-Kilobit per Second (Kbit/s) Point-to-Point Service

On the low end of WAN point-to-point services is the 56-/64-Kbit/s service. There are 9600-Kbit/s leased lines but they are becoming less common. For companies requiring relatively inexpensive communication
services, the 56-/64-Kbit/s service is generally adequate. Some areas, such
as western Europe, supply links with full 64Kbit/s service. Other areas,

such as North America and Japan, actually supply only 56-Kbit/s service because of management overhead imposed on the communication link.

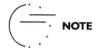

> **Service providers use a digital service number to refer to digital signaling speeds. 64-Kbit/s service is referred to as "DS-0." Refer to Chapter 8 for a listing of digital service numbers.**

NOTE

There are two "flavors" of 56-/64 Kbit/s services: switched and dedicated. A switched 56-/64-Kbit/s service offers dial-up, on-demand service. Costs are based on actual usage time. A dedicated 56-/64-Kbit/s service, however, offers dedicated services that are charged at a flat monthly rate. Unlike dial-up services, dedicated services do not require call setup; for this reason, the connection is faster.

When selecting a point-to-point WAN link, keep in mind that there is a significant difference in speed between a LAN (using between 4 and 10 megabits per second) and a WAN communicating at 56 kilobits per second. Users are often surprised with the drastic difference in response time across a WAN and a LAN.

TI/EI Service

Significantly more expensive than the 56-Kbit/s service, the T1/E1 service offers transmission speeds up to 1.544-Mbit/s for some areas (such as the United States and Japan) and 2.048-Kbit/s for areas that follow the CCITT standard (such as the United Kingdom, Mexico, and Europe).

T1 service is equivalent to 24 DS-0 (64-Kbit/s) channels and is more suitable for links requiring faster throughput than 56-/64-Kbit/s.

Fractional TI Service

Some long-distance telephone companies sell portions of a T1 link for companies requiring greater throughput than 56-Kbit/s links but without the budget for a full T1 link. Fractional T1 services are available in increments of 56-/64-Kbit/s.

T3/E3 Service

T3/E3 services are significantly more expensive than a T1/E1 rate and utilize optical fiber or microwave lines.

T3 service offers the equivalent of 672 DS-0 (64-Kbit/s) circuits—a 44.736-Mbit/s digital transmission rate. E3, offered by companies following the CCITT standard, provides a 34.368 Mbit/s digital rate.

Figure 6.7 depicts a corporate-wide internetwork configured for a manufacturing company that utilizes both 56-Kbit/s and T1 services. From the corporate headquarters in San Francisco, to the distribution plant in Detroit, the company has installed a T1 link. Four separate 56-Kbit/s links have been installed to connect the west coast branch offices to the corporate office in San Francisco. The selection of WAN links was based on the frequency of communication and required transmission speeds.

Packet-Switched Networks

On packet-switched networks, user data is segmented and transmitted via shared circuits to the destination. Each packet carries information used to route the packet through the network. Packet-switched networks are usually the most practical solution for connecting multiple sites and for providing easy access, reliable connection services, and redundant routes.

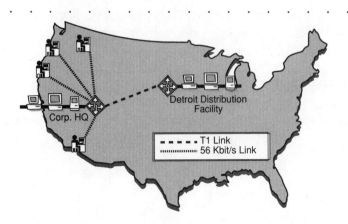

X.25 NETWORKS

X.25 networks provide connection-oriented services for internetworking multiple sites. X.25 networks provide transmission speeds ranging from 9.6-Kbit/s to 56-/64-Kbit/s. Even higher speeds are available in some countries where X.25 networks are even more popular than in the U.S. X.25 is the most cost-effective method for connecting multiple sites that require consistent access and limited data transfers (such as electronic mail and short transactions). X.25 is one of the most utilized WAN schemes worldwide.

Because packet-switched customers are charged based on the amount of data sent across the network, X.25 is not cost effective for high-volume communications. For example, if a company maximizes use of a dedicated 56-/64-Kbit/s line over several hours of the business day, the cost of dedicated lines would be much less than the costs incurred on a packet-switched network.

CompuServe is an example of a large X.25 network. Users dial-in to local CompuServe PADs (Packet Assembler/Disassemblers) from thousands of locations throughout the world. Because of the nature of X.25 networks, they are easy to expand.

 NOTE

One example of an X.25 network is depicted in Figure 6.8. A large international retail chain requires the ability to exchange electronic mail and sales information. Notice that the links into the X.25 "cloud" vary in speed from 9.6-Kbit/s to 19.2-Kbit/s. Since multiple sites can simultaneously transmit to the main office, the corporate office (number 4) is connected to the domestic and international X.25 networks using higher speed lines than the local offices.

To date, X.25 has been an excellent choice for networks with lower bandwidth and lower volume requirements. Modern requirements of LAN-to-LAN wide area network connectivity, however, require facilities that accommodate the high-speed bursts of data characteristic of LAN communications. Frame relay meets these needs and is well suited to address the problems of bursty LAN communications and unpredictable traffic patterns.

▶ · ◀

FIGURE 6.8

An international organization uses two X.25 networks to share information.

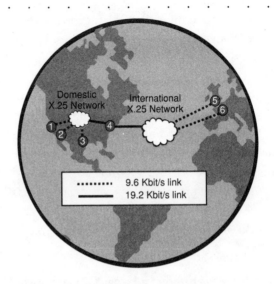

FRAME RELAY

Frame relay is a logical successor to X.25. Like X.25, it is a data-only protocol (not suited for voice or video), and it is a packet-oriented network-access protocol. Frame relay is more efficient and less costly than X.25 while still maintaining the multi-point and redundant route capability of X.25. Frame relay supports transmission rates up to 2 Mbit/s.

On a frame relay network, the responsibility of error detection and correction is placed on the end stations, not the network switches. This is acceptable since many protocols, such as TCP/IP and now Novell's IPX/SPX, use their own error-checking mechanism. Frame relay operates on the principle that "less is more"—less overhead means more throughput. In a packet-switched network, it may be necessary to cross several links in an end-to-end transmission. Elimination of lower level error checking at each switch greatly improves throughput.

An increasing number of service providers are offering frame relay as an option for interconnecting networks. This increasing availability of frame relay will enable businesses without high-speed private WANs to effectively interconnect their LANs.

This chapter has focused on wide area internetworking options using point-to-point and packet-switched networks. You should now be familiar with common WAN types and some configuration options. Chapter 7 examines various WAN designs, configurations, and common implementations using point-to-point links.

CHAPTER 7

Implementing
Point-to-Point WANs

Compared to packet-switched networks point-to-point WAN links are dedicated links and are characterized by high speed and high throughput. You should consider them whenever your requirement is a high volume of real-time data. This could be LAN data or, in the case of high-speed, dedicated links, real-time voice and/or imaging (video) data. Point-to-point links are ideal for real-time voice and imaging data transmissions because these data types cannot tolerate any delay during transmission, as can occur with packet-switched services.

 NOTE

Point-to-point links implemented through satellite links are susceptible to a good deal of latency. This latency can cause considerable delays. If your needs are such that delay is not acceptable, check with your service provider to ensure that your links will not experience delays of this nature.

Designing Point-to-Point Links

To design and implement a point-to-point WAN link, answer the following questions about the link responsibilities:

▶ What type of information will be transported across the links (voice, data, and/or imaging)?

▶ What are the throughput requirements for the links?

▶ How critical are the links to business operations?

The following sections introduce the basic information required to answer these questions.

DETERMINING DATA TYPE

Data can be categorized into three groups: LAN, voice, and imaging. Point-to-point links are well suited to carry all three types. Packet-switched WAN services are not suited for voice and imaging but do well for low-volume LAN data.

Though WAN links are usually associated with computer communication, more and more companies are finding cost savings by incorporating voice and image data over their WAN links. Linking PBXs over these links can provide faster, less expensive voice communication between remote sites. Add imaging (real-time video) and you can use teleconferencing to cut down on the expense of traveling to remote locations for meetings and training.

Incorporating voice and/or imaging over WAN links requires a multiplexor (MUX). A MUX (time division or statistical) combines multiple signals over the same point-to-point link. Figure 7.1 shows two sites connected by a point-to-point link and using MUXs to multiplex data, voice, and imaging over the same link.

Determine whether or not your point-to-point link will need to carry voice or imaging. Ask yourself if you have a situation in which you are making a large volume of long distance calls to your remote offices over standard telephone or 800 services. If so, you may be able to realize substantial savings by having those calls carried over your WAN links. Likewise, teleconferencing has proven itself in terms of saving travel costs to meetings and for training.

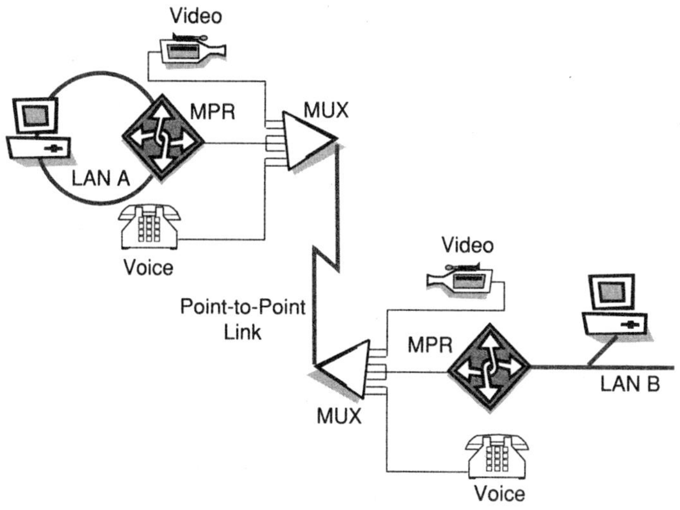

FIGURE 7.1

MUXs combine LAN data, voice, and imaging over the same point-to-point link.

If there is no need for voice or data, and depending on the LAN data volume and delay requirements, you may want to implement or recommend a packet-switched service (discussed in Chapter 8).

DETERMINING THROUGHPUT REQUIREMENTS

Data throughput requirements can be estimated from known LAN throughput. Using a protocol analyzer such as LANalyzer for Windows, you first determine the average utilization of the applications that will be using the WAN link. You make this utilization determination based on the applications throughput on the LANs to be connected. With this information you can determine approximately what percentage of this utilization will be WAN crossover traffic.

NOTE

When approximating the amount of throughput required on a WAN link, be sure to include enough extra bandwidth to accommodate occasional high bursts in WAN traffic and to provide room for future growth. About one third of normal average throughput is recommended. For example, you would add about 12Kbps onto an estimated 35Kbps throughput requirement for a total recommended average throughput of 47Kbps. Always estimate high; it is better to have too much than not enough.

For example, Figure 7.2 shows two LANs connected by a point-to-point WAN link. The average throughput of the applications that will use the WAN link on LAN A is 200Kbps; LAN B is 500Kbps. You estimate that the application will transmit data across the link approximately 5 percent of the time. This means that LAN A's average throughput requirements will be approximately 10Kbps (5 percent of 200Kbps). LAN B's average requirements will be approximately 25Kbps for a combined total of a 35Kbps average throughput requirement for the link.

NOTE

Determining throughput requirements, in addition to studying trends, depends a great deal upon knowing the characteristics of the protocols that will be transporting data between networks. Chapter 9 deals with these protocol-specific issues.

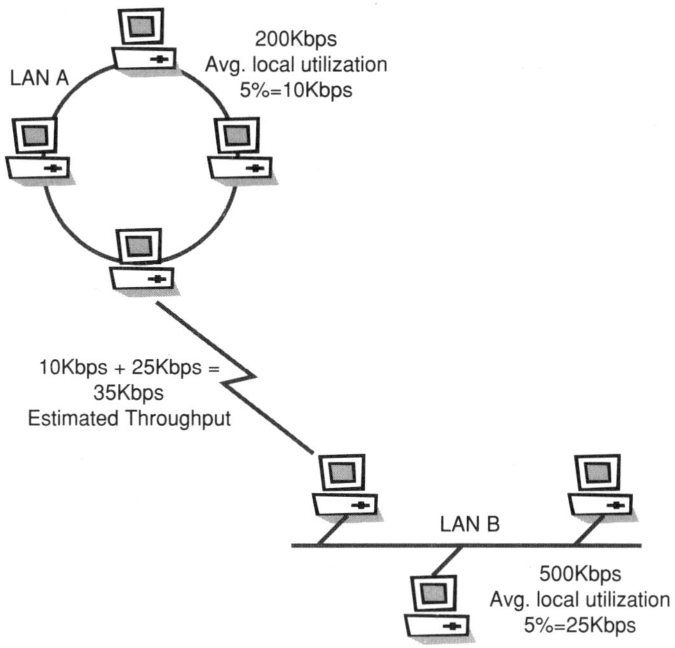

FIGURE 7.2

*Determining LAN
application utilization in
order to estimate WAN link
throughput requirements*

CRITICAL LINKS AND REDUNDANCY

Before ordering point-to-point services, you need to determine how critical the links are to day-to-day business operations. In other words, how critical is link downtime to the revenues of your company? Some types of businesses rely more on WAN links than others. For example, financial institutions and real-time order entry and travel reservation businesses have a very low tolerance for link downtime. Every minute their communication link is down costs them thousands of dollars. These types of business will probably require some type of fault-tolerant redundancy built into their WAN links along with additional management and monitoring capability.

Businesses that are not as affected are those in which each remote site is not as dependent on the WAN links. They typically use the links for e-mail, occasional file transfer, or other batch-type process communication. Because these businesses can tolerate longer downtimes, redundant links and sophisticated managing and monitoring equipment may not be necessary.

A representative design for fault-tolerant point-to-point links is discussed in the design scenarios at the end of this chapter.

Exploring the Available Point-to-Point WAN Link Services

A number of point-to-point WAN services are available from local exchange carriers (LECs) and interexchange carriers (IXCs). In this chapter you will learn about the capabilities of the following currently available digital point-to-point services and how to implement them based on throughput, cost/performance, and fault tolerance:

- ▸ Dataphone digital services (DDS)

- ▸ Switched 56Kbps

- ▸ T-carrier services (T1/E1, fractional T1, T3/E3)

DATAPHONE DIGITAL SERVICES

Dataphone digital services (DDSs) are dedicated digital point-to-point links available from most LECs and IXCs that provide virtually error-free transmission up to 56Kbps. DDS is also available at lower data rates from 2.4Kbps to 19.2Kbps. These lower data rates are known as subrate services. DDS's reliability is due to the fact that DDS is carried over T-carrier channels. (T-carriers are discussed later in this chapter.)

Implementing DDS

DDS is a synchronous service. This means you will have to connect to the LEC's line with a synchronous modem or DSU/CSU. In most cases, these are owned by you as part of your customer premise equipment (CPE).

LANs are connected to a DDS through a remote bridge or router. Figure 7.3 shows a typical 56Kbps DDS link configuration using a NetWare

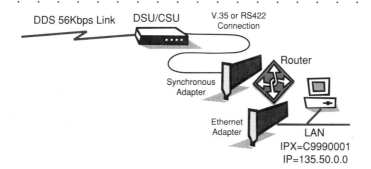

FIGURE 7.3

Standard DDS 56Kbps link to LAN connection using a NetWare MultiProtocol Router, showing example IPX and IP network addresses

MultiProtocol Router (MPR) and a DSU/CSU. The router is attached to the LAN by way of an Ethernet LAN adapter. The DDS connection requires that a synchronous adapter be installed in the router. The synchronous adapter attaches to the DSU/CSU with a V.35 or RS422 cable connection.

DDS subrate LAN connections are similar to the 56Kbps service connections. The difference is that subrate services may use a lower speed RS232C connection between the router's synchronous adapter and the DSU/CSU or synchronous modem.

> **If a remote bridge is used to connect LANs, the LANs and the WAN link all become the same network and would share a single network address for each protocol. Bridges were designed to connect LAN link segments (Token Ring, Ethernet, and so on) and do not provide the services needed to reliably and efficiently connect LANs into internetworks. Routers were designed specifically for this purpose. Use bridges only to connect networks using unroutable protocols (SNA, DEC LAT, and so on).**

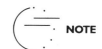

NOTE

DDS Price/Performance

DDS is a relatively (compared to T-carrier services) low-cost digital service. It provides reliable high-throughput point-to-point services with data rates up to 56Kbps.

DDS is tariffed on a monthly basis and pricing is based upon the distance of the link. You will be billed by the IEC or IXC for DDS service depending on whether your service is intra- or interLATA. The monthly rate is the same regardless of how much data is transmitted or how much time the link is used. This means you pay for the link even when you are not using it. Also, there is always an additional charge for the IEC's local loop. The local loop is your service connection to the LEC's central office (CO). In most cases you will be responsible for purchasing and managing the CPE (DSU/CSUs and so on). Some service providers do supply CPE, but this is rare. Check with your local provider for specifics of their services. Figure 7.4 illustrates the DDS tariff responsibilities.

NOTE

A LATA (Local Access and Transport Area) is typically the area serviced by a local exchange company. (After they were initially set up, vendors have been allowed to expand their area or even buy out other vendors, so this is not always the case.) If you are purchasing service within a LATA, you will purchase everything from the LEC. This is known as intra-LATA service. If your WAN needs require that you go between LATAs, you will use an inter-exchange carrier, or IXC, and your service would be referred to as inter-LATA. The LEC is required to provide connections to IXCs at the central office. This is called The Point of Presence (POP).

DDS tariff responsibilities

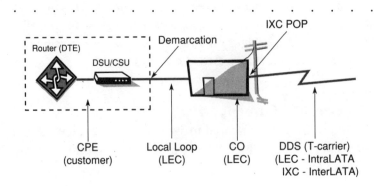

When ordering DDS services, you need to provide the vendor with the following information:

- Data rate requirements (subrate or 56Kbps)
- Area codes of the sites to be connected

DDS Design Scenarios

Following are some typical DDS service design scenarios. These scenarios are intended to provide you with examples of WAN needs assessments and DDS solutions. Be aware that these are examples and the prices shown are based on average DDS service pricing at the time of this writing. Check with your local provider for exact pricing.

- DDS Design Scenario 1: L,S and H, Attorneys at Law

Need: L,S and H has two law offices located in a large city. They are currently transmitting legal document text files between the two offices through a dial-up link and modem at 9600bps. The document load has increased substantially and legal assistants are waiting unacceptable amounts of time for the modem link to be free. In addition, the offices have recently upgraded to a legal document software that allows them to include digital images of evidence. This extra throughput requirement has made their existing link obsolete. Both offices use a NetWare 3.11 LAN operating system and servers.

Solution: A DDS subrate service of 19.2Kbps would allow L,S and H to transmit text and graphics files that average about 1.3MB per file in about a minute and a half each. This is acceptable since they transmit, at most, five documents an hour. Figure 7.5 shows the equipment configuration at both sites. The DDS service was purchased from the LEC, so the local loop charge is incorporated in the monthly tariff.

Table 7.1 shows initial installation (LEC) and equipment (CPE) costs and monthly tariffs for local loop and DDS subrate service for L,S and H, Attorneys at Law.

FIGURE 7.5

*Equipment configuration for
the L, S and H, Attorneys at
Law DDS link*

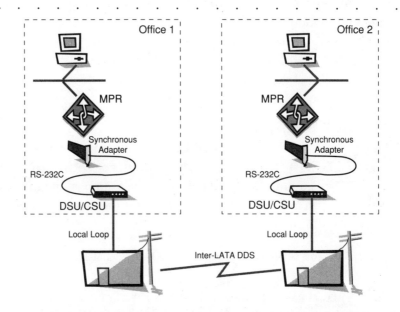

TABLE 7.1

*L, S and H Link Component
and Network Costs*

Components	Hardware/ Software Costs	Local Loop Installation	DDS Monthly Charges
Novell MPR software (2 @ $995)	$1,990.00		
486 PCs (2 @ $3,000)	$6,000.00		
Novell Synchronous/+ NIC (2 @ $1,195)	$2,390.00		
DSU/CSU (2 @ $700)	$1,400.00		
Local Loop (LEC)		$600.00	
19.2Kbps DDS monthly tariff (LEC)			$100.00
Total hardware and installation costs	$11,780.00	$600.00	
Total recurring monthly charges			$100.00

▸ DDS Design Scenario 2: JJ Beene Wholesalers

Need: JJ Beene Wholesalers is a catalog sales company. All of their sales are phone orders. They have three sales locations and one warehouse location. Sales offices are located in Denver, Colorado; Portland, Oregon; and Seattle, Washington. The warehouse is in Portland. Phone orders taken in Denver and Seattle were previously sent via postal services to Portland, where they were processed. This meant customers had to wait a minimum of two weeks for delivery. Competition from another wholesaler made the JJ Beene company realize that if they didn't speed up the delivery time to the customers they could not compete.

Solution: JJ Beene installed order-entry software in all of the sales offices. This software allows orders to be sent over WAN links to an order-processing computer in the Portland warehouse as soon as the order is entered at any of the sales offices.

JJ Beene order takers handle about 1500 calls an hour, 24 hours a day, from all over the world. Company-hired consultants determined that the average data rate from the Denver and Seattle sales offices to Portland would average approximately 20 to 30Kbps with bursts to 45Kbps during peak traffic times. For JJ Beene, dual 56Kbps DDS links from Denver to Portland and Seattle to Portland were the WAN solution. One link from each location was leased from one vendor, the other from another vendor. This dual-link system from different vendors provided redundancy in case of a link failure. The new system cut minimum delivery time to customers to a couple of days.

Figure 7.6 shows the equipment configuration for the JJ Beene DDS WAN. Note the redundancy in the routers and DSU/CSUs. This is to ensure that there is no single point of failure.

Table 7.2 shows the initial installation and equipment costs and local and IXC monthly tariffs for the JJ Beene WAN.

FIGURE 7.6

*DDS equipment
configuration for the
JJ Beene point-to-point
DDS solution*

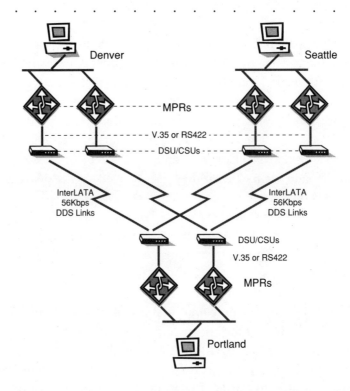

TABLE 7.2

*JJ BEENE WAN Link
Component and
Network Costs*

Components	Hardware/ Software Costs	Local Loop Install	IXC DDS Install	Local Loop Monthly	IXC DDS Monthly
Novell MPR software (6 @ $995)	$17,910.00				
486 PCs (6 @ $3,000)	$18,000.00				
Novell Synchronous/+ NIC (6 @ $1,195)	$7,170.00				
DSU/CSU (6 @ $700)	$2,100.00				
Portland (local loop X 2)		$800.00		$210.00	
Seattle (local loop X 2)		$740.00		$196.00	
Denver (local loop X 2)		$760.00		$200.00	
Portland - Seattle (X 2)			$350.00		$560.00
Portland - Denver (X 2)			$350.00		$1,000.00
Total hardware and installation costs	$45,180.00	$2,300.00	$700.00		
Total recurring monthly charges				$606.00	$1,560.00

SWITCHED 56KBPS SERVICES

Switched 56Kbps service is used primarily as a backup to 56Kbps DDS or to provide a test link for temporary file transfer or management. They are both digital services, with one difference: DDS is a dedicated channel circuit (T1 channels are discussed later in this chapter), and switched 56Kbps is not. This means that when your link is idle, the vendor will use the 56Kbps channel for other users. As soon as your link goes active, whatever 56Kbps channel is available is "switched" to your link. Chances are you will not be using the same circuit every time. For this reason switched 56Kbps services do not have as high a reliability rating as DDS services. However, because the vendor can use the same circuit for a number of users, the services are not as expensive. If your WAN needs are such that reliability is not critical, you can save on monthly tariffs.

Digital services reliability is measured in error-free seconds (EFS) over 24 consecutive hours. DDS services typically run between 99.960 percent and 99.990 percent EFS. Switched 56Kbps service is somewhat less, at about 99.920 percent to 99.970 percent.

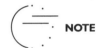 NOTE

Implementing switched 56Kbps service is the same as 56Kbps DDS. Use switched 56Kbps as a lower cost backup to DDS 56Kbps services, or if reliability is not critical, you can order switched 56Kbps as the primary service. Throughput considerations are the same as for DDS.

T-CARRIER BASED WAN LINKS: T1-E1/T3-E3

T-carrier was developed by AT&T to fulfill a need to transmit more than one phone conversation over a pair of wires. It seems that underground cable conduits in large cities had become filled. There was no more room for cable, yet the demand for telephone service was growing. They had a choice: Either enlarge the conduit, allowing more room for cables, or figure out a way to move more than one conversation through a pair of copper wires. AT&T opted for the latter, and T1 was born.

T1 uses two pairs of wires to transmit 24 conversations. One pair of wires is for transmitting, the other for receiving. This makes T1 a full duplex (simultaneous transmit and receive) transmission facility. T1 transmits 24 conversations over two pairs of wires using a technology known as time division multiplexing (TDM). With TDM the 24 conversations are sampled one at a time, 8000 times a second. Each sampling is given an 8-bit value. Samplings are transmitted over the wire in the order in which they were sampled. A single set of 24 samples is called a *frame* (see Figure 7.7). As each frame arrives at the other end it is de-multiplexed into the individual conversations.

FIGURE 7.7

T1 technology showing frame, channels, and data rates

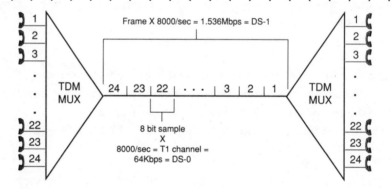

Figure 7.7 shows a single frame, or 24 samples, multiplexed across the T1 connection. Imagine that happening 8000 times a second. That means that each conversation would have an 8-bit sample transmitted 8000 times a second. Eight bits times 8000 times a second is 64,000 bits per second, or 64Kbps. This 64Kbps is the data rate for one conversation, or *channel,* of a T1 link. But remember that there were 24 channels, and 24 times 64Kbps is 1.536 million bits per second, or 1.536Mbps. In actuality, the T1 data rate is 1.544Mbps. This is due to an extra bit, known as a framing bit, that is transmitted with each frame. One extra bit per frame times 8000 frames per second is an extra 8Kbps, which makes up the difference.

T1 was originally designed for voice, but because it uses a digital signal and each sample is 8 bits or 1 byte, T1 is ideal for transmitting computerized data. We said that each channel has a data rate of 64Kbps. In reference to

T1 data rates, this rate is known as digital signal level 0, or DS-0. It is the building block of all T1-related services. The data rate of all 24 channels, or 1.536Mbps, is known as DS-1.

In North America, Australia, and Japan the actual data rate per T1 channel available to the user is 56Kbps. This is because 1 bit per channel may be used for signal management and is not considered reliable.

T1 frames are multiplexed together into superframes to create services with even higher data rates. This is known as the T-1 digital hierarchy. T3 and T4 are currently the most popular high data rate services. The table below shows the different data rate levels of North American T-carrier digital hierarchy.

T-1 through T-2 facilities may use copper wire. T-3 and T-4 require fiber-optic or other high-speed transmission facilities.

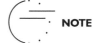

NOTE

SIGNAL LEVEL	FACILITY	# OF T1'S	# OF T1 CHNLS	DATA RATE (MBPS)
DS-0	N/A	N/A	1	0.064
DS-1	T-1	1	24	1.544
DS-1C	T-1C	2	48	3.152
DS-2	T-2	4	96	6.312
DS-3	T-3	28	672	44.736
DS-4	T-4	168	4032	274.760

CCITT T-Carrier Services

In Europe, South America, Mexico, and other countries that use CCITT standards, T1 service is known as E1. It has 32 64Kbps channels for a total data rate of 2.048Mbps. Two of the channels are used for management and signaling requirements. This leaves 30 channels at a full DS-0 data rate, giving E-1 customers a full 64Kbps per channel.

The data rate difference between E1 and T1 services is such that they are not directly compatible. Most IXCs offer some T1 translated services to

CCITT E1 areas. Presently, though, X.25 remains the service of choice between North America and Europe. Like T-1, E-1 is multiplexed into superframes to provide higher data rate services. The following table shows the E-1 digital hierarchy.

SIGNAL LEVEL	FACILITY	CHANNELS	DATA RATE (MBPS)
0	N/A	1	0.064
1	E-1	30	2.048
2	E-2	120	8.448
3	E-3	480	34.368
4	E-4	1920	139.264
5	E-5	7680	565.148

Now that you understand the fundamentals of T1, let's examine the point-to-point services built upon this technology.

T1 Services Defined

Full T1 service is a high-throughput, flexible, reliable, and readily available point-to-point service. Given the 24 separate channels, you can easily multiplex LAN data, voice, and imaging with a single service connection.

The basic hardware connections for T1 service are the same as for DDS. (In fact, DDS services use T1 links.) LAN connections require a remote bridge or router. The router must have a synchronous adapter connected to a DSU/CSU by way of a V.35 or RS422 cable.

T1's channels offer a flexibility in the type of data transmitted. Using a MUX to multiplex different inputs into the 24 channels, you can simultaneously transmit LAN data, voice, and imaging, or the data from two or more LANs can be carried over the T1 link at the same time. MUXs have DSU/CSU functionality built in.

Figure 7.8 shows a typical T1 configuration using a MUX. A typical MUX will allow you to select the number of T1 channels that will be used for each data input. In the diagram the LAN is using the majority of the channels.

> **The multiconnections shown for the various data inputs in Figure 7.8 are for demonstration purposes only. In actuality, a MUX could have only one of each data type connected, and the number of channels assigned to each is user programmable.**

 NOTE

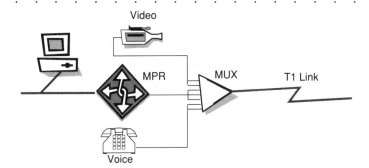

A type of MUX known as a *statistical multiplexor,* or *STAT MUX,* automatically allocates channels to the various inputs as needed. For example, if the LAN in Figure 7.8 is the only input that is transmitting, the MUX would allocate all of the channels for its use. If someone started using the voice service, the MUX would free up channels to handle it.

T-1 Price/Performance   T-1 services are costly. In addition to high monthly tariffs based on distance, they require a high initial investment in equipment and installation/connection charges. Maintaining and managing T1 services requires that you have sophisticated test and management equipment and the technical staff to operate it. Still, T1 can be cost effective if your company has the data volume required to keep a T1 service busy.

Planning Your T1 Internetwork   Given the complexity and cost of T1 services, they should not be implemented without extensive research and planning. There are two important things to keep in mind as you design your T1 internetwork (or any internetwork design, for that matter):

▸ Don't make cost the number one priority when purchasing equipment and services. Low-grade equipment and services will cost you more in the long term in downtime and repair costs.

▸ Plan for the future. Successful businesses and their internetworks are never static. They will continue to grow and change. Build flexibility for growth into your T1 internetwork.

Research your T1 needs and requirements thoroughly. You may wish to seek the advice of a seasoned internetworking veteran if this is your first time. Here are some of the issues to consider and research:

▸ What are the throughput requirements between each site? (If you haven't guessed by now, this is somewhat important.) Are DS-1 data rates justified? Will data rates higher than DS-1 (DS-3 or DS-4) be required?

▸ How critical will the links be to your business operations? Will some form of backup be required? You may wish to consider not only redundant T1 links but redundancy in vendors as well.

▸ Does your PBX support T1 connections? This will make integrating voice much easier. Check with your PBX vendor.

▸ Is the technical expertise at your company such that you may require an outside consultant? You may consider contract consulting to help with the initial design and implementation of your T1 internetwork. Many internetworking resellers or T1 vendors can supply this type of help.

▸ Will you need to hire or train existing technical staff to manage and maintain the T1 equipment and links? In most cases you will be responsible for managing and diagnosing the T1 link. You will need technically competent staff to do this.

▸ Where will the T1 equipment be located? T1 CPE should be in a climate-controlled room. Check to make sure there is an ample supply of power available. You should also consider security issues when determining a suitable location.

▸ Does the telephone wiring in your building meet the T1 specifications? T1 connections require two pairs of unshielded twisted-pair telephone wiring. However, many times the wiring does not have the proper number of twists per foot, or junction boxes and cable splicing are not up to standards for quality. You may want to consider having a T1 vendor inspect your wiring for compliance with T1 specifications.

Once you have researched your needs, you will have to plan and design the T1 internetwork. This is where you actually determine the type of equipment that will be necessary to fulfill your needs, the location of the equipment, and the management scheme you will use to support your links. In addition to the T1 interconnecting equipment (MUXs, DSU/CSUs, routers, and so on), there are also management and troubleshooting equipment considerations. Many vendors provide T1 diagnostic analyzers and management software.

Part of the planning and design process should include the hiring or training of support personnel. The importance of on-site monitoring and managing of your T1 equipment and services cannot be overstated.

Once you have researched and planned your T1 internetwork, you will have to purchase T1 CPE and services.

Purchasing the T1 CPE and Services   Once you have determined your needs and have designed the T1 internetwork, you will have to purchase the CPE. T1 is a mature technology. This means that vendors have been developing and selling T1 hardware for a number of years. It also means there are a lot of them, thus providing a large range of products to choose from.

You can research equipment by talking directly with the vendors or by contacting an internetworking reseller. A good reseller can not only help you determine the best equipment for your needs but can also help with design, implementation, and T1 vendor negotiations.

When purchasing the CPE, look for vendor reputation (warranty coverage, response to in-warranty failures, and so on), and equipment features that meet your design requirements. For example, you may have decided on a management scheme for your T1 links using SNMP protocol. Therefore, the equipment you purchase should support some type of SNMP agent compatible with your management design specifications.

A number of LECs as well as IXCs offer T1 services. Some common T1 vendors are

AT&T

Wiltel

MCI

US Sprint

Obtain proposals from as many as you can. Most vendors are willing to spend a good deal of time talking to you about your needs. Here are some issues to be aware of before you start negotiations with vendors:

▶ Many vendors offer discounts if you can guarantee to purchase the service for a specified number of months. The longer the time you can guarantee, the lower the price.

▶ Depending on your location, T1 circuits may not be readily available. You may have to wait a number of weeks after ordering before they are installed.

▶ You will have to contact both an IXC and an LEC for interLATA T1 services—the IXC for the T1 service, the LEC for the local loop connection. If your T1 services will be intraLATA, the LEC may be able to supply both.

T1 Design Scenarios

Following are two design scenarios involving the design and implementation of T1 services. First is a simple (if such a thing is possible for T1) design scenario, followed by a more complex one.

▶ Design Scenario 1: K. Watt Electronic Component Mfg

Need: K. Watt Electronic Component Manufacturing has two manufacturing locations. One is in Dallas, Texas, the other in Los Angeles, California. Each location employs about 800 people. Costs for phone service and travel between sites for meetings are becoming a problem. K. Watt executives have decided on T1 service to allow them to incorporate voice and teleconferencing facilities as well as replace the 56Kbps LAN data services they currently have.

Solution: The K. Watt Information Services (IS) department, along with a hired outside internetworking consultant, decided on the design shown in Figure 7.9. As you can see, there is no redundancy in T1 links or CPE. This is because the T1 link itself is not critical to business operations. In other words, K. Watt can tolerate a fair amount of T1 downtime for repairs. Voice communication can fall back on the company's 800 services, and teleconference meetings can be rescheduled. LAN data transfer will still happen over backup switched 56Kbps links.

Rather than hiring experienced T1 technicians, K. Watt put three of its IS technicians through a T1 diagnostic and management certification course sponsored by a T1 diagnostic equipment manufacturer.

Table 7.3 shows the initial equipment and installation costs and the monthly tariffs for the K. Watt company.

▶ Design Scenario 2: Cash, Kash, and Cache Investment Consultants

Need: CK&C Investment consultants specialize in buying and selling investment securities. They have offices in New York, Chicago, and San Francisco.

FIGURE 7.9

K. Watt T1 link design

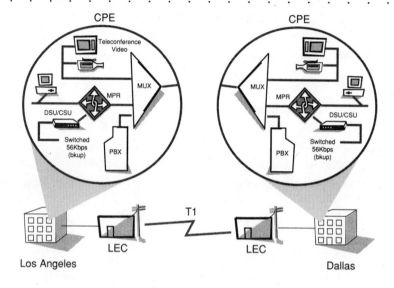

TABLE 7.3

K. Watt WAN Link Component and Network Costs

Components	Hardware/ Software Costs	Local Loop Install	IXC Install	Local Loop Monthly	IXC Monthly
Novell MPR software (2 @ $995)	$1,990				
486 PCs (2 @ $3,000)	$6,000				
Novell Synchronous/+ NIC (4 @ $1,195)	$4,780				
T1 MUX (2 @ $4000)	$8,000				
56Kbps DSU/CSU (2 @ $700)	$1,400				
Teleconference Equipment (2@$10,000)	$20,000				
Los Angeles (T1 and 56Kbps)		$1,000		$640	
Dallas (T1 and 56Kbps)		$760		$420	
Los Angeles - Dallas (T1 service) $2,000 base + 1200 miles @ 3.30/mi			$350		$5,960
Los Angeles - Dallas (switched 56Kbps)			$350		$670
Total hardware and installation costs	$42,170	$1760	$700		
Total recurring monthly charges				$1,060	$6,630

A large amount of voice and LAN data throughput is required between sites as CK&C buys and sells stocks and securities by computer on both coasts. Any WAN links would be critical to business operations.

Solution: Figure 7.10 shows how a redundant T1 internetwork was implemented. CK&C decided on a mesh topology, or the "triangle" approach. Each site has dual connections with a link to every other site. If any link fails, communication will still happen through another route. For example, if the link goes down between Chicago and New York, Chicago can still communicate with New York by way of its link to San Francisco and the San Francisco–to–New York link.

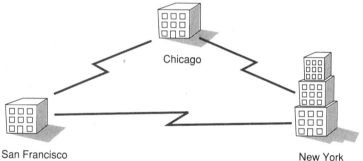

Chicago

San Francisco

New York

FIGURE 7.10

How a redundant TI internetwork was implemented

Implementing redundant T1 links would not make much sense without redundant MUXs. (Redundancy for the PBX and router may also be considered.) One advantage of the mesh topology approach is that the redundant equipment is active and in use rather than sitting idle, waiting for a failure. Figure 7.11 shows the equipment requirements for each of the CK&C sites.

CK&C's T1 internetwork was important enough to justify the hiring of specialists to manage and maintain the equipment. Table 7.4 shows the initial equipment and connection costs and the monthly tariff for the CK&C T1 internetwork.

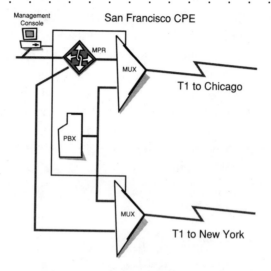

F I G U R E 7.11

Equipment requirements
for each CK&C site

T A B L E 7.4

CK&C WAN Link Com-
ponent and Network Costs

Components	Hardware/ Software Costs	Local Loop Install	IXC Install	Local Loop Monthly	IXC Monthly
Novell MPR software (3 @ $995)	$2,985				
486 PCs (3 @ $3,000)	$9,000				
Novell Synchronous/+ NIC (6 @ $1,195)	$7,170				
T1 MUX (6 @ $4000)	$24,000				
Chicago local (X2)		$950		$840	
New York local (X2)		$1,050		$1,320	
San Francisco local (X2)		$900		$800	
Chicago - New York (T1 service) $2000 base + 820 miles @ 3.30/mi			$350		$4,706
Chicago - San Francisco (T1 service) $2,000 base + 2000 miles @ 3.30/mi			$350		$8,600
San Francisco to New York (T1 service) $2,000 base + 2,800 miles @ 3.30/mi			$350		$11,240
Total hardware and installation costs	$43,155	$4900	$1050		
Total recurring monthly charges				$2,960	$37,852

FRACTIONAL T1 SERVICES

Perhaps your business requires higher data rates than 56Kbps DDS but the required data rates do not justify the expense of full T1 services. To meet this need a number of T1 vendors offer fractional T1 services, or FT1. FT1 allows you to purchase two or more T1 channels. Data rates increment by DS-0 data rates. For example, four channels would provide a data rate of DS-0 × 4, or 256Kbps. Planning and designing an FT1 connection is the same as for T1.

FT1 cost is less than full T1 service up to about 8 to 12 channels. (It varies with distance and the vendor.) This is the break-even point. After that it becomes more cost effective to have full T1 services.

You have seen how point-to-point links can provide high throughput with minimum delay over private dedicated circuits. They are ideal for high-volume data-transfer situations that require voice and imaging in addition to computer data. You have also learned that point-to-point links (especially T1, T3, and so on) are very expensive and require a high level of technical expertise to implement and maintain. In Chapter 8 you will discover other available WAN service options that are not as expensive and that do not require the on-site technical expertise.

Implementing
Packet-Switched WANs

Packet-switched WAN services, like X.25 and frame relay, provide low (DS-0 and below) to high (DS-1) throughput at a relatively low cost (as compared to T1 services). Lower cost is achieved because switching resources are shared between subscribers.

A disadvantage of packet-switched links (currently) is that they tend to be slower than point-to-point links. By "slow" we mean on the order of a few seconds, or even fractions of a second. However, when you are talking over the phone or communicating with voice and image in a teleconference, those small delays make communicating difficult and often confuse users. Until faster methods of packet-switched services are available to overcome this delay, packet-switched services are considered unacceptable for real-time voice and imaging.

Packet-switched services may not currently be suited for voice and real-time imaging, but with lower relative pricing and throughput up to DS-1, packet-switched circuits are ideal for computer data traffic. When you are copying a file, waiting fractions of a second or even a couple of seconds over the speed of the LAN is tolerable.

Packet-switched services support a logical multiplexing of connections from one point to many points without dedicated circuits. Logical multiplexing allows you to have more than one logical connection from a site to multiple sites using a single connection to the provider. For example, Figure 8.1 shows site A with packet-switched connections to three other sites. Using logical multiplexing, a router at Site A could have a TCP/IP connection to Site B, an IPX connection to Site C, and an AppleTalk connection to Site D.

The cloud in Figure 8.1 represents the packet-switched network of the service provider. It is typically referred to as the public data network (PDN). Some providers call their networks value-added networks (VANs). VANs usually offer additional services such as e-mail and Bulletin Board Service (BBS).

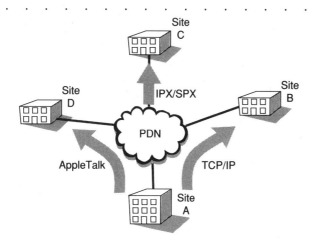

FIGURE 8.1

*Packet-switched networks
provide logical multiplexing.*

X.25 and Frame Relay Described

There are two common packet-switched services available as of this writing: X.25 and frame relay. X.25 is an old technology available throughout most of the world. Frame relay is a newer technology and is currently not available in all parts of the world. In this chapter you will first learn about each of these packet-switched technologies and then learn how to design and implement them.

X.25

X.25 was developed by CCITT in the early 1980s and was later adopted by the International Standards Organization (ISO). It was developed during a time when most transmission lines were copper and conditioned for voice frequencies. Transmitting data over this type of medium was inefficient at best. To cope with this environment, the X.25 protocol was given a substantial amount of error-recovery capability.

Figure 8.2 shows the major phases of an X.25 connection. First, special packets are transmitted to establish the route between end stations or data-terminating equipment (DTE). In this case the DTEs are Novell MultiProtocol

Routers. These packets contain the address of the destination end station. Connections made based on addresses contained in the packet are said to be point-to-many-point connections because, depending on the address, the connection could be made to any end station attached to the network (cloud). All packets transmitted in both directions will use the established route. This type of point-to-many-point connection over a route established by a connection sequence is known as a *switched virtual circuit* (SVC).

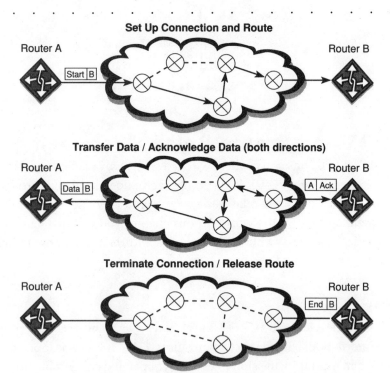

FIGURE 8.2

The three phases of an
X.25 connection:
(1) Establish route,
(2) Transfer data,
(3) Clear connection

Once the route has been established the transfer data phase begins. Every packet transmitted is checked for errors. All packets received are acknowledged by the DTE. Special management packets request retransmission of any corrupted packets. Last, the connection is terminated using special connection-termination packets.

This process of establishing routes and providing built-in error recovery became known as connection-oriented, or guaranteed, delivery. Guaranteed delivery has a price, though: throughput. It takes a substantial amount of overhead to guarantee delivery of packets and it is paid for in throughput.

Transmission technology has grown more reliable since X.25 was developed. Faster, more reliable media, like fiber optics, are now widely available. Networking protocols have put the burden of responsibility for error recovery on the end stations and not the network. Thus, new packet-switching technologies, like frame relay, do not need to guarantee delivery of packets and therefore are not handicapped with the overhead.

Based on these facts you might think that X.25 has outgrown its usefulness as a WAN link. Well, not yet. X.25 is a good solution for the following:

- ▸ International communication

- ▸ Small transactions (credit card verification, ATM, and so on)

- ▸ Terminal-to-host traffic (with PAD local echo)

Frame relay is not currently available in most parts of the world, and we saw in Chapter 7 how T1 and E1 are not compatible. This means that to date, X.25 is still the only WAN transmission method that is readily available on a global basis. You can call your local WAN or VAN vendor today and order an X.25 connection to just about anyplace in the world. True, it is outdated technology and not the fastest transmission method available, but it still plays an important part in global communication.

X.25 is good for communications that require small transactions such as credit card verification and automated teller machine transactions. This is because X.25 can carry data in the packets that set up the route.

Because it is a low-volume communication, terminal-to-host traffic works well with X.25. Terminal traffic is made up of single characters or small blocks of data. Because of this, X.25 requires a packet assembler-disassembler (PAD) to group characters together to form a packet (see Figure 8.3). The

PAD also provides polling for the terminals so the host does not have to poll the terminals across the network.

The PAD should provide local echo to the terminals. A terminal sends a character and relies on the host to echo back a character to paint the screen. Without local echo from the PAD, the delay in communication from the terminal to the host while the PAD collects enough characters to make a packet—transmits the packet, waits for a response packet, disassembles the characters— is usually unacceptable for the user.

NOTE

FIGURE 8.3

X.25 terminal-to-host connection

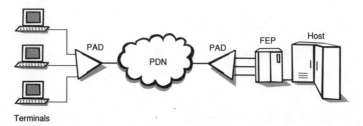

What X.25 is not good for is client/server connections where a large throughput is required. Those types of applications are better suited for frame relay. Terminal-to-host communication produces small, fixed-size packets. Client/server communication produces a large number of variable-size bigger packets. In addition, client/server connections are not as tolerant of delays between requests and replies as terminal-to-host.

X.25 is actually one protocol in a family of protocols. Most of these are CCITT protocols, but a few are ANSI specifications. These protocols span the bottom three layers of the OSI model and address only the connections between the DTE and DCE. They do not cover the internal switching of the PDN. Figure 8.4 shows a diagram of the components of an X.25 connection and the major X.25 protocols.

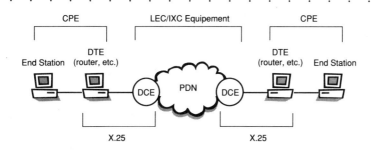

FIGURE 8.4

Components and protocols
of an X.25 WAN link

OSI Layer	X.25 Protocol
Network	X.25
Data Link	Link Access Protocol-Balanced (LAPB)
Physical	X.21, X.21bis, RS232, V.35, RS422

FRAME RELAY

Frame relay is a packet-switched technology derived from X.25. It is basically X.25 without the overhead. Because of the reliability of today's transmission media there is no longer the need for the overhead of connection-oriented guaranteed delivery found in X.25. The responsibility for what little error recovery is required is put on the end stations. This is not a problem since most networking software was developed to handle error recovery (OSI Transport Layer services).

Because it does not have to deal with the overhead associated with guaranteed delivery services, frame relay can provide a much greater throughput for a lower price than X.25.

The X.25 overhead that is stripped away to make frame relay faster represents the OSI network-layer services. This leaves no provision for addressing the destination network. Because of this, frame relay is currently not a point-to-many-point service like X.25. To compensate for this lack of addressing capability, frame-relay addressing is programmed into the vendor's switches (routers) when you order the service. This creates a permanent virtual circuit (PVC) and is currently the only way frame-relay services can be ordered. This means you must order PVCs to all the desired remote sites when you order the service.

Designing a Packet-Switched WAN

Designing a packet-switched WAN is much the same as designing a point-to-point link. Many issues, such as the much-talked-about throughput, are the same. However, the differences in the inherent features and the way services are provided require a somewhat different approach to designing packet-switched links.

DETERMINING THROUGHPUT REQUIREMENTS

When estimating the throughput requirements for point-to-point links between multiple sites, you knew there would be a dedicated link between any two sites. You simply (well, somewhat simply) determined how much each site would be transmitting to the other, and your task was complete. In other words, you could figure throughput for each link independently of the others. With packet-switched links between multiple sites, things become a little more complex.

Figure 8.5 shows a multilocation packet-switched WAN. The first thing you will notice is that there is only one link from each site to the cloud. You determine the total throughput to and from each site to each remote site before ordering the service. You may find that each site requires a different data rate.

Let's examine how you would estimate the average throughput for one site in a multiple-site packet-switched network. Site A in Figure 8.5 has a total estimated average throughput to all other sites of 67Kbps. This can be determined by pretending there is a point-to-point link between A and the other sites. First, determine throughput requirements from A to each of the sites, as you would for a point-to-point link; then add them together.

Add the throughput from each remote site to Site A. In the example, the estimated average throughput from other sites to Site A is 50Kbps.

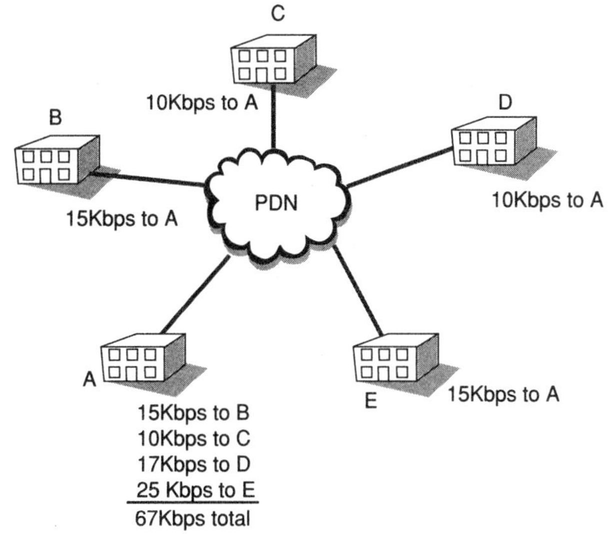

FIGURE 8.5

Example of determining
throughput requirements
for a packet-switched
WAN link

Therefore, you would order a packet-switched service with a total average throughput of 117Kbps (67Kbps + 50Kbps) for Site A.

What, you may ask, about the one-third extra bandwidth for the growth factor used when ordering point-to-point links? Packet-switched networks can provide momentary extra bandwidth, so having extra bandwidth to handle occasional traffic bursts is not a problem. You will learn about some of the options available to you when we discuss how to order X.25 and frame-relay services later in this chapter.

X.25 AND FRAME-RELAY HARDWARE REQUIREMENTS

X.25 and frame relay require the same customer premise equipment (CPE):

▶ Data Terminating Equipment (DTE)—a router, bridge, or other intermediate device that supports X.25 protocol

▶ An RS232, RS422, X.21, or V.35 connecting cable

▶ A synchronous modem or DSU/CSU to connect the DTE to the local loop

Figure 8.6 shows typical customer premise equipment for a packet-switched network using a Novell MultiProtocol Router, a Novell synchronous/+ link adapter, and a DSU/CSU.

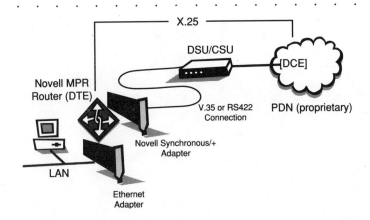

FIGURE 8.6

Typical packet-switched customer premise equipment

PURCHASING X.25 SERVICES

X.25 can be purchased as a switched virtual circuit (SVC) or as a permanent virtual circuit (PVC). It is available at data rates up to 56Kbps (64Kbps in Europe). SVC is a point-to-many-point service and allows you to connect to any DTE connected to the network. A PVC is a virtual circuit permanently established from one site to another. PVCs are usually less expensive and may be desirable in situations in which you are expecting to communicate on a fairly consistent basis with only a particular site. This saves the time needed to establish and clear a route.

NOTE

Remember that the X.25 throughput you pay for includes the management overhead for guaranteed delivery, and this must be factored into your average throughput requirements. This overhead is almost 100 percent of your required throughput! So if you require 19.2Kbps you should order a 38.4Kbps X.25 link.

X.25 is not a tariffed service. It is offered mostly through value-added network vendors that specialize in X.25 services (CompuServe and BT Tymnet, for example). Service costs can be and often are negotiated. Common practice is that you will be billed monthly for a local loop access and a port charge. The local loop is the connection to your premise and the port charge is a connect charge to the vendor's switch. These charges are usually combined. In addition, you will be billed monthly for either your usage, based on kilopackets, or by the access time, usually by the hour. Check with your vendor for specifics about their X.25 service options.

PURCHASING FRAME-RELAY SERVICES

Frame relay currently provides packet-switched services from 56Kbps to DS-1 (1.544Mbps). It is currently available only as a PVC. You will need to provide the vendor with the sites to be connected and the throughput requirements of each.

The throughput requirement will determine the committed information rate (CIR) of each site. The CIR is the throughput guaranteed by the vendor and is what your monthly tariff is based on. For this reason it is a good idea to estimate on the low side for throughput because frame-relay vendors, in most cases, allow you to transmit bursts above the CIR for short periods of time. For example, you may have a CIR of 56Kbps. This is what you pay for monthly. However, you may actually be transmitting bursts of traffic up to 64Kbps or even higher from time to time. Some frame-relay vendors even allow you to order periods of higher throughput on an as-needed basis.

Frame relay provides a much higher throughput for the price compared to X.25 and is ideal for client/server and LAN-to-LAN communications. This is because frame relay does not have to support the high overhead for link management that X.25 does and because vendors use high-speed, high-reliability links such as fiber optics and microwave.

The more sites you are connecting to your frame-relay network, the more cost effective it becomes. This is due to the frame relay's tariff structure. For example, Figure 8.7(a) shows a frame-relay PVC between two sites, A and B. It has been determined that 64Kbps are required for data throughput between the sites. Therefore, each site purchases a CIR of 64Kbps, which costs about $1200 per month each, for a combined cost of $2400 for a 64Kbps link between Sites A and B.

NOTE   **The frame-relay tariffs quoted in this example are for demonstration purposes only and should not be used as a basis for purchasing frame-relay services. Check with your vendor for current tariffs.**

In Figure 8.7(b), a PVC between Site A and Site C has been added. It will also require 64Kbps throughput to Site A. So Site C purchases a CIR of 64Kbps at $1200 per month. Site A adds another 64Kbps to its CIR to accommodate Site C. But notice that even though Site A's CIR has doubled, the cost went up only $220, from $1200 to $1420. Now there is a combined data rate of 128Kbps between Sites B and C to Site A at a combined monthly cost of $3820. You can see that even though the data rate between the remote sites and Site A has doubled, the cost has not.

In Figure 8.7(c) Site D has been added. Again, it will require a PVC to Site A with a CIR of 64Kbps at $1200 per month. Site A will again have to increase its CIR by 64Kbps to accommodate Site D. Notice that Site A now has a CIR of 192Kbps at a monthly tariff of only $1600. This frame-relay network now has a combined data rate of 192Kbps between Sites B, C, and D to Site A at a total monthly tariff of $5200. You can see how the tariff structure of frame relay can save you money on internetworks with multiple sites.

In addition to the CIR, you will have to factor in the monthly local loop and port connect charges from your LEC.

MANAGING AND MONITORING PACKET-SWITCHED LINKS

The only parts of a packet-switched link that are dedicated to you are the CPE and local loop connection to the LEC. This is also your single point of failure. If the link is critical enough to justify redundancy, the local loop and CPE are the only parts you have to worry about. If equipment fails in the

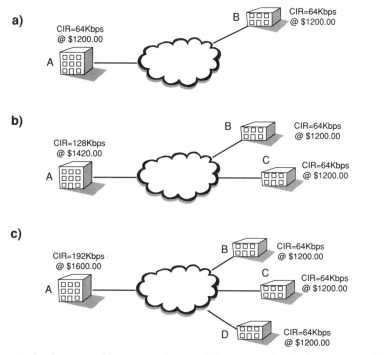

FIGURE 8.7

*Calculating frame-relay CIR
and monthly tariffs*

packet-switched network, connections will automatically be rerouted by the vendor. This is in contrast to T1 services, for which you lease a dedicated link from point to point.

Most DTEs (routers, bridges, and so on) and DSU/CSU vendors are offering built-in management capabilities, typically of the SNMP variety. For example, Novell's MultiProtocol Router (MPR) has management and monitoring capability accessible through Novell's NetWare Management System (NMS) console. Because the MPR uses standard SNMP and SNMP-compliant enterprise MIBs, it can also be managed and monitored by other vendors' SNMP-compliant management stations. Check with equipment vendors before purchasing to evaluate their particular management capabilities.

Other vendors offer X.25 and frame-relay diagnostics equipment for troubleshooting connections between the DTE and the vendor's DCE. Many of these can be monitored remotely via a sideband asynchronous link.

The asynchronous link allows the management station to maintain communication with the WAN equipment in spite of network failure.

You can see that packet-switched services are ideal for low-cost, low-to-high-speed, terminal-to-host, and LAN-to-LAN WAN communication. As packet-switched technology advances and the speed at which they operate increases, it will become common for voice and imaging data to move across packet-switched links. In addition, the time is close at hand when high-speed packet-switched WAN technologies such as cell relay will provide throughput speeds in excess of 2 gigabits per second up to the LAN desktop. This technology will help us create a truly global network.

CHAPTER 9

Implementing Multiprotocol Wide Area Internetworks

In this chapter you will learn the do's and don'ts of implementing networking protocols over wide area links—specifically, TCP/IP, IPX/SPX (NetWare), and AppleTalk protocol suites. But first, a word about connecting networks into wide area internetworks.

The network layer of the OSI model outlines services and responsibilities for routing data between networks. IP (of TCP/IP), IPX, and AppleTalk's DDP are network-layer protocols. Their job is to route packets of data across multiple networks independent of the underlying network media (Ethernet, Token Ring, and so on). To do their job these protocols operate from end stations and a device known as a router. They have an overall view of the entire internetwork. They routinely check their information against that of other routers, make decisions about the best routes to a particular destination, and alert other routers and end stations of possible routing problems. That is the job they were designed to do.

The data-link layer of the OSI model outlines services and responsibilities for moving data between devices connected to a common link. Ethernet, Token Ring, LLC, and HDLC are data-link layer protocols. Their job is to move data between devices connected to a common link segment. A bridge is a data-link layer device. They were designed to load balance link segments that have exceeded the capabilities of the media (distance, number of devices, and/or traffic load tolerances) by acting as a repeater (increase the distance and device limitations) and by filtering link-level traffic (isolate and control traffic between segments).

Routers were designed for internetworking. Bridges were designed for connecting LAN link segments. Routers should be used whenever possible to connect networks. Bridges should be avoided except in a couple of instances where routers cannot do the job:

> ► In those rare cases when you have data to move between networks and it does not support a network-layer protocol (SNA, for example, but even it can be routed using the X.25 and QLLC protocols), it is highly recommended that you use a brouter until such time as all protocols have routing capabilities. A brouter

will act as a router, with data that supports a network-layer protocol and a bridge for those that do not.

▸ You may want to use bridges because they are typically less expensive than routers. However, the difference in the overall cost of your internetwork is insignificant and should not be a factor.

Although the SNA suite of protocols does not support routing, there are a number of protocols being developed to provide SNA routing. The Qualified Link Level Control (QLLC) protocol allows SNA to be routed over X.25 links. An emerging protocol known as Advanced Peer-to-Peer Network (APPN), together with an older protocol, LU6.2, allows SNA to be routed dynamically.

 NOTE

Figure 9.1 shows the internetwork according to a router and according to a bridge. You can see that a bridge's view of the internetwork is very limited.

FIGURE 9.1

Routers and bridges have different perspectives of the internetwork.

Link 1   Link 2
Me

Bridge

Network 1   Network 2
Network 3
Network 4   Network 5
Me

Router

If you have to use a bridge to connect networks, remember this: Networks connected by a bridge become the same network and must share a common network address. Figure 9.2 illustrates networks connected by bridges.

FIGURE 9.2

Networks connected by bridges become the same network and must share a common network address.

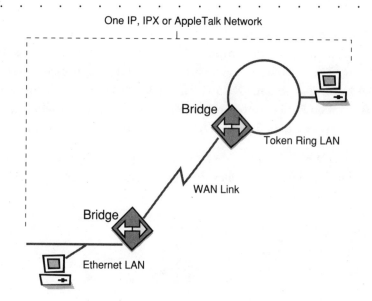

Routing Protocols

Before a discussion of the specifics of TCP/IP, IPX/SPX, and AppleTalk WAN optimization, you need to understand some basic concepts about routers and routing protocols in general. For the most part, routing protocols require the most research when you are implementing multiprotocols over WAN links. You will be introduced to the tasks required of all routers, some ways the internetwork is affected by these tasks (good and bad), and general recommendations about how to optimize their impact on internetwork performance. The section on specific protocols discusses other upper-layer protocols that can affect WAN performance, in addition to specific routing protocols.

ROUTING TASKS

For routers to do their job—namely, to route packets as efficiently as possible across internetworks—they all have common route administration tasks that may need to be done, regardless of the protocols they support. Those tasks are

- ▸ Building a routing database (required)

- ▸ Maintaining the routing database (required)

- ▸ Alerting other routers on the internetwork to detected changes in routes (required)

- ▸ Alerting other routers and end stations of congested routes or undelivered packets (optional)

- ▸ Distributing the traffic load over all routes; load balancing (optional)

Three of the five tasks listed above are required. They have to be done by any router supporting any network-layer protocol. With that in mind, your job as an administrator is to make decisions about purchasing, installing, and configuring routers so they can accomplish those tasks with as little impact as possible on the performance of the internetwork.

Every router has to build and maintain a route database. This task is accomplished by route support programs, based on routing protocols, that run on the routers. Routing protocols have names like Routing Information protocol (RIP), Open Shortest Path First (OSPF), Novell Link Service protocol (NLSP), and Route Table Maintenance protocol (RTMP). Each network-layer protocol has its associated routing protocol(s).

Routing databases are typically created dynamically when the router is first powered up. The router, with help from its neighbor routers, gathers information about the network from which it creates its routing database. This initial information-gathering requires that the router use broadcast packets.

Once the database has been created, it must be maintained. If the router receives information from another router (usually by way of a broadcast packet) of a route change, the router must update its route table and notify other routers down the line about the change (again using a broadcast type packet). The time it takes for the route change information to be dispersed to all routers on the network is known as *convergence time*. The shorter the convergence time, the better.

Most common routing support protocols will broadcast periodically for the purpose of letting all other routers know that they are still alive and functional and that there are no changes in the routes they know of—again, with broadcast packets.

Alerting routers and end stations of possible congested routes is a service to the internetwork, but it usually requires that some packets be broadcast. Perhaps you have noticed that a side effect of each feature is the generation of broadcast traffic.

ROUTING IMPACT ON INTERNETWORK PERFORMANCE

Creating and maintaining routing tables, alerting routers of route changes, and other optional services can create a substantial amount of broadcast traffic. On a LAN, with plenty of throughput to spare, this is usually not a problem. Over WAN links with limited throughput it is a potential problem.

You know there are certain tasks a router must perform and that those tasks require the router to inject traffic on the internetwork. If you are an internetwork designer or administrator, the trick is to purchase and configure routers such that an acceptable compromise is reached between router functionality and traffic over the WAN links. You want the routers to operate as efficiently as possible without injecting too much traffic doing it.

As you deal with this compromise problem, be aware that where routing protocols are concerned, there are some things you can control and some things you can't. In the following sections we will try to point out which is which.

SOME GENERAL RECOMMENDATIONS FOR OPTIMIZATION

Most of the things you can control in optimizing routing protocols deal with creating and maintaining the route tables. This depends a great deal on the implementation of the protocol (how the software was implemented) and which routing algorithm was used (link-state or distance vector; see Chapter 3).

You have a choice of which routing algorithm to use. The link-state algorithm provides a more reliable routing database and faster convergence but typically creates slightly more traffic in doing so. The distance vector algorithm provides less reliable routing database information and is slower to converge, but it typically creates less traffic. The benefits of link-state far outweigh any slight increase in traffic it may induce.

The biggest factor you can control in optimizing your routing protocols is choosing the proper router implementation. For example, if you purchase a router implementation that does not let you restrict periodic route database updates over the WAN link, your routers may broadcast periodic updates to each other as often as every 30 seconds or even more frequently. (AppleTalk does so every 10 seconds!) This is in addition to any immediate broadcasts for changes in routes. As demonstrated in Figure 9.3, you want to have only changes in routes or router status broadcast over WAN links.

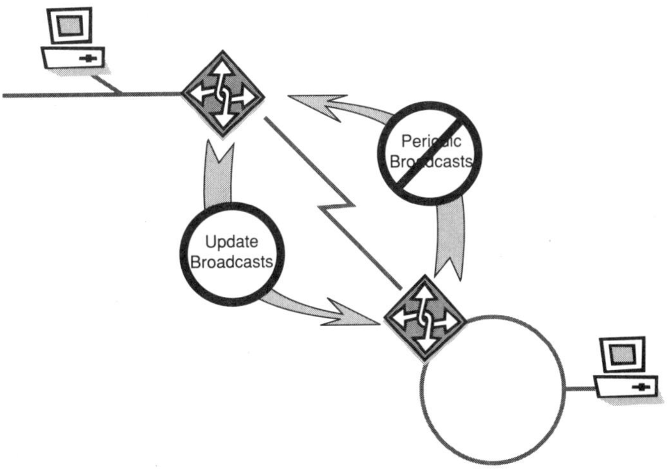

FIGURE 9.3

Try to eliminate periodic routing broadcasts across WAN links.

NOTE

This chapter describes how protocols behave over **WAN** links and offers some suggestions on how best to optimize them. But most of what you can and cannot do is based on the implementation of those protocols. Study the products and discuss routing and higher layer protocol implementation, characteristics, and options with the vendor before making a purchasing decision.

Optimizing Protocols over WAN Links

Now that you have a general idea of what optimizing routing protocols is about, let's examine three common networking protocol suites. They are

- ▶ TCP/IP
- ▶ IPX/SPX (NetWare)
- ▶ AppleTalk

INTERNET PROTOCOL SUITE (TCP/IP)

TCP/IP is a full-featured internetworking protocol suite. The TCP/IP network-layer protocol is the Internet protocol (IP). Routing protocols developed for IP are the Routing Information protocol (RIP) and Open Shortest Path First (OSPF). RIP is based on a distance vector algorithm and OSPF is based on link-state.

TCP/IP has been around since the late 1970s. It has gone through a lot of refinements for WAN applications since then. It is robust and optimized for WAN use.

Both TCP/IP routing protocols are robust, optimized, and reliable. RIP has been around a long time (it was one of the first distance vector protocols) and is a mature protocol with a lot of vendor support. RIP was typically implemented to broadcast periodic updates every 30 seconds. If you choose to use RIP, check with the router vendor to see if this can be suspended for your WAN links.

The OSPF is relatively new and is gaining widespread acceptance. Being a link-state protocol, it provides the advantages of more reliable routing information and a faster convergence time.

There are two major types of IP connections using two different transport-layer protocols. A connection using the Transmission Control protocol (TCP) is connection oriented and provides a guaranteed delivery of packets. TCP creates and manages a virtual connection. It takes overhead in the form of added throughput to provide this type of service. Figure 9.4 shows how TCP adds traffic over the WAN link to acknowledge receipt of data (guaranteed delivery) and to set up and tear down the virtual connection. Some TCP/IP applications that use TCP are

▸ File transfer applications using the File Transfer protocol (FTP)

▸ Terminal emulation applications using the TELNET protocol

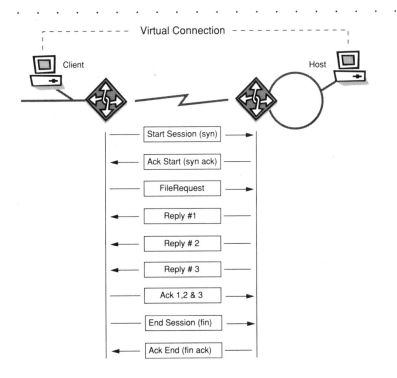

FIGURE 9.4

TCP virtual connection over a WAN link

A WAN consideration when using a TCP connection is timeouts. This parameter determines how much time can elapse between an end station receiving a packet from the remote host before it times out and drops the connection. If the WAN link is too slow this could cause a problem. If you are experiencing timeouts you may wish to increase the timeout interval (software implementation permitting).

The other type of TCP/IP connection is connectionless and uses the User Datagram protocol (UDP). This protocol does not create a virtual circuit, nor does it require acknowledgments. As such it uses much less throughput than a TCP connection. Figure 9.5 shows how UDP can transfer the same number of packets as the TCP connection in Figure 9.4 with much less management overhead. With UDP connections, it is the responsibility of the upper-layer protocols (Session and above) on the end stations to recover lost data.

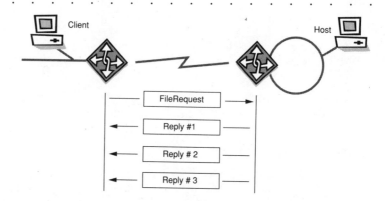

F I G U R E 9.5

UDP data transfer over a
WAN link

Some applications that use the UDP protocol are

- ▸ Network File System (NFS)

- ▸ Message-handling systems using the Simple Mail Transfer protocol (SMTP)

- ▸ Management products using the Simple Network Management protocol (SNMP)

Because there is no virtual connection, there is no connection timeout associated with UDP. However, be aware that the application, even though it is using a UDP connection, may have a timeout for a response from the remote host.

IPX/SPX (NETWARE)

The Internet Packet eXchange/Sequenced Packet eXchange (IPX/SPX) protocols were derived from the Xerox Network System (XNS) Internet Datagram protocol (IDP) and Sequenced Packet protocol (SPP). They were adapted by Novell in the early 1980s to provide network-layer connectionless (IPX), and connection-oriented (SPX) transport for NetWare or, more specifically, NetWare Core protocol (NCP). Since then they have been used for a variety of NetWare server processes.

IPX is the network-layer protocol, and its routing support protocols are the Routing Information protocol (RIP; similar but not the same as the IP RIP) and the Novell Link Service protocol (NLSP). RIP is a distance vector protocol and NLSP is link-state.

Until recently, RIP was implemented with a periodic update every 60 seconds. The Novell MultiProtocol Router (MPR) has a feature that lets you set RIP for broadcast on updates only. Check router vendors that support IPX and RIP for that option. NetWare servers that are doubling as IPX routers will still use RIP with periodic updates (unless they have the Multi-Protocol Router software loaded). This is fine for LAN routing applications, but it is not recommended that servers be used as WAN routers.

NLSP is the latest routing support protocol from Novell and is based on the link-state algorithm.

In addition to RIP, there is another protocol used by NetWare servers and routers. It is called Service Advertising protocol (SAP). Servers use SAPs to advertise themselves and their services to other servers. Workstations use SAP broadcasts to find servers. The SAP protocol must travel across WAN links so NetWare servers can find each other on an internetwork; thus, they are broadcast by routers across WAN links. SAP broadcasts should be treated the same as RIP broadcasts; periodics are fine on LANs but are to be avoided across WAN links. The Novell MultiProtocol Router has an option for broadcasting SAPs across WAN links only when the routers detect a change (a server has come up or gone down).

NetWare 4.0 has a built-in directory service. Workstations will find servers, and servers will learn about other servers, through the directory services. This will eliminate the necessity for the SAP protocol.

In terms of NetWare and WAN links, it is important to know about NCP. NCP is the protocol that provides file, print, and other services to client workstations. It acts as a connection-oriented guaranteed delivery upper-layer protocol. To accomplish this, NCP uses a method known as "ping-ponging." That means the server and workstation engage in a request/reply conversation. The workstation sends a packet with a request, and the server sends back a packet with a reply. Requests and replys are interleaved this way throughout the connection. For example, Figure 9.6 shows that when the workstation requests a file transfer, the workstation sends a packet with a request for a portion of the file. (The amount that will fit in the packet is determined by workstation/server negotiation.) The server will read that much of the file and send it to the workstation. The workstation will then request another slice of the file, and so on.

This type of ping-ponging creates quite a bit of traffic. On a LAN, it is not a problem. But over a WAN link, the delays resulting from throughput congestion can cause the connection to timeout. There are a couple of things you can do to avoid this:

  ▸ First, and most important, try not to execute programs over the WAN link. Programs should be executed locally (either from the user's local drive or a server on the local network). Use the WAN link only for transferring files. Be especially careful about LOGIN.EXE since users will often try to log in to a remote server. If you suspect this might happen, put LOGIN.EXE on their local drive or a search drive mapped to a local server.

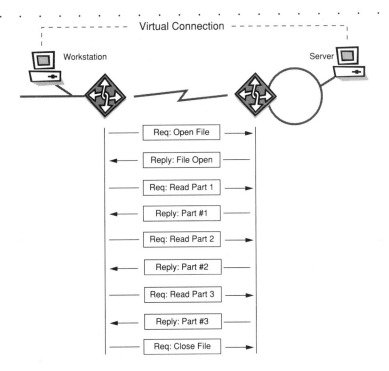

FIGURE 9.6

NCP virtual connection
using the ping-pong method
to guarantee delivery

- ▸ Second, use the Packet Burst protocol to transfer large files. Packet Burst lets the server send a stream of packets before the work-station acknowledges them. This cuts down on the number of packets transmitted across the link.

Figure 9.7 shows how the Packet Burst protocol can cut down on the number of packets transmitted across the WAN link during the same NCP file transfer as shown in Figure 9.6. Packet Burst currently works only on large (over 512K) file transfers. It does not help when executing programs across the network.

NCP file transfer using
Packet Burst

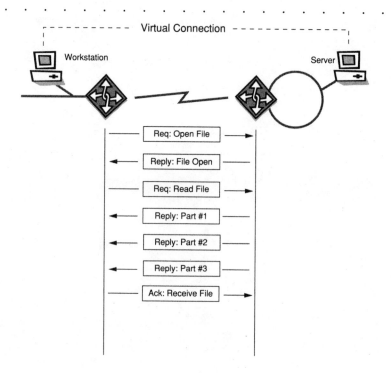

APPLETALK

Implementing AppleTalk over wide area links requires consideration of all the issues of local area internetworking and a few special considerations. Chapter 4 addressed the following AppleTalk features and the implications for local internetworks:

▶ In addition to routing services, AppleTalk routers locate resources and supply startup information services for nodes.

▶ AppleTalk nodes constantly change the value of A-ROUTER.

▶ AppleTalk makes extensive use of broadcast and multicast addresses.

▶ Zones are assigned to networks so that resources can be logically grouped for easy location by users. A single zone may span more than one network, and more than one zone may exist on a single network.

▶ Apple computers running system v7.0 or higher are capable of peer-to-peer networking (and resource advertisement).

These features increase in importance when implementing an AppleTalk wide area link because of the additional bandwidth constraints. If you have integrated the design suggestions of Chapter 4 in your local area design, you have a good start at maximizing the efficiency of your WAN.

Adding wide area links may require rethinking network design issues at each of the sites being joined to the enterprise network. One of these issues is addressing.

AppleTalk Addressing Issues for Wide Area Networks

One of the most obvious addressing issues that must be investigated when joining local area networks is duplicate network addresses. As LANs are added to the internetwork, it must be assured that the rules for network addressing are followed across the WAN. With AppleTalk networks this includes zone-naming conventions. Keep in mind these important considerations:

▶ All networks must have unique network numbers, even across a WAN. (For an exception to this rule, see the section "Special AppleTalk Routing" at the end of this chapter.)

▶ Routers must agree on network number and zone name affiliations.

▶ A zone should never span networks across wide area links.

It is very common for administrators to use nice round numbers when assigning network addresses. If two local area internetworks are to be joined by a wide area link when two of the networks being joined are using the same address, you must be sure to change the router configurations, including specifying which zones are associated with which network numbers.

NOTE

Whenever network numbers and zones are reconfigured, it is necessary to bring down the AppleTalk internetwork for a period of 10 minutes. This should be done across all wide area links as well. The 10-minute "down time" will result in the aging and removal of all zone and network addresses from all AppleTalk nodes. (Some routers may still route other protocols while the AppleTalk protocols are being reset.)

Certain zone names are found on many networks. When the same name (Sales, for example) exists on two networks that are to be joined by a wide area link, you must reconfigure your network so that all devices on both sides of the WAN won't be advertised in a single zone. It may seem that keeping the Sales zone in both sites and simply changing the router configurations to reflect that the Sales zone now resides on more networks would work fine, but this would cause the Sales zone to span the wide area link. This results in broadcasts to all networks sharing the selected zone. Whenever a user tries to find a "Sales" resource (such as a printer or file server), the wide area link is used to forward all requests and replies. If many resources reside across the link, significant traffic will be generated.

Figure 9.8 illustrates how networks should be reconfigured to avoid addressing conflicts and shows zones spanning the wide-area link.

Bridging the Wide Area

AppleTalk protocols should never be bridged across a wide area link. Since some protocols cannot be routed, you may need to design your network to ensure that some protocols are bridged while others are routed. You can integrate your bridging/routing solution with your backbone topology through proper choice and placement of internetworking devices. Consider

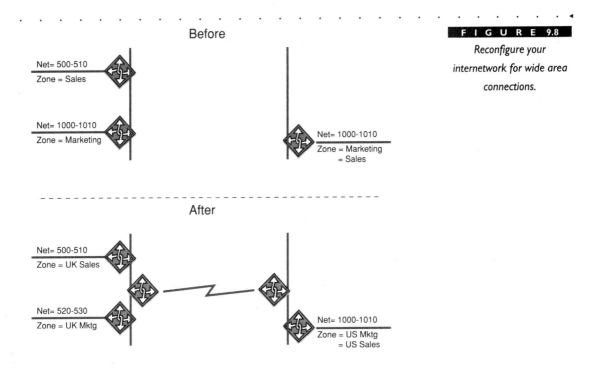

FIGURE 9.8

Reconfigure your internetwork for wide area connections.

the following options when it is necessary to bridge some protocols:

- ▸ Use a device that does bridging and routing for your wide area link (brouter).

- ▸ Use a router to isolate AppleTalk nodes from the wide area bridge.

- ▸ Whenever possible, group devices using the same protocol onto the same network. Some of the new modular wiring schemes (such as 10Base-T) make this easier than you might guess.

Figure 9.9 shows possible placement of bridges, routers, and brouters. Notice that AppleTalk is always separated from the wide area link by a router, and nonrouting protocols always have a path to the wide area

FIGURE 9.9

*Device selection and
placement depend on
which protocols are on
the network.*

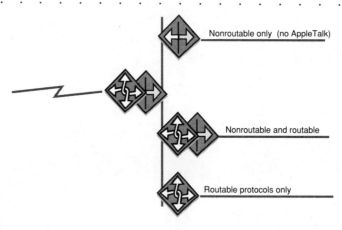

Nonroutable only (no AppleTalk)

Nonroutable and routable

Routable protocols only

through a bridge. This arrangement reduces the AppleTalk utilization of the wide area link.

Minimizing Wide Area Traffic

Link utilization could be significantly reduced if it were not necessary to pass all of the RTMP traffic. This could be accomplished in two ways. One way is to send routing information only when a change in routes is detected. The other is to configure a static routing configuration for the link and restrict all traffic except for traffic destined for a specific address across the link.

AppleTalk Update-Based Routing Protocol (AURP)

Chapter 4 discussed the RTMP protocol and the traffic that resulted from the 10-second RTMP updates. This is not usually a problem in local area networks where high bandwidth is available, but wide area links are generally much slower and more expensive. AURP was developed to meet the demands of wide area links. AURP does not send routing information except when changes to the routing table are detected. Since AURP is compatible with RTMP, it is possible to configure the LAN side of the router with RTMP and the WAN side with AURP. If AURP is used, all interfaces on the

WAN link should be configured for AURP only. See Figure 9.10 for an example of an internetwork using AURP.

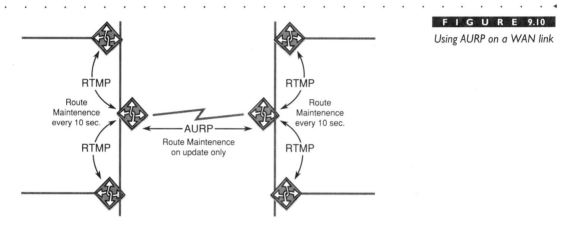

AURP also supplies important additional features for wide area networking. One of the most important features of AURP is tunneling.

Protocol Tunneling   AURP allows AppleTalk information to be transmitted across non-AppleTalk networks. This is done through a process known as *tunneling*. The router using AURP places AppleTalk packets inside the header of another protocol. This is commonly done for TCP/IP internetworks or point-to-point links using the Point-to-Point protocol (PPP). For example, an AppleTalk network connecting to another AppleTalk network across the Internet would require tunneling. Figure 9.11 illustrates how AppleTalk data packets and routing information can be passed across a TCP/IP network.

AURP provides the flexibility to route AppleTalk over the WAN, but when this means connection into a large enterprise such as the Internet or a multinational enterprise network, it may be necessary to use routers implementing specialized proprietary functions or some of AURP's optional facilities.

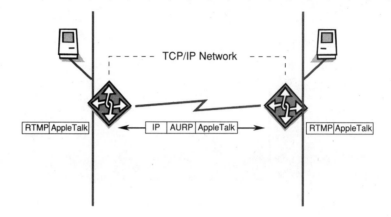

Special AppleTalk Routing

When connecting to very large internetworks you may not wish to load up your local internetwork with information about the larger internetwork. It may also be useful to enable links on demand and close down links that are rarely used. Some routers can provide you with options to meet these needs.

Optional AURP Features   Chapter 4 discussed AppleTalk filtering as a desirable router option. AURP can decrease WAN traffic and provide extra security by implementing network hiding or device hiding through filtering. An exterior router can hide networks from the WAN by exporting only a subset of its local internetwork's routing information. The router can also hide individual devices by not forwarding Name Binding protocol (NBP) LkUp-Reply packets from that device. The administrator should be able to select all ports or individual ports to hide information from.

On-Demand Links   There are some situations that require wide area access, but only occasionally. A branch office that needs access to the home office resources only a few times a day can save money and maximize the use of network resources if it implements on-demand routing. This type of routing would utilize static routing information to advertise the presence of exterior networks even though no route currently exists. When a user tries to access information about the external network, a connection is established and communication proceeds as usual. Of course, users would experience delays when trying to access the remote resources until the link was reestablished, but if use of the link is infrequent this may be acceptable.

Implementing advanced features like on-demand routing or network and device hiding can affect router and network performance. If possible, use routers that are easily reconfigured and scaled to higher performance platforms.

Earlier chapters showed how proper configuration (for example, use of a backbone) and proper selection of internetworking devices are critical to optimizing performance. This chapter has pointed out that these issues are even more critical when confronting the bandwidth restrictions of wide area links. To optimize the performance of your WAN link, it is necessary to implement specialized protocols and router functions to reduce traffic and minimize routing and management overhead.

CHAPTER 10

Internetworking Blueprints:
Wide Area Networks

This chapter focuses on three WAN internetworks that use routers to connect two or more remote offices. These design scenarios include a checklist of WAN components (Network-at-a-Glance), a brief description of the design scenario company and its network requirements, one or more key features of the network, and finally, one or more blueprints of the WAN configuration. The WAN blueprints include network addresses and link types wherever possible. (Network addresses have been changed to ensure privacy of network information for the design scenario participants.)

The three design scenarios in this chapter include the following types of WANs and key features:

- ▸ Branch office WAN

- ▸ ISDN-based WAN

- ▸ Mainframes and minis on the WAN

- ▸ Load balancing across routers

- ▸ Video, voice, and data on the WAN

- ▸ Prioritizing WAN transmissions

- ▸ Mixing WAN topologies

- ▸ Fault tolerance

 NOTE

The final design scenario in this chapter details Novell's WAN. The Novell WAN consists of multiple protocols and international links as well as data, voice, and video connectivity.

Design scenario participants were supplied with a Design Scenario Questionnaire that required a simple overview of their network components, protocols and link types, needs assessment, and reason for internetworking. The participants were asked to submit a blueprint of their WAN layout—a necessity for WANs. These design scenarios illustrate the need for WAN blueprints to keep abreast of network configuration changes, possible bottlenecks, and enhancements.

Design Scenario #1: Configuring a Branch Office WAN

Businesses often need to connect many smaller branch offices with each other and/or with a headquarters. Examples of businesses with this need include banks, hotel chains, sales and retail outlets, travel agencies, and any business having multiple outlets (chains) or warehouses. This design scenario focuses on the Arabella chain of hotels. By connecting the hotel LANs into a WAN, the Arabella could offer customers immediate confirmed reservations at any of the hotels and supply information on hotel facilities for guests or conventions.

NETWORK-AT-A-GLANCE

Listed below are the company name and the major hardware and software compenents that needed to be included in the network.

Company:	Arabella Hotel Consult GmbH
Number of servers:	12
Number of clients:	300
Network type:	Ethernet
Routers:	12 NetWare MultiProtocol Routers
Protocols:	IPX/SPX over ISDN
Applications:	Databases, electronic mail, and business-specific software for hotels

NETWORK DESCRIPTION

Arabella has a number of hotels located in cities such as Munich, Frankfurt, and Mallorca. They internetworked their LANs to connect the various branch offices and build a central reservation system that served all the hotels in the Arabella group. The network also allowed Arabella to create a centralized sales information system that can be accessed from any hotel in any location. The network configuration was designed as an ISDN network because of the lower costs of ISDN and the minimal amount of data exchanged between the sites.

KEY FEATURE: ISDN-BASED WAN

The router connections to the ISDN network are accomplished with a special configuration of the NetWare MultiProtocol Router. The NetWare Multiprotocol Router for ISDN (MPR for ISDN) was developed in cooperation with AVM Computersysteme Vertriebs GmbH for use in Europe and, eventually, worldwide. The MPR for ISDN platform is scaleable from ISA to EISA and MCA platforms. (Arabella routers currently are Compaq 486 33Mhz computers with ISA buses.) The ISDN adapter can provide two B-channels (74Kbits each), and up to four adapters can be installed in an MPR. Features of the ISDN controller include

- ► Configurable inactivity timer: The physical connection can be cleared down and restored while maintaining a continuous logical connection. B-channels are reestablished in 1 to 2 seconds transparent to the user.

- ► Channel on demand: This mechanism activates a second B-channel whenever the first active data channel reaches full load.

- ► Monitoring utilities: ISDN monitoring provides statistics, current connection data and rate information, and a trace function.

- ► Data compression: Compression ratios of 4:1 and more can be achieved.

Additional features of MPR utilized by Arabella include the familiar MONITOR, RCONSOLE, and CALLMGR utilities. SAP filtering was initiated so only the most involved servers advertised across the WAN, thus reducing WAN traffic. Arabella uses SNMP as a management tool and is able to query the SNMP agents in NetWare for additional monitoring.

As shown on the blueprint diagram in Figure 10.1, this network consists of two main offices—one in Munich, another in Frankfurt. The Munich office is the coordinating location for communication occurring in hotels located in Munich, Spitzingsee, and Lengries. The Frankfurt office is the coordinating office for communication occurring in hotels located in Frankfurt, Dusseldorf, and Mallorca. The centralized reservation system and sales information can be accessed from any hotel through the ISDN routing system. Because the company is based in Germany, Arabella had to contact the local ISDN vendor for configuration, pricing, and service. The local vendor is the German PTT: Telekom.

After the decision to integrate the existing LANs into a WAN was made, two weeks were spent defining the project, planning the implementation, and determining what the economic factors were. This was followed by eight weeks of testing and revisions. After this, only two LANs were brought

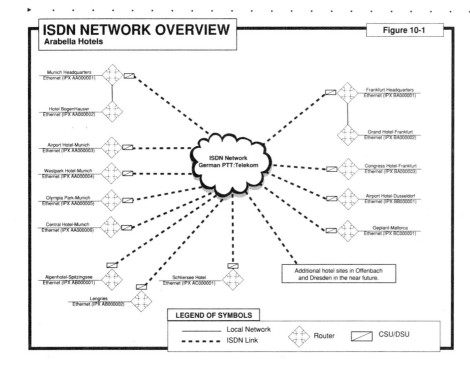

FIGURE 10.1
WAN design scenario #1: Arabella Hotels—ISDN network overview

on-line for a "real world" test before integrating the other LANs into the internetwork. Novell, AVM, Compaq, and Telekom were already known to Arabella and were chosen because of successful experiences in previous situations.

Design Scenario #2: Linking Mainframes and Minis into the WAN

This design scenario focuses on Avery-Dennison's Token Ring and Ethernet networks that were internetworked by Trellis Communications, Inc., of Walnut, California. This WAN connects a variety of platforms and protocols.

NETWORK-AT-A-GLANCE

Listed below are the company name and the major hardware and software compnents that needed to be internetworked.

Company:	Avery-Dennison
Number of servers:	50+
Number of clients:	2000+
Network type:	Token Ring and Ethernet
Protocols:	IPX/SPX, AppleTalk, TCP/IP
Applications:	Electronic mail, data sharing, mainframe-based applications

NETWORK DESCRIPTION

Avery-Dennison's WAN connects nine separate offices through 56Kbs links using the PPP (Point-to-Point protocol). Avery-Dennison uses the internetwork to share data and peripherals among the offices. When installing the internetwork, special attention was paid to the load on the cabling system—routers were used to alleviate cabling bottlenecks whenever possible.

This WAN is used to connect NetWare LANs, OS/2 networks, IBM 3090s, IBM System 38s, AS/400s, and several RS6000s. The 56Kbs link vendor is Wiltel Communications. This network consists of two types of routers: Newport Systems v.30 routers and NetWare MultiProtocol Routers.

KEY FEATURE: LOAD BALANCING ACROSS ROUTERS

As shown on the blueprint diagram in Figure 10.2, this network consists of two primary types of routers: Newport and NetWare MultiProtocol Routers. The Newport routers are HDLC/Compression routers used for the HDLC traffic. The NetWare MultiProtocol Routers, however, are dedicated to routing the LAN protocols such as IPX/SPX and TCP/IP. Because of the low volume of traffic across the IPX WAN, 56Kbs lines were sufficient.

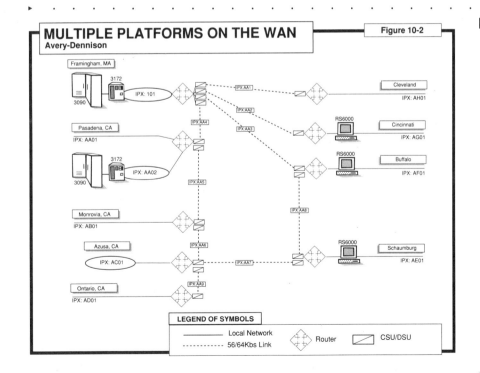

MULTIPLE PLATFORMS ON THE WAN
Avery-Dennison

Figure 10-2

FIGURE 10.2

*WAN design scenario #2:
Avery-Dennison—IPX
Internet blueprint*

Figure 10.3 displays the same sites and physical layout for the internetwork; however, this figure displays the logical IP internetwork, with the associated IP addresses. Notice that Pasadena, CA, is not part of the IP internetwork.

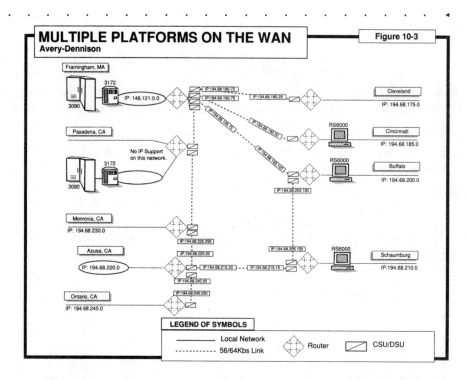

MULTIPLE PLATFORMS ON THE WAN
Avery-Dennison

Figure 10-3

The Avery-Dennison internetwork is actually larger than illustrated here. It is sometimes useful to view only the portion of the network involved in certain types of operations, such as the case where several sites' primary operations all involve using the same client/server applications or the same mainframe database. Figure 10.4 shows the portion of the Avery-Dennison internetwork concerned with AS/400 access. This portion of the network utilizes data compression techniques to maximize throughput across the wide area links.

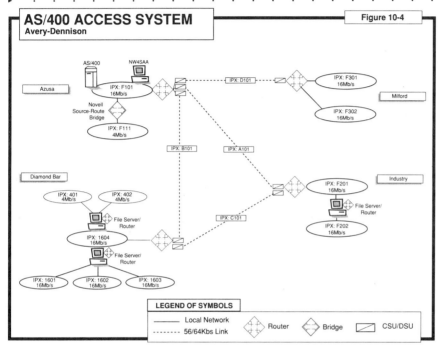

AS/400 ACCESS SYSTEM
Avery-Dennison

Figure 10-4

WAN design scenario #2:
Avery-Dennison—AS400
Access System blueprint

Trellis Communications Inc. used Novell's PERFORM2 and PERFORM3 to benchmark network performance. Trellis recommends "real world" testing of fault-tolerant features, noting that a vendor's definition of fault tolerance may be limited to reestablishment of a physical or virtual communication channel. Applications using the communication channel must be tested to see if sessions can be maintained through this process.

Design Scenario #3: Video, Voice, and Data across the WAN

The Novell WAN is an enterprise-wide hybrid network consisting of a private line TDM (Time Division Multiplexor) network and public X.25 networks that currently connect multiple international and domestic sites for data, voice, and video communication. The basic structure of Novell's network is shown in Figure 10.5.

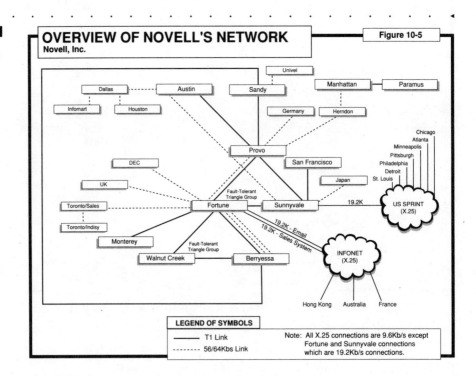

OVERVIEW OF NOVELL'S NETWORK
Novell, Inc.

Figure 10-5

LEGEND OF SYMBOLS

——— T1 Link

------- 56/64Kbs Link

Note: All X.25 connections are 9.6Kb/s except Fortune and Sunnyvale connections which are 19.2Kb/s connections.

NETWORK-AT-A-GLANCE

Listed below are the company name and the major hardware and software components that needed to be included in the internetwork.

Company:	Novell, Inc.
Number of servers:	500+
Number of clients:	6000+
Network type:	Ethernet (10BaseT), FDDI, Token Ring

| Protocols: | IPX/SPX, AppleTalk, TCP/IP, OSI |
| Applications: | Electronic mail, data sharing, telephone system, video teleconferencing, order entry |

NETWORK DESCRIPTION

Novell's private network is used to connect major locations for multi-protocol and multi-application support ranging from order entry to software development. The private network is highly reliable and robust; however, it is expensive and cannot be justified at all locations. Therefore, the X.25 technology was selected for smaller sites at remote locations. The X.25 performance, however, can be erratic and throughput can be inconsistent. The X.25 connections from Infonet and US Sprint are used to connect sales offices to the corporate network for single protocol (IPX) and single (electronic mail or VAX access) applications.

KEY FEATURE: DATA, VOICE, AND VIDEO NETWORK

The Novell private WAN supports voice, video, and data traffic on common facilities. The main application on the Novell private network is data sharing. (Refer to the next Key Feature for more information on the assignment of priorities to data communications.)

The Data Network

Routers are used to connect the LAN to the muxes or DSU/CSUs. Remote routers are used to connect logical networks such as IPX/SPX, TCP/IP, and AppleTalk. These routers are the key to data communication over the WAN. On the WAN side of the routers, there are numerous V.35 serial interfaces that allow it to connect into the DSU/CSUs or muxes. On the LAN side, there are numerous Ethernet or Token Ring interfaces that allow the router to connect to the LANs.

Novell uses a mixture of routing devices including Cisco and NetWare MultiProtocol Routers. The Cisco routers are used in areas where high-performance and high-capacity links are required. These routers are used to provide LAN and WAN connections. The Cisco routers, however, are very expensive and cannot be justified for all locations. To reduce the cost of the entire WAN, NetWare MultiProtocol Routers have been used throughout the network. These NetWare MultiProtocol Routers can support up to 16 high-speed synchronous interfaces with a total aggregate bandwidth of 4 T1s.

The public data network connects remote sales offices to the main Novell network for electronic mail and order inquiry purposes. This public network consists of an X.25 international network provided by Infonet and an X.25 domestic network provided by US Sprint. The basic internetwork is shown in Figure 10.5.

Two network providers were selected because it was found that although Infonet has a very good installed base and the best cost in the international market, its presence in the U.S. is limited; therefore, its X.25 domestic cost is the most expensive. At the time the Novell network was configured, analysis of the X.25 domestic network providers showed that US Sprint, which acquired Telenet, the original and oldest X.25 network provider, had the largest installed base as well as the most flexibility in both technical offerings (both dial-up and dedicated X.25) and price.

The domestic offices are tied together through a combination of T1 lines and 56/64Kbs lines, as shown in Figure 10.5. The main Novell offices (Sandy, Provo, Fortune, Sunnyvale, Monterey, Walnut Creek, and Berryessa) are connected via T1 lines.

VOICE NETWORK

The voice network consists mostly of AT&T equipment that runs on top of the Novell private WAN. The voice traffic was placed on the private network to maximize the capital investment in the private network equipment and facilities and to reduce the long-distance cost over the public lines. The voice traffic is considered secondary to the data, and if data is moved to a redundant route due to a link failure, voice is bumped off to make room for the data traffic.

When the private voice connection at locations with the AT&T Distributed Communication System (DCS) is bumped off or disconnected, the voice traffic is routed to the public voice networks offered by AT&T SDN (Software-Defined Network) or MCI V-Net (Virtual Network). Whenever a phone call is made, the switch uses AAR (Automatic Alternate Route) to select the least-cost route to use. This means the private network is the first choice, followed by either SDN or V-Net. The last choice is via Pacific Bell Co. (Central Office).

Normally, each phone conversation takes up a full time slot or 64Kbs of bandwidth. To better utilize the WAN link facilities, however, 32Kbs compressed voice channels are implemented to reduce the amount of bandwidth required for a phone conversation to 32Kbs. This means that a single time slot can support two phone conversations. Voice compression is implemented on the muxes with the use of compressed voice card interfaces.

The Video Network

Video-Net is Novell's videoconferencing network. Video-Net is a star topology with the Fortune site at the center, where the Compression Lab, Inc. (CLI) Multi-Point Control Unit (MCU) is located. Video traffic is considered secondary to the data and is bumped to make room for data traffic if a link failure occurs.

The Novell Video-Net consists of CLI codecs (Fortune, Austin, Provo, and Monterey) that are connected through the T1 facilities. These codecs are connected to the MCU that is capable of providing three simultaneous conferencing connections or one single eight-way conference. Connections between remote sites and the MCU are made via the muxes.

At each site, the mux is connected to a codec via a pair of RS449 short-haul modems. The modems are simply used to extend the length of the RS449 cable beyond the 2500 feet standard over two pairs of voice grade, unshielded, twisted-pair cable. Because of the limited capacity available at the muxes, only five time slots (or 320Kbs) were assigned to video connections between Austin-Fortune and Provo-Austin and only three time slots (or 112Kbs) were assigned to the Monterey-Fortune connection.

KEY FEATURE: PRIORITIZING WAN TRANSMISSIONS

Different priority levels (such as high, normal, and low) are assigned to each channel group. When link failure occurs, the 745 T1 switch uses the channel's priority levels to determine how to reroute them. On the failed link, only channel groups with high priority are rerouted. On the available links, channel groups with low priority are bumped to make room for the high-priority rerouted traffic. Normal priority channels cannot be bumped or activate bumping. The reroute process takes about 15 seconds for the first channel group and 2 seconds for the subsequent channel groups.

Currently, all data channel groups are set to high priority. Video and voice channel groups have low priority. This means that when a link fails, voice and video traffic will be bumped to make room for data traffic.

KEY FEATURE: MIXING WAN TOPOLOGIES

Novell's network consists of private leased lines from various carriers and covers 21 sites—3 international and 18 domestic. To provide network redundancy, the major and critical domestic sites are connected through a mesh topology. The smaller, less critical sites and international locations are connected by point-to-point private lines.

The Mesh Network

Novell's mesh network consists of eight T1s and one 56Kbs line and covers seven sites located at Fortune Drive, Berryessa, Walnut Creek, Sunnyvale, Provo, Sandy, and Austin. This portion of the private network has dynamic network redundancy and automatic hardware backup. This mesh network was organized into a group of "triangles," each of which connects three sites. This ensures that if one of the lines, or a "side" of a triangle, fails to operate, the other lines can take over. Figure 10.5 shows the Provo/Sunnyvale/Fortune and Fortune/Walnut Creek/Berryessa triangles.

At the heart of this network are AT&T Acculink 740 and 741 muxes and AT&T 745 T1 switches. The muxes multiplex the lines into channel groups; each channel group can carry voice, video, or data.

Point-to-Point Network

The Novell point-to-point network consists of two T1s and nine 56Kbs lines and covers 11 sites (6 domestic and 5 international). Most of the sites on the point-to-point network are less critical sales offices that cannot justify the high cost associated with a redundant network (hardware and line cost). In addition, there is also an "island" WAN made up of a T1 connecting the Paramus and Manhattan sales offices.

This portion of the network has no rerouting capability.

 NOTE

The international sites connected to this network are located at Bracknell, UK; Dusseldorf, Germany; Tokyo, Japan; Toronto/Indisy; and Toronto/Sales. The domestic sites are located at Dallas, Houston, Herndon, San Francisco, and Monterey.

For their assistance with the design scenarios in this section, the authors give special thanks to Larry Shiable (Trellis Communications, Inc.), J. Hock (Arabella Hotel Group), Dorothe Faxel (Audiovisuelles Marketing und Computersysteme GmbH), Gordon Jones and Bach Nguyen (Novell, Inc.).

 NOTE

As networks grow larger and become internetworks, network management becomes both more important and more complex. Chapter 11 will guide you in selecting a management scheme for your network and provides details of the SNMP protocol as a standards-based management tool.

PART 3

Managing and Troubleshooting an Internetwork

Internetwork management is a consideration that should be addressed during the planning stage of the internetwork. Once the internetwork has been configured and installed, setting up a reliable method for managing and troubleshooting the internetwork (including devices and links) is an absolute necessity. This, unfortunately, is the most likely aspect of the internetwork to be left out of the planning stages. Often, the internetwork management system is left out because of budget restraints or the perception that an internetwork management system is a luxury, not a necessity.

CHAPTER II

Overview of Internetwork Management Options

This chapter first addresses the simple network management options, such as blueprinting network addresses and physical layouts. Next it examines the various options available for remote access management, centralized and distributed management systems, and SNMP-based management consoles. Since management systems are often considered a luxury, we next examine justification for network management and monitoring and troubleshooting systems. Finally, we delve into the many options for managing and monitoring the internetwork devices, such as routers, communication equipment, and the communication link.

Blueprinting the Network

During the design and installation of the internetwork, a simple "blueprint" of the devices, protocols, and physical layout should be created. This blueprint should be a requirement of all network cable installers and WAN service providers. The blueprint can be relatively simple and still give a complete picture of the entire internetwork and the protocols in use. Figure 11.1 shows a sample internetwork blueprint that details the basic internetwork infrastructure and IPX addresses of a company that has offices in San Francisco, Dallas, and New York.

Many network integrators create and maintain a network blueprint to provide new account representatives with a quick reference of the customer's network layout. This blueprint idea is the basis behind many management console displays that present logical maps of the internetwork. These management consoles and logical maps are discussed later in this chapter.

 NOTE

For more examples of internetwork blueprints, refer to Chapters 5 and 10.

Next we examine several options for managing the devices on the internetwork.

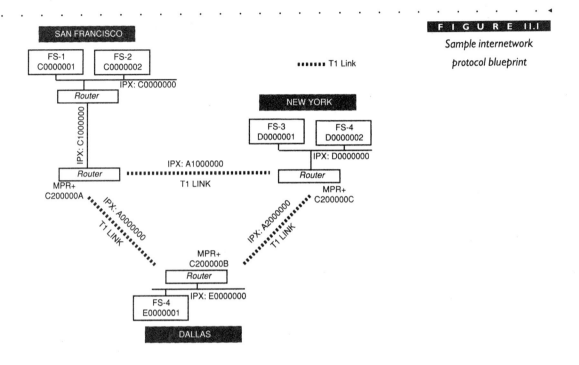

FIGURE 11.1

*Sample internetwork
protocol blueprint*

Internetwork Management Options

The type of management option you select may be determined based on cost and/or available technology. For example, remote access is often bundled with routers and network servers and is therefore less expensive than dedicated management systems. Vendor-specific remote access, however, does not generally provide an automatic alarm system or internetwork mapping, which are available with many dedicated management systems. This section examines simple remote access options, some standard NetWare monitoring utilities, and management console options that utilize the Simple Network Management protocol (SNMP), the *de facto* standard for internetwork management.

IN-BAND AND OUT-OF-BAND COMMUNICATION

Many internetworking devices provide an RS232 port that can be used for configuration and management. When the device is managed through the RS232 port, it is using out-of-band or out-of-channel management. The term *out-of-band* means that the communication channel that carries user data is not used to carry management information. This accounts for some confusion in the use of 56-/64-Kbs leased lines. The actual line speed is 64Kbs, but phone companies reserve 8Kbs of bandwidth for out-of-band management of the link. An RS232 connection allows use of a completely separate communication link for transmitting management information. *In-band* management usually provides easier access and setup and a faster communication channel, but it has two major drawbacks. In-band management uses network bandwidth that would otherwise be available for user data, and if the main data channel is down, the managed network device is unavailable for diagnosis or reconfiguration. Ideally a device allows the use of in-band management if network bandwidth utilization permits and the use of out-of-band management for periodic remote monitoring or when the network is down. Keep in mind that if periodic management updates are sent from the RS232 port via dial-up connections, the management software should support calls to the console upon detection of an alarm. Otherwise, problems will go unnoticed until the next periodic update.

REMOTE ACCESS

Remote access software allows you to access, or "take over," a device from a remote location. For example, NetWare's RCONSOLE software is used to access the NetWare Server console or NetWare MultiProtocol Router from another PC on the network. Figure 11.2 shows the remote-access options, RCONSOLE, ACONSOLE, and XCONSOLE, that are discussed in this section.

RCONSOLE

Based on NetWare's Sequenced Packet Exchange (SPX) protocol, RCON-SOLE is a utility that allows a NetWare DOS client access to the router or

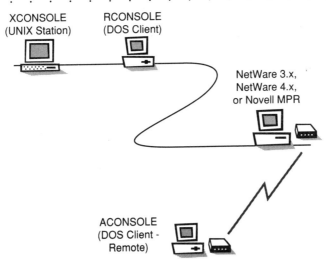

FIGURE II.2

The remote access utilities
RCONSOLE, ACONSOLE,
and XCONSOLE

server console. This utility supplies in-band monitoring and management and requires a physical connection to the network and specific NLMs to be run on the server/router (REMOTE.NLM and RSPX.NLM). RCONSOLE (included in NetWare 3.x, NetWare 4.x, and the NetWare MultiProtocol Router) can be password protected to restrict access to authorized network administrators.

ACONSOLE

ACONSOLE provides out-of-band access to the same monitoring and management functions as RCONSOLE, but over an asynchronous line. To use ACONSOLE, you must connect a modem to a server or router COM port and another modem to a remote PC. Special NLMs must be run at the server or router as well (REMOTE.NLM and RS232.NLM) and can be password protected to restrict access to authorized network administrators.

XCONSOLE

XCONSOLE is the most recent remote-access software developed and is included with NetWare NFS and the NetWare MultiProtocol Router.

XCONSOLE allows a UNIX workstation to take over the console using TCP/IP as the communication protocol. XCONSOLE requires a physical connection to the network and can be password protected to restrict access to authorized network administrators.

These remote-access programs are used to view the many monitor utilities that are included in NetWare. The next section focuses on the monitoring utilities that are inherent to the NetWare MultiProtocol Router.

MONITORING UTILITIES

Monitoring utilities included in the NetWare MultiProtocol Router provide information on IPX/SPX, TCP/IP, AppleTalk, and OSI communication.

MONITOR.NLM is a NetWare-loadable module that reports the status of connections, memory, and communication to the NetWare MultiProtocol Router. One area of special interest is the LAN Driver Information area, where you can monitor the status of the WAN links on a port-by-port basis. NetWare users should be familiar with the statistics presented in MONITOR. TCPCON is the SNMP console for TCP/IP communication including IP forwards, TCP and UDP receives, and known routes and route costs. ATCON is the AppleTalk console that displays statistics on AppleTalk services on the network and routes known, as well as configuration information. ISOCON is the management console for the OSI communication stack. This console provides information on data rates, error rates, and utilization.

X.25 DIAGNOSTIC TOOL: CPECFG

The NetWare MultiProtocol Router also includes a special diagnostic tool for X.25 links: CPECFG. The CPECFG (Customer Premises Equipment Configuration) utility is a remote communication device control tool used to configure and troubleshoot communication devices on X.25 links. CPECFG provides a terminal interface to a DSU/CSU management port and uses the router or server serial (COMx) port for out-of-band communication with the local DSU/CSU. In-band communication across the X.25 link can be used to manage the remote device. Figure 11.3 shows how CPECFG is used to monitor local and remote communication devices by opening up a management and troubleshooting "highway."

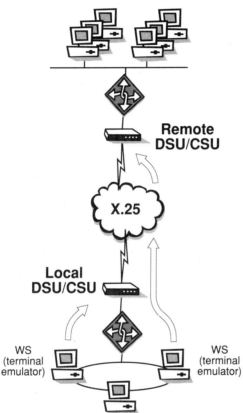

FIGURE 11.3
CPECFG opens
management and
troubleshooting"highways."

As shown in Figure 11.3, a workstation using a standard NASI (Novell Asynchronous Services Interface) certified utility, such as Procomm or CrossTalk, can monitor DSU/CSU devices on the local or remote LAN.

Sophisticated management systems, often an afterthought to the network planning and installation phases, help alert the network administrator to possible problems before they occur. These management systems often utilize SNMP (Simple Network Management protocol), the *de facto* standard for internetwork management. The next section focuses on SNMP-based management solutions and manager/agent types of management systems in general.

An Introduction to SNMP

In April of 1989, the Simple Network Management protocol (SNMP) became an Internet-recommended standard (RFC 1098). Originally assigned as a means of managing TCP/IP and Ethernet networks, SNMP proved to be a simple yet well-architected protocol for managing multivendor network systems.

SNMP was designed to use any network medium (Ethernet, Token Ring, ARCNET, FDDI, and so on). SNMP was also designed to be entirely transport independent, enabling management information to be exchanged using a variety of protocols (IPX/SPX, TCP/IP, and OSI). It seems evident that over the next several years, SNMP will continue its rise in support and use.

SNMP was designed with four basic components:

▸ SNMP manager

▸ SNMP agent

▸ SNMP commands

▸ Management Information Base (MIB)

Let's take a closer look at the functions and features of an SNMP-based management system.

THE SNMP MANAGER

An SNMP manager application resides on one or more network management stations on the network, as shown in Figure 11.4. This figure

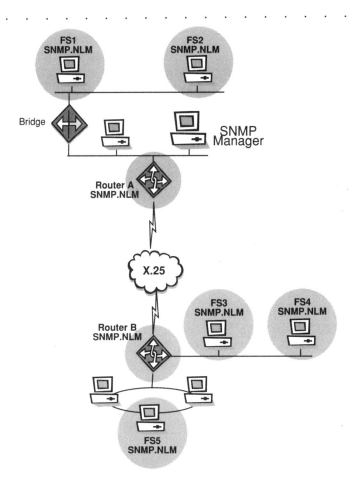

FIGURE II.4

*One or more SNMP
management stations
reside on the
SNMP-managed
internetwork.*

illustrates an internetwork that consists of three Ethernet networks and one Token Ring network. These networks are connected across an X.25 link.

The SNMP manager gathers, tracks, and displays management information. This management information is obtained by querying SNMP agents. For example, Novell's NetWare Management System console is an SNMP manager. The NetWare Management System console creates logical "maps" of network devices, tracks cabling system statistics, and displays alarms on devices when unusual or error conditions occur. Most SNMP managers can also set alarm thresholds and change settings on SNMP agents.

THE SNMP AGENT

SNMP agents respond to SNMP manager queries and send "trap" messages when alarms or unusual conditions occur. These trap messages, in turn, cause the SNMP manager to display an alarm on the management console.

SNMP agents are responsible for tracking information about the device they are loaded on. For example, NetWare's TCPCON NLM is an SNMP management console that communicates with a management agent NLM called SNMP.NLM. Figure 11.5 depicts the relationship between TCPCON and SNMP.NLM.

In Figure 11.5 the SNMP manager NLM is loaded on FS3. This NLM queries the SNMP agent NLMs (SNMP.NLM) on servers FS1, FS2, FS4, FS5, FS6 and Router A and Router B. If SNMP.NLM is loaded on FS3, then FS3 can also be managed by TCPCON. When you load TCPCON.NLM and select another server as a host, the SNMP manager and agent use SNMP commands to communicate.

SNMP COMMANDS

There are very few SNMP commands—four, in fact. These commands are

- GET (request and reply)
- GET NEXT
- SET
- TRAP

The GET Command

The GET command is used by an SNMP manager to request information from an agent and by an agent when responding to a request. Figure 11.6 shows a sample communication using the SNMP GET command. The SNMP manager software, TCPCON.NLM, has transmitted a GET request to the agent. The agent software, SNMP.NLM, transmits a GET reply in response.

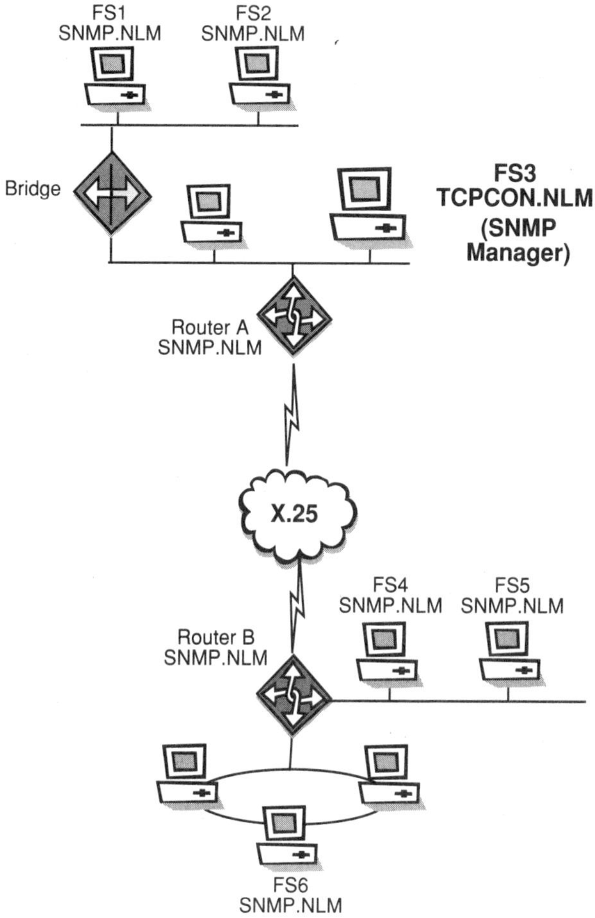

FIGURE 11.5

*TCPCON communicates
with SNMP.NLM, the
SNMP agent.*

The GET NEXT Command

The GET NEXT command is used to create a table or listing of information. For example, an SNMP manager may request the entire routing table from an SNMP agent. As shown in Figure 11.7, the SNMP manager issues GET NEXT requests to obtain the entire routing table. The SNMP agent replies with GET responses until the entire routing table has been reported to the manager.

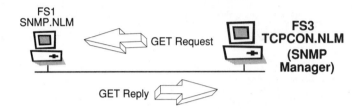

F I G U R E 11.6

The GET command is used
to exchange management
information.

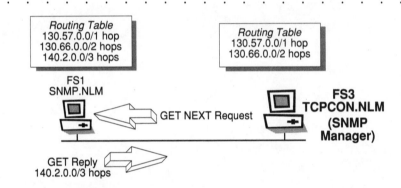

F I G U R E 11.7

The GET NEXT command
is used to gather a table
or list of information from
an agent.

The SET Command

The SET command is issued by a manager to change information maintained by the agent. For example, an authorized manager may issue a SET command changing an entry in the agent's routing table, as shown in Figure 11.8.

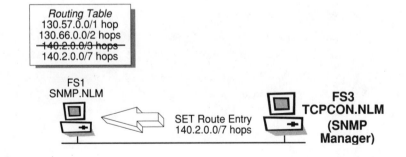

F I G U R E 11.8

The SNMP manager issues
a SET command to change
a routing entry in the
agent's routing table.

The TRAP Command

SNMP agents sometimes send information without an SNMP manager's request. This type of unsolicited communication is called a *trap message*. SNMP agents send trap messages to the manager when a network event has occurred, as shown in Figure 11.9. The network event could be an alarm threshold that has been exceeded or a device that has become unavailable on the network, or perhaps there was an unauthorized attempt to access the agent's information (authentication failure). The SNMP manager's reaction to a trap message is implementation specific. For example, the SNMP manager software may display an alarm message when trap messages are sent to the manager and keep the trap messages in a log for future reference.

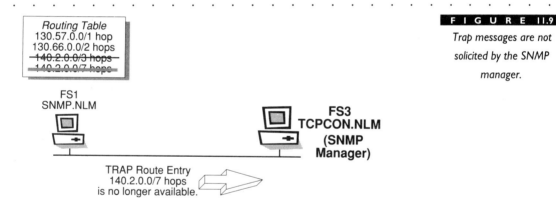

FIGURE 11.9

Trap messages are not solicited by the SNMP manager.

THE SNMP MANAGEMENT INFORMATION BASE (MIB)

A Management Information Base (MIB) is simply a database of objects that can be tracked by an agent. MIB objects may include routes known and the number of packets transmitted and received. Not all MIBs are created equal, however, and this can add to the confusion when selecting an SNMP management system. When an SNMP manager queries an SNMP agent, they must both utilize the same MIB in order to exchange information, as shown in Figure 11.10.

FIGURE 11.10

SNMP managers and agents must support the same MIB.

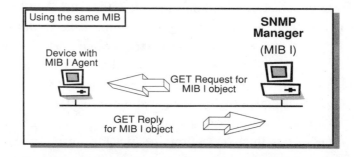

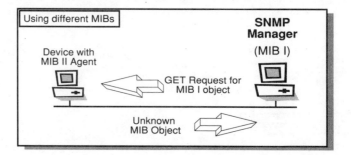

There are two primary types of MIBs:

- Internet-standard MIBs

- Private-enterprise MIBs

Internet-Standard MIBs

Internet-standard MIBs are defined in an RFC (Request for Comment). There are currently two commonly used Internet-standard MIBs: MIB I and MIB II.

MIB I lists 14 different objects and is defined in RFC 1156. MIB II, the successor to MIB I, lists 172 manageable objects and is defined in RFC 1213.

The RMON (Remote Monitoring) MIB was drafted in November 1991 (RFC 1271). Management consoles supporting RMON are not as common as MIB I or MIB II but it is gaining in popularity as more vendors support the MIB in their devices. The RMON MIB contains nine distinct groups of information that may be tracked. These groups are

- ▶ Statistics

- ▶ History

- ▶ Alarm

- ▶ Host

- ▶ HostTopN

- ▶ Matrix

- ▶ Filter

- ▶ Packet capture

- ▶ Event

If a vendor wants to use the RMON MIB, it can select the object group that it would like to track. The vendor, however, does not need to support all nine groups. Each group includes objects relating to that group. If a vendor chooses to implement only six of the groups, they must recognize all objects in each of the six groups.

The RMON MIB provides additional flexibility that is not currently available with MIB I, MIB II, or most of the enterprise MIBs in use today.

Private-Enterprise MIBs

Private-enterprise MIBs are either proprietary or open.

A proprietary MIB is often sold as a package with a vendor's manager and agent software. The MIB is developed specifically for that vendor's equipment and is generally not available for third-party development—it is not considered an "open" solution. Because of this limitation, you may be tied to the vendor's entire management solution. You may have to purchase a separate SNMP manager to query other MIBs on your network.

Open MIBs are developed by a vendor with MIB contents supplied to third-parties for development. This enables a third-party company to create other management solutions that work in conjunction with the open MIB. With device-specific management options and third-party development, support, and enhancements, an open MIB is often the most flexible and appropriate management database for SNMP-managed objects.

How MIB Objects Are Defined

If you ever read a MIB document, you may be confused to find that 1.3.6.4.1.23.2.1.2.16 is the Novell Enterprise MIB identifier for Ethernet local collisions. This format is a subset of an International Standards Organization (ISO) specification called Abstract Syntax Notation One (ASN.1).

You generally do not need to be concerned with ASN.1's object identifiers; however, it may help in translating MIB documents. For more information on ASN.1, refer to Chapter 8 of *The Open Book: A Practical Perspective to OSI* by Marshall T. Rose (Prentice Hall, 1990).

Limitations of SNMP

There are two primary limitations of SNMP: relatively weak security features and the "ping-pong" nature of getting large amounts of data.

SNMP SECURITY

The only security implemented in SNMP is in the form of "community names," which are similar to passwords. When an SNMP manager requests information from an SNMP agent, it includes a MonitorCommunity name with its request. If the agent recognizes the name sent, it responds with the required data. If the agent does not recognize the name, it cannot authenticate the requesting manager and does not reply. When an SNMP manager wants to use the SET command to change the value of an editable MIB object, such as a route hop count, the manager sends a ControlCommunity name with the SET request. Once again, the agent checks the manager's authorization to change MIB object values. If the authentication succeeds, the agent changes the MIB object value.

The security system for SNMP is weak because the community names are sent in plain ASCII text across the network and can be read with any wiretapping device.

GETTING LARGE AMOUNTS OF DATA

SNMP managers transmit one request for each MIB object value. For example, an SNMP manager sends numerous GET requests to obtain an entire table of information from the agent. This makes the SNMP communication less effective than if it could make a single request for the entire table of information.

These limitations of SNMP have been addressed in the successor to SNMP, SNMP II. One necessary enhancement included in SNMP II is a more robust security system. Community names are sent in encrypted form rather than plain ASCII text on the network. SNMP II also includes a GET BULK command that enables the manager to make a single request for a large amount of information and receive the information in a stream of replies without having to reissue the request. This feature will enhance SNMP communication significantly. SNMP II also features manager-to-manager communication, allowing multiple SNMP managers on the network to share information and ensure that management information is synchronized across multiple managers.

Now that we've examined SNMP managers, agents, MIBs, and future enhancements, let's take a look at a product that manages NetWare servers, routers, cabling segments, hubs, and third-party devices.

NetWare Management System

The NetWare Management System consists of a console and management agents that reside on NetWare servers, as well as third-party agents for network devices such as hubs or the Compaq System Pro. The NetWare management system builds a map of network devices and communicates to the various agents on the network to obtain management information. The agents, in turn, send messages to the management console to alert the manager to unusual events or error conditions on the network. Figure 11.11 shows the basic architecture of the NetWare management system.

F I G U R E II.II

Basic architecture of the NetWare management system

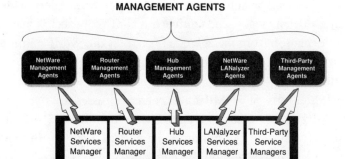

MANAGEMENT AGENTS

MANAGEMENT CONSOLE

Using the NetWare management system, an administrator can view a map of network devices and see associated alarms indicating that an unusual event, such as a server low on memory, has occurred.

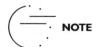

NOTE

For more information on the NetWare Management System, contact your local Novell Authorized Reseller or ask your local Novell Authorized Education Center (NAEC) about the NetWare Management System course (Course 730).

This chapter has focused on the management of the internetwork. A well-researched, easy-to-use, robust management system is imperative for a large internetwork. There are a variety of SNMP-based management systems available in the market today. As discussed in this chapter, special attention should be paid to the MIB used and the openness of the management platform. Management systems should be included in the planning stage of the internetwork to ensure adequate funding and configuration time. Evaluate your management software based on the following considerations:

- ► Support of SNMP and the standard MIBs

- ► Ability to map and document your internetwork

- ► Third-party support for monitoring a variety of devices

- ► Ability to integrate new enterprise MIBs (such as a MIB compiler)

As you add devices to your network, you should consider how they will fit into your management scheme. Important management considerations include the following:

- ► Support of the standard MIBs

- ► Use of an enterprise MIB that your management console can support

- ► In-band and out-of-band monitoring options

Including management considerations in the selection of your internetworking devices will help you achieve the maximum performance your network is capable of.

Appendices

Vendor Directory and WAN Installation Checklist

This appendix provides a list of service providers and product vendors worldwide. There are two separate directories contained in this appendix:

- ► PDN (Public Data Networks) and carriers
- ► DSU/CSU and modem vendors

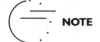 **NOTE** **Because of the dynamic nature of the industry, some of the contact names may have changed.**

At the end of this appendix we've included a WAN installation checklist. This checklist is extremely valuable if you are installing your first WAN.

PDN and Carrier Directory

The following list is provided to aid in selecting and contacting a PDN or carrier service.

U.S. CARRIERS

ACCUNET Packet Service

800-222-0400

AT&T

408-452-3719

AT&T International

Syracuse NY

Tel: 315-442-3500

Fax: 800-446-3856

BT Tymnet

Contact: International Support Center

Tel: 703-356-6995

Fax: 703-556-3212

CompuServe, Inc.

614-457-8600

GEIS

301-340-4000

Infonet

El Segundo CA

Contact: Ms. Laura Andrus

Tel: 213-335-2872

Fax: 213-335-2876

MCI International

Piscataway NJ

Tel: 908-885-4040

Fax: 908-980-7629

Metropolitan Fiber

708-218-7200

Pacific Bell

415-811-2900

Southern Pacific Telecom

415-541-2000

Southwestern Bell

314-247-4613

US Sprint International

Reston VA

Contact: E. Goldstein

Tel: 703-689-6000

Fax: 703-689-5177

US Sprint

913-854-2118

Willtel

800-364-5113

INTERNATIONAL CARRIERS

Antigua

Cable and Wireless Ltd.

St. Johns

Contact: Mr. Carl Roberts

Tel: 809-462-0840

Fax: 809-462-0843

Telex: 2149

Argentina

Empresa Nacional de Telecommunicationes Gerencia de Servicios
Internacionales

Buenos Aires

Contact: Mr. Armando Parolari

Tel: 54-1-49-0913

Telex: 390-18372

Australia

Telecom

Australia Melbourne

Contact: Corporate Customer Division

Tel: 61-3-664-9924

Fax: 61-3-664-9999

Austria

Radio Austria

A.G. Vienna

Contact: Mr. Gerhard Zandler

Tel: 43-222-50145-0

Fax: 43-222-50260

Telex: (47) 114731

Belgium

Regie del Telegraphes et de Telephones

Brussels

Contact: Mr. Mano Bultinck

Tel: 32-3-313-3489

Fax: 32-3-317-9481

Bolivia Entel

Bolivia

Contact: Mr. Juan José Peralta Cataldi

Tel: 591-2-35-2001

Brazil

Brazil Empresa Brasileira de Telecommunicacoes

S.A. Rio de Janeiro

Contact: Mr. Arne Sampaio Freinsilber

Tel: 55-21-216-8328

Telex: (391) 2121810

Canada Telecom

Canada Ottawa

Contact: Customer Assistant Center

Tel: 613-781-6829

Fax: 613-781-5392

Chile

Chile Empresa Nacional de Telecommunicaciones

S.A. Santiago

Contact: Mr. Jean Paul Porre Beckett

China PLTELCOM

Beijing

Contact: Mr. Zeo Feng

Tel: 86-6010757

Fax: 86-6010717

Telex: (716) 222180

Curacao

Curacao Landsradio Telecommunication Administration

N.A. Willemstad

Contact: Ing R.A.C. Bernadina Btw.

Tel: 59-9-9631111 Ext. 306

Fax: 59-9-9631321

Telex: 1075 LRNA

Egypt

Telecommunication Organization of Egypt

Cairo

Contact: Mr. M.A. Hegazy

Tel: 20-2-775-085

Telex: (927) 92100

El Salvador

El Salvador Administracion Nacional de Telecommunication

Contact: Mr. C. Zaveleto

Tel: 503-71-71-71

Finland

Finland Telecom

Finland Helsinki

Contact: Mr. Tauno Stjernberg

Tel: 358-0-704-2373

Fax: 358-0-704-2659

Telex: (857) 123434

France

France Telecom International

Paris

Tel: 33-1-4564-3629 Ext. 260

Germany

Deutsche Bundespost Telekom

Bonn

Contact: Mr. Herbert Muller

Tel: 49-228-181-9330

Fax: 49-228-181-8872

Hong Kong

Hong Kong Telecom

Contact: Mr. K.S. Mak

Tel: 852-808-6474

Fax: 852-824-0033

Telex: 70907 MUTCH HX

Ireland

Telecom Eireann

Dublin

Contact: Mr. Pat Cleary

Tel: 353-1-77-8222

Fax: 353-1-774941

Telex: (852) 90936

Israel

Ministry of Communications

Jerusalem

Contact: Ms. Zvia Nathan

Tel: 972-2-208362

Fax: 972-3-204328

Telex: (922) 25269

Italy

ItalCable

Rome

Contact: Mr. Valerio Pella

Tel: 39-6-47-70-4425

Fax: 39-6-47-70-4596

Telex: (843) 611146

Ivory Coast

Intelci Abidjan

Contact: Mr. Abi

Tel: 225-34-64-71

Telex: (969) 23790

Japan

Nippon Telephone and Telegraph Corp.

Tokyo

Tel: 81-3-3509-8044

Fax: 81-3-3593-1794

Luxembourg

Luxembourg Administration des P. et T.

Section T, L-2020 Luxembourg

Tel: 352-4765-1

Fax: 352-475110

Telex: 3450 GENTLLU

Mexico

Mexico Telefonos De Mexico

Mexico City

Contact: Mr. Jesus A. Ramirez Cordero

Tel: 52-5-530-2099 or 52-5-591-0299

Telex: (383) 170932

Netherlands

PTT Telecom

Netherlands The Hague

Contact: Mr. Albert Straatman

Tel: 31-70-34-39263

Fax: 31-70-34-39747

New Zealand

New Zealand Telecom

New Zealand Wellington

Tel: 64-4-496-6132

Fax: 64-4-496-6125

Telex: 791-31688

Norway

Norweigian Telecommunications

Administration Oslo

Tel: 47-2-48-8304

Fax: 47-2-36-0103

Telex: (856) 71203

Panama

Panama Instituto Nactional de Telecommunicaciones

Panama City

Contact: Sales and Marketing

Tel: 507-64-0271

Fax: 507-63-6525

Telex: (368) 2660

Saudi Arabia

Saudi Arabia Cable and Wireless

Saudi Arabia Ltd. Riyadh

Contact: Mr. Barrie Littlefair

Tel: 966-1465-7092

Fax: 966-1465-6426

Telex: 401691 CBLWIR SJ

Singapore

Singapore Telecom

Singapore

Contact: Mr. Tan Kee Joo

Tel: 65-730-3633

Fax: 65-733-8191

Telex: RS21246

South Africa

Telecommunicational Commercial

Pretoria

Contact: Mr. G. Van Miekerk

Tel: 27-12-293-1156

Telex: (99960) 320924

Spain

Compania Telefonica Nacional de Espana

Madrid

Contact: Mr. Francisco Linares

Tel: 34-1-248-81-20

Telex: (831) 277774

Sweden

Swedish Telecom

Stockholm

Contact: Customer Support

Tel: 46-8-7806228

Fax: 46-8-407-853

Telex: 12020

Switzerland

Direction Geneerale de PTT

Berne

Contact: Mr. P. Laesser

Tel: 41-31-62-4374

Fax: 41-31-62-2549

Telex: (845) 911010

Taiwan

International Telecommunications Administration

Taipei

Contact: Ms. T.F. Leng

Tel: 886-2-344-3770

Fax: 886-2-321-1804

Telex: (785) 26665

Telco Norte

Contact: Mr. Dominic

St. Jean Telcor Sur

Contact: Mr. J.L. Martin de Bustamante

Tel: 54-1-334-5771

Thailand

The Communications Authority of Thailand

Bangkok

Contact: Mr. Vichien Bhenchsonggram

Tel: 66-2-233-5380

Telex: (86) 70046

U.K. British Telecom International

London

Contact: Sales

Tel: 44-71-250-8719

Fax: 44-1-831-9959

Telex: (851) 21601

U.S.S.R.

Institute for Automated Systems

Moscow

Contact: Prof. Oleg L. Smirnov

Tel: 7-095-229-7846

Fax: 7-095-229-3237

Telex: 411809

Yugoslavia

GenTel

Belgrade

Contact: Jose Lajavec

Tel: 38-61-311-230

Telex: (862) 31913

DSU/CSU and Modem Vendors

ALCATEL Network Systems

2912 Wake Forest St.

Raleigh NC 27609

Tel: 800-877-6060 or 916-850-6000

Fax: 919-850-6409

Channel banks, modems (specialized), multiplexors/T1 products

Astrocom Corporation

120 W. Plato Blvd.

St. Paul MN 55107-2092

Tel: 612-227-8651

Fax: 612-227-0703

Multiplexors/T1 products

AT&T Paradyne

8545 126th Ave., N.

P.O. Box 2826

Largo FL 34649-2826

Tel: 800-482-3333 Ext. 448 or 813-530-2000

Fax: 813-530-2109

Channel extenders, conversion equipment, modems (specialized), modems (voiceband), multiplexors/T1 products

Avanti Communications Corporation

115 Norwood Park South

Norwood MA 02062

Tel: 800-535-3550

Tel: 617-551-3333

Fax: 617-769-0942

Modems (specialized), multiplexors/T1 products

CYLINK Corporation

110 S. Wolfe Rd.

Sunnyvale CA 94086

Tel: 408-735-5800

Fax: 408-720-8294

Modems (specialized)

Digicom Systems, Inc.

188 Topaz St.

Milpitas CA 95035

Tel: 800-833-8900 or 408-262-1277

Fax: 408-262-1390

Modems (specialized)

Dowty Communications, Inc.

55 Carnegie Plaza

Cherry Hill Industrial Center

Cherry Hill NJ 08003

Tel: 800-424-4451 or 609-424-4451

Fax: 69-424-8065

Modems (specialized), multiplexors/T1 products

Develcon Electronics

515 Consumers Rd., Ste. 500

Willowdale, Ontario, Canada M2J 4Z2

Tel: 800-667-9333 or 416-495-9303

Fax: 408-745-6250

Multiplexors/T1 products

Digital Link Corporation

252 Humboldt Court

Sunnyvale CA 94089

Tel: 800-441-1142 or 408-745-6200

Fax: 408-745-6250

Multiplexors/T1 products

IBM

Old Orchard Rd.

Armonk NY 10504

Tel: 800-426-2468 or 914-765-1900

Data communication (modems, LAN hardware, muxes)

Kentrox Industries, inc.

P.O. Box 10704

Portland OR 92710-0704

Tel: 800-733-5511 or 503-643-1681

Modems (specialized)

Larse Corporation

P.O. Box 56138

4600 Patrick Henry Dr.

Santa Clara CA 95052-8138

Tel: 408-988-6600

Fax: 408-986-8690

Modems (specialized)

MICOM Communications Corporation

P.O. Box 8100

4100 Los Angeles Ave.

Simi Valley CA 93062-8100

Tel: 800-642-6687 or 805-583-8600

Fax: 805-583-1997

Modems (specialized), multiplexors/T1 products

Motorola Codex

20 Cabot Blvd.

Mansfield MA 02048

Tel: 800-446-6336 or 508-261-4000

Fax: 508-261-1203

Channel banks, modems (specialized), multiplexors/T1 products, telecommunications equipment, ISDN, terminal adapters

Multi-Tech Systems, Inc.

2205 Woodale Dr.

Mounds View MN 55112

Tel: 800-328-9717 or 612-785-3500

Fax: 612-785-9874

Modems (specialized), multiplexors/T1 products

NEC America, Inc.

110 Rio Robles

San Jose CA 95134

Tel: 800-222-4NEC Ext. 1276 or 408-433-1250

Fax: 214-437-8912

Modems (specialized)

Network Equipment Technologies, Inc.

800 Saginaw Dr.

Redwood City CA 94063

Tel: 415-366-4400

Fax: 415-366-5675

Modems (specialized), multiplexors/T1 products

Racal-Milgo

1601 N. Harrison Parkway

Sunrise FL 33323-2899

Tel: 800-722-2555 or 305-846-1601

Fax: 305-846-4942

Channel banks, modems (specialized), multiplexors/T1 products

Racal-Vadic

1708 McCarthy Blvd.

Milpitas CA 95035

Tel: 800-482-3427 or 408-432-8008

Fax: 408-434-0188

Modems (specialized), multiplexors/T1 products

Scitec Communication Systems, Inc.

26 Valley Rd.

Middletown RI 02840

Tel: 800-343-0928 or 401-849-4353

Fax: 401-849-8020

Modems (specialized), multiplexors/T1 products

UDS Motorola

5000 Bradford Dr.

Huntsville AL 35805-1993

Tel: 800-451-2369 or 205-430-8000

Fax: 205-830-5657

Modems (specialized), multiplexors/T1 products

Ven-Tel, Inc.

2121 Zenker Rd.

San Jose CA 95131

Tel: 4098-436-7400

Fax: 408-436-7451

Modems (specialized)

Verilink Corporation

145 Baytech Dr.

San Jose CA 95134

Tel: 800-543-1008

Tel: 408-945-1199

DSU/CSU

WAN Installation Checklist

This list is provided to aid in designing a WAN solution. If you are in doubt about the steps listed, hire a qualified WAN consultant to implement your proposed solution.

DISCOVERY STAGE

Plenty of time should be allotted to the discovery stage. This is the stage during which the link type and performance requirements are set.

- ▶ Conduct user survey.

- ▶ Conduct needs assessment study.

- ▶ Define application requirements.

- ▶ Contact international system design consultants.

- ▶ Determine site locations.

- ▶ Determine site modifications.

- ▶ Develop time line for project.

- ▶ Finalize system design.

- ▶ Propose solution to management.

- ▶ Obtain budgetary approval.

- ▶ Assemble project team.

IMPLEMENTATION PLANNING STAGE

Keep a diary of your daily and weekly progress during the implementation planning stage. This helps ensure that loose ends are dealt with.

- Develop requirements for equipment/services bids.

- Obtain government regulation guidelines for each country, including PTTs (Public Telephone and Telegraph) and Customs.

- Investigate customs and holiday schedule for each country, and incorporate into schedule.

- If possible, contract with local in-country integrators to assist in the final schedule.

- Assign corporate in-country contract for project-tracking responsibility at that location.

EQUIPMENT PLANNING STAGE

During the equipment planning stage, ask vendors for referrals. (Ask industry contacts for recommendations on equipment and service providers.)

- Evaluate necessary hardware.

- Determine potential vendors, both local and international.

- Obtain required PTT certification documents for equipment from vendors.

- Obtain VERIFICATION documents from the PTT on the equipment.

- Determine which communication gear can be purchsed or brought in from outside the country in question.

- Acquire permits, government approvals, and network addresses.

- Send out bid requests to all vendors and service providers.

- Select bids and award contracts.

- Mock up network in-house for application testing.

▸ Document network and publish.

▸ Develop cut-over schedule and publish.

▸ Purchase or lease test gear for circuit and network troubleshooting.

IMPLEMENTATION STAGE

During the implementation stage, be certain to test the network connection thoroughly with the service provider.

▸ Coordinate equipment delivery dates with all vendors.

▸ Coordinate service installation dates with all PTTs and carriers.

▸ Run loopback tests with all telecom personnel, end point to end point, to ensure proper circuit operation at each location.

▸ Install pilot location end to end and test applications for one week minimum to locate and repair problems and establish performance benchmark.

▸ Complete installation of remaining sites on a scheduled basis, test each one, and allow for fine-tuning of network parameters.

▸ Select a team member to act as the central contact for all internetworking issues.

▸ Follow up with all vendors to ensure no loose ends remain.

▸ Complete and publish network user documentation.

▸ Implement user training.

▸ Complete and sign off project documentation.

Glossary

Aconsole Novell NetWare utility that allows a workstation to use a modem to call a remote NetWare server or router and to manage the server through the transfer of screen and keystroke information.

active hubs ARCnet hubs that amplify the signal. Used to send signals to devices on an ARCnet LAN at a greater distance (2000 feet) than is possible with a passive hub (100 feet).

adapter Hardware, typically an interface card, installed in a computer, that connects the computer to other hardware or devices.

address Identifier assigned to networks, stations, and other devices so that each device can be separately designated to receive and reply to messages.

Address Resolution protocol *See* ARP.

advertising Process by which services on a network inform other devices on the network of their existence. NetWare uses the Service Advertising protocol (SAP) to do this.

AFP AppleTalk Filing protocol. Protocol that allows distributed file sharing across an AppleTalk network.

agent The part of a networked system that performs information preparation and exchange on behalf of a software entity.

aging Process used to remove old entries (such as routing and server information) from tables.

alarm Audible or visible warning signal that tells a network administrator an error has occurred or there is a critical situation on the network.

alert Alarms sent by management devices to management consoles to inform administrators of thresholds reached and other discrepancies on the network.

alternative route Secondary communication path to a destination; used when the primary path is unavailable.

American National Standards Institute *See* ANSI.

American Standard Code for Information Interchange *See* ASCII.

analog Signal that varies as a sine wave to change frequencies, phase, or amplitude for transmitting data, voice, and so on.

ANSI American National Standards Institute. Nonprofit organization in the U.S. that defines standards in many industries. Supported by over 1000 trade organizations, professional societies, and companies and affiliated with the Consultative Committee for International Telegraphy and Telephony (CCITT) and the International Organization for Standardization (ISO).

AppleTalk Protocol suite developed by Apple Computer that can be used by Apple and non-Apple computers for communicating and sharing resources such as printers and file servers.

AppleTalk Filing protocol *See* AFP.

application layer Layer 7, the highest layer of the Open Systems Interconnection (OSI) model; provides network access to users.

ARCnet Proprietary token-bus networking architecture developed by Datapoint Corporation in the mid-1970s. Licensed by third-party vendors, it is a popular networking architecture in smaller installations. Relatively fast (2.5Mbps) and reliable and supports coaxial, twisted-pair, and fiber-optic implementations.

ARP Address Resolution protocol. Internet protocol that dynamically maps Internet addresses to physical (hardware) addresses on local area networks. Limited to networks that support hardware broadcast.

ARPANET Packet-switched network developed in the early 1970s; the first network in the Internet.

ASCII American Standard Code for Information Interchange. An 8-bit code for data transfer that was adopted by ANSI to ensure compatibility among data devices.

asynchronous transfer mode See *ATM*.

asynchronous transmission Data transmission method in which each character is individually synchronized, usually by means of start and stop elements. The gap between characters is not a fixed length.

ATCON Diagnostic tool used in Novell NetWare environments; provides information about a server's or router's AppleTalk stack and about other AppleTalk networks on the internetwork.

ATM Asynchronous transfer mode. Very high-speed method of transmission that uses fixed-size "cells" of 53 bytes to transfer information over fiber; also known as cell relay.

B channel Full-duplex 64K channel in an Integrated Service Digital Network (ISDN).

backbone network Primary connectivity mechanism of a hierarchical distributed system. Ensures that all systems that have connectivity to an intermediate system on the backbone have connectivity to one another.

bandwidth Carrying capacity of a circuit, usually measured in bits per second (bps) for digital circuits or hertz (Hz) for analog circuits.

baseband Network technology that uses a single frequency; requires all stations attached to a network to participate in every transmission.

baud Unit of signaling speed defined as cycles per second, which equals bits per second only if 1 bit is transmitted per cycle. Bits per second is more accurate, but baud is a more common term.

baud rate Number of signal changes in one second.

beaconing In Token Ring networks, the state that results when a severe error condition occurs, preventing communication until the error condition is resolved.

binary Numbering system using 0's and 1's.

BISDN Broadband Integrated Service Digital Network. Communication standard that handles high-bandwidth applications such as video, voice, data, and graphics.

bit Binary digit; either a 1 or a 0.

bit-oriented protocol Communication protocol that moves bits across a data link without regard to the meaning of those bits—for example, the high-level data-link control (HDLC) protocol.

bit rate Rate at which bits (binary digits) are transmitted over a communication line. Normally expressed in bits per second (bps).

bits per second (bps) Number of bits transmitted or received in 1 second.

block Set of continuous bits or bytes that make up a definable quantity of information, such as a message.

BNC connector Connector for coaxial cable that locks when one connector is inserted into another and rotated 90 degrees.

BOC Bell Operating Company. In the U.S., one of 22 local telephone companies spun off from AT&T and reorganized into seven regional Bell operating companies (RBOCs).

bridge Device that connects two or more physical networks, forwarding frames between networks based on information in the data-link header. Because it operates at the data-link layer, it is transparent to the network-layer protocols.

broadband Characteristic of any network that multiplexes multiple, independent network carriers on a single cable. Allows several networks to coexist on a single cable. Traffic from one network does not interfere with traffic from another network because conversations happen on different frequencies.

broadcast (noun) Packet delivery service in which all hosts on a network receive a copy of any frame that is designated for broadcast.

broadcast (verb) Sending the message to all nodes.

brouter Device that routes some protocols and bridges others.

buffer Memory area or electronic register where data is stored temporarily while awaiting disposition. Compensates for differences in data-flow rates (for example, between a terminal and its transmission line). Also used as a data backup mechanism, holding data that may be retransmitted if an error is detected during transmission.

burst Method of data transfer in which information is collected and sent as a unit in one high-speed transmission. LAN traffic is usually considered bursty traffic because it has short intervals of intense activity with lulls between.

bus topology Linear LAN used by Ethernet networks.

byte Group of 8 binary digits operated on as a unit; also known as a character or octet.

byte-oriented protocol Protocol that uses a whole byte to communicate control information.

cache High-speed memory section that holds blocks of data the CPU is currently working on; designed to minimize the time the CPU spends accessing memory.

call Request to establish communication with another network node; also, the resulting communication session or the virtual circuit over which it is conducted.

call setup time Length of time required to establish a switched call between data terminal equipment (DTE).

carrier Analog signal at a fixed amplitude and frequency that is combined with an information-bearing signal to produce an intelligent output signal suitable for transmitting data. *See also* carrier frequency.

carrier frequency Basic frequency or pulse repetition rate of a signal. Does not convey any information until it is modulated by another signal that imparts intelligence.

CCITT Consultative Committee for International Telegraphy and Telephony. Group within the International Telecommunications Union (ITU) that defines data communication standards.

cell relay *See* ATM.

central office Local exchange carrier's office, where the central office switch is located. A central point where trunk lines converge.

central office switch Device in the central office that provides the power, routing, and signaling functions for local phone lines.

central office trunk Local loop between central offices.

channel Path for transmitting electromagnetic signals; synonym for "line" or "link."

channel bank Equipment that multiplexes low-speed analog or digital channels into a high-speed composite channel.

channel service unit *See* CSU.

character Group of eight binary digits operated on as a unit; also called a byte or octet.

checksum Numeric computation that combines the bits of a transmitted message; also, the resulting value. The value is transmitted with the message; the receiver recalculates the checksum and compares it to the received value to detect transmission errors. *See also* CRC.

circuit Any path that can carry an electrical current.

circuit switching Procedure for establishing a connection between two end devices. Once connected, it uses a nonshareable path through the network.

client Node or workstation on a network that requires services from a server.

client/server model   Configuration that uses distributed intelligence to treat both the server and the individual workstations as intelligent, programmable devices.

CLNP   Connectionless Network protocol. Open Systems Interconnection (OSI) protocol that provides the OSI Connectionless Network Service (delivery of data). CLNP is the OSI equivalent of the Internet IP protocol.

clocking   Time synchronization of communication information.

CLTP   Connectionless Transport protocol. Provides end-to-end transport data addressing and error detection but does not guarantee delivery or provide flow control. The Open Systems Interconnection (OSI) equivalent of the User Datagram protocol (UDP) datagram service.

cluster controller   IBM or IBM-compatible device for attaching 3270 or 3270-class terminals. It can be channel-attached to a host system or it can communicate with the host via the Synchronous Data-Link Control (SDL) protocol or, in some cases, a bisync link to a host-attached communication controller.

CMIP   Common Management Information protocol. Open Systems Interconnection (OSI) network management protocol.

CMOT   Common Management Information protocol over TCP. Network managers can use CMOT to manage TCP/IP networks.

coaxial   Type of cable that uses two conductors: a central, solid wire core surrounded by insulation and, surrounding that, a braided-wire conductor sheath. Well suited for networking because it can accommodate high bandwidth but is relatively resistant to interference.

collision   What happens when two devices transmit data at the same time, resulting in a loss of data.

common carrier   Organization that provides regulated telephone, telegraph, telex, and data communication services. Usually denotes U.S. and Canadian telephone companies but can also refer to telecommunication organizations in other countries. *See also* PTT.

communications controller   Machine directly attached to a host computer that processes communication to a host; also known as a front-end processor.

compression   Method of compacting data for more efficient transmission.

concentrator   Device with a single bus and multiple connections to computers; provides a star-wired LAN topology.

congestion   Excessive traffic on the network.

connection-oriented   Model of interconnection in which communication proceeds through three well-defined phases: connection establishment, data transfer, and connection release.

connectionless   Model of interconnection in which communication takes place without first establishing a connection.

Connectionless Network protocol   *See* CLNP.

Connectionless Transport Protocol   *See* CLTP.

CONS   Connection-oriented network service; for example, X.25.

console   Monitor and keyboard from which the server or host activity can be viewed and controlled.

contention   Situation that occurs when processors want to use the same communication lines. Each processor must send a request to transmit; if the channel is busy, the processor must wait.

convergence   Synchronization process that a network goes through immediately after a route change happens on the network.

convergence time   Time required for routing information to propagate throughout the network.

CPE   Customer-premises equipment. Devices used at a customer site, either leased or owned, including telecommunication equipment.

CPECFG   Novell NetWare utility, installed on the NetWare MultiProtocol Router, that expands remote control of data communication equipment.

CRC   Cyclic redundancy check. Sophisticated checksum algorithm; uses a complex mathematical formula that employs division and addition to detect errors.

crosstalk   Interference caused by a signal transferring from one circuit to another.

CSMA/CD   Carrier Sense Multiple Access with Collision Detection. Access method used by local area networking technologies such as Ethernet.

CSU   Channel service unit. Digital signal processor that performs transmit and receive filtering, signal shaping, longitudinal balance, voltage isolation, equalization, and remote loopback testing for digital transmission. Functions as a guaranteed safe electrical circuit, acting as a buffer between the customer's equipment and a public carrier's wide area network. CSUs prevent malfunctioning digital service units (DSUs) or other customer-premises equipment (CPE) from disabling a public carrier's transmission system. The design of a CSU must be certified by the FCC. *See also* DSU.

customer-premises equipment *See* CPE.

cyclic redundancy check *See* CRC.

DARPA Defense Advanced Research Projects Agency. The U.S. government agency that funded ARPANET.

DAS Dual-attached station. Fiber Distributed Data Interface (FDDI) that supports a dual, counter-rotating ring.

data channel *See* channel.

data circuit-terminating equipment Device that terminates a communication circuit. (For example, a PC connected to a modem is the terminating point of that circuit.) Also, communication equipment installed to establish and maintain circuits at a customer site.

data communication equipment *See* DCE.

data-link control *See* DLC.

data-link layer Second of seven layers of the Open Systems Interconnection (OSI) model. Involved in both packaging and addressing information and in controlling the flow of separate transmissions over communication lines.

data rate Speed at which data bits are transmitted and received. Usually measured in bits per second (bps).

data service unit *See* DSU.

datagram One packet of information and associated delivery information that is routed through a packet-switching network.

Dataphone Digital Service *See* DDS.

DB-9 A 9-pin connector defined in the ISO standard and RS-449 standard; used with the secondary channel of the RS-449 interface.

DB-25 Standard plug and jack set used in RS-232C wiring; it has a 25-pin connector, with 13 pins in the top row and 12 pins in the bottom row.

DB-37   A 37-pin connector defined in the ISO standard and RS-449 standard; used with the primary channel of the RS-449 interface.

DCE   Data communication equipment. Devices that establish, maintain, and terminate a data communication session; they also provide encoding or conversion.

DDN   Defense Data Network. Comprises MILNET and several other U.S. Department of Defense networks.

DDS   Dataphone Digital Service. AT&T's four-wire, digital communication service that operates at speeds from 2400bps to 56Kbps on a point-to-point connection.

DECnet   Set of networking protocols developed by Digital Equipment Corporation primarily for use in their VAX computers to exchange messages and other data.

dedicated circuit   Leased communication circuit that goes from a user's site to a telco point of presence. A clear, unbroken communication path.

dedicated line   Communication line that is not dialed. *See also* leased line.

default route   Path that network data travels if there is no explicit routing information to direct it.

demodulation   Process of recovering information from a previously modulated carrier frequency.

demultiplex   One common input and several outputs; opposite of multiplexing. *See also* MUX.

destination address   Address in a packet identifying which station is to receive it.

destination node   In the Open Systems Interconnection (OSI) model, represents the host computers at each end of a connection. In a packet-switching network, the node attached to the DTE that is receiving the data.

device driver   Software or firmware that translates operating system requests into a format that is recognizable by specific hardware, such as adapters.

dial-up   Access to a telephone circuit that requires a manual or automatic dial to establish connection.

digital   Representation of information using 1's and 0's.

digital circuit Special lines provided by common carriers that transmit data directly in square-wave form without modulation.

Digital Network Architecture *See* DNA.

digital PBX Private telephone switch that manages internal voice and data traffic.

digital service unit *See* DSU.

digital signal Discontinuous signal that is discrete intervals apart—for example, +15 volts and −15 volts.

digital transmission Data transmitted in a square-wave form rather than modulated over analog circuits.

digitize To convert analog voice or other analog information to 1's and 0's (digital form).

directory services Network service that provides information about an entity of interest. Like an electronic phone book to help network clients find services. There are several designs, including the X.500 standard, the Domain Name System, and Novell's NetWare Directory Services.

distance vector algorithm Class of routing algorithms that derive best-path information from best-path information present in adjacent nodes. IP RIP and IPX RIP are distance vector protocols.

DIX Digital, Intel, and Xerox. Ethernet specification jointly promoted by the three companies; it became the IEEE 802.3 standard. Also, an AUI connector for thick Ethernet (DB-15).

DLC Data-link control. Protocols that govern packet information, including destination address, source address, and control information.

DNA Digital Network Architecture. Developed by Digital Equipment Corporation as its network architecture.

drop Position of a multipoint line where a tap is inserted, enabling the network administrator to connect a device.

drop cable Cable used in thick Ethernet to attach a media attachment unit (MAU) to a network device. The maximum distance is 50 meters.

DS-0 Digital service-0. Standard that specifies the electrical characteristics for 64Kbps data transmission; also referred to as fractional T1. Fractional T1 bridges the gap between 56Kbps DDS service and full T1.

DS-1 Digital service-1. Standard specifying the electrical characteristics for 1.544Mbps data transmission over four wires—for example, in T1 transmission.

DSU Digital service unit. Device between a user's data terminal equipment (DTE) and a common carrier's digital circuits. Formats data for transmission on public carrier wide area networks and ensures that the carrier's requirements for data formats are met.

DTE Data terminal equipment. For X.25, customer-premises equipment such as terminals and computers that connect to data communication equipment (DCE) in a packet-switched network.

dual homing Configuration that enables a computer to be connected to more than one physical data link. Provides link redundancy.

dumb terminal Simple CRT and keyboard with limited capabilities such as display and edit functions; may provide printer ports.

dynamic routing Routing that changes automatically as your network changes.

E1 Facility used to transport 30 voice channels at 64Kbps (for a total of 2.048Mbps); also known as CEPT.

EBCDIC Extended Binary Coded Decimal Interchange Code. Coding scheme used by IBM computers.

EDI Electronic data interchange. Technology that allows users to transfer information such as orders and invoices from one computer to another using a network.

EGP Exterior Gateway protocol. Routing protocol used by gateways in an internet, connecting autonomous networks; used in the Internet core system.

EISA Expanded Industry Standard Architecture. Bus standard that is compatible with earlier Industry Standard Architecture (ISA).

encapsulation Technique used by network-layer protocols in which a layer adds header information to the protocol data unit from the preceding layer. Also used in "enveloping" one protocol inside another for transmission (for example, IP inside IPX).

encryption Scrambling or coding of data for security.

end node   Node that serves as an originator and the final destination of network traffic but does not relay traffic originated by other nodes.

end system   Open Systems Interconnection (OSI) system containing application processes that can communicate through all seven layers of the OSI model. Equivalent to an end node.

enterprise-wide network   Internetwork that connects a corporation's local and remote sites.

equalization   Process of reducing frequency and phase distortion of a circuit by introducing time differences to compensate for the difference in attenuation or time delay at the various frequencies in the transmission band.

error detection   Process of determining whether one or more bits have changed from a 1 to a 0, or vice versa, during transmission.

error detection and correction   Process of determining which bits changed from a 1 to a 0, or vice versa, during transmission, and changing the bits back to their original form.

ES-IS   End-System-to-Intermediate-System protocol. Open Systems Interconnection (OSI) protocol that allows end systems and intermediate systems to communicate; also allows end systems to communicate with one another in the absence of an intermediate system.

Ethernet   A 10Mbps baseband LAN developed by Xerox Corporation in 1976. Uses a bus topology (configuration) and relies on the CSMA/CD access method.

EtherTalk   AppleTalk packets encapsulated to run on Ethernet cables.

even parity   Error detection method that requires an even number of 1's in each byte.

explorer frame   Frame used in Token Ring source-route bridging to determine the best route to other network devices. There are two types of explorer frames: the all-routes explorer, sent along every route between two hosts, and the spanning-tree explorer, sent only along the spanning tree.

Exterior Gateway protocol   *See* EGP.

facility   Optional field within an X.25 packet that enables users to request special services from the network at either subscription or call-setup time.

FCC   Federal Communications Commission. The U.S. government agency that regulates all interstate communications.

FCS   Frame check sequence field. In a high-level data-link control (HDLC) protocol, the part of the frame containing the cyclic redundancy check (CRC error-checking bits).

FDDI   Fiber Distributed Data Interface. Standard developed by the American National Standards Institute (ANSI) for high-speed (100Mbps) fiber-optic connections.

FDM   Frequency division multiplexing. Multiplexing method in which devices continually share the bandwidth of a link by dividing the communication circuit into many separate channel frequencies.

FDX   Full duplex. Capability to transmit in both directions at one time.

Federal Communications Commission   *See* FCC.

FEP   Front-end processor. Performs many of the functions, such as processing and control, required to operate a data communication network.

Fiber Distributed Data Interface   *See* FDDI.

fiber-optic cable   High-bandwidth transmission medium that allows data to be transmitted by modulating a light through a special glass or plastic fiber.

file server   Shared storage device for local area network users, typically in the form of a personal computer that has a high-volume disk and is attached to the network.

file transfer   Process of moving or transmitting a file from one location to another.

filter   To selectively discard packets of a certain type.

filtering rate   Rate at which packets are checked and discarded.

firmware   Group of software instructions that are set, permanently or semipermanently, into read-only memory.

flag   Field that is repeated at the beginning and end of a synchronous data-link control (SDLC) or high-level data-link control (HDLC) frame. Always has a bit pattern of 011111110.

flooding   Propagation of information or discovery packets throughout an entire network.

flow control   Hardware or software mechanism, such as a buffer, that manages data transmissions when the receiving device cannot accept data.

four-wire communication   Communication over two pairs of wires, one send pair and one receive pair.

fractional T1   *See* DS-0.

fragment   One piece of a packet that has been divided by fragmentation.

fragmentation   Process in which a datagram is broken into smaller pieces to fit the size requirements of the physical network it is transmitted across.

frame   Block of data sent using a protocol, such as high-level data-link control (HDLC) or link access procedure balanced (LAPB); or a group of bits representing data from many channels, as in T1 communication.

Frame relay   Switching interface and network that operate with variable-length packets such as X.25, but with less processing time, supporting the bursty data of high-speed networking.

frequency   Pitch or tone, or number of cycles per second of a wave—for example, a sine wave.

frequency division   Local area network contention method based on the frequency division multiplexing technique. Designates and defines frequency slots for transmission.

frequency division multiplexing   *See* FDM.

FTAM   File Transfer, Access, and Management. The Open Systems Interconnection (OSI) remote file service and protocol.

FTP   File transfer protocol. TCP/IP application protocol that supports file transfers.

full duplex   *See* FDX.

gateway   Internetworking device that operates from the network to application layers of the Open Systems Interconnection (OSI) model. Sometimes used as a synonym for router.

group address   Address that includes more than one station.

hardware address   Address that is preprogrammed on a network interface card. *See also* physical address; MAC.

HDLC   High-level data-link control. Bit-oriented, synchronous protocol that applies to the data-link layer of the Open Systems Interconnection (OSI) model.

header   Information at the beginning of a packet defining control information, including addressing and control.

HMI   NetWare Hub Management Interface.

hop   Intermediate step within an internetwork.

hop count   Routing metric used to measure the distance between a source and a destination; each hop equals the transmission of a packet across one router.

hub   Concentrator or repeater at which node connections meet in a star topology.

hub card   Multiport card that is placed in a server or router to provide direct connection to workstations on the network. Hub cards duplicate the function of a concentrator or hub on a 10Base-T network.

HUBCON   NetWare Loadable Module (NLM) that manages NetWare Hub Services.

ICMP   Internet Control Message protocol. Used to handle errors and control messages at the IP layer; part of the IP protocol.

IEC   Interexchange carrier. Long-distance telephone companies.

IEEE   Institute of Electrical and Electronics Engineers. A professional organization for engineers in the U.S. that publishes standards and belongs to the American National Standards Institute (ANSI) and the International Organization for Standardization (ISO).

IEEE 802.1   Standard that provides an overview of local area networks, methods for connecting networks, and systems management.

IEEE 802.2   Logical link control standard for local area networks.

IEEE 802.3   CSMA/CD bus media access control.

IEEE 802.4   Token-bus media access control.

IEEE 802.5   Token Ring media access control.

IEEE 802.6   Metropolitan area network (MAN) media access control.

IEEE 802.7   Advisory subcommittee on broadband transmission in local area networks.

IEEE 802.8   Advisory subcommittee on fiber optics in local area networks.

IEEE 802.9   Advisory subcommittee on integrating voice and data in local area networks.

IETF   Internet Engineering Task Force. Internet Activities Board (IAB) task force, with more than 40 working groups; responsible for solving the short-term engineering needs of Internet.

IGP   Interior Gateway protocol. Protocol used to exchange routing table information between collaborating routers in the Internet. The Routing Information protocol (RIP) and the Open Shortest Path First (OSPF) protocol are examples of IGPs.

in-band signaling   Transmission signaling information interleaved with the data at some frequency or frequencies that lie within a carrier channel normally used for information transmission.

INETCFG   NetWare Loadable Module (NLM) that simplifies the installation of Novell internetworking products by allowing a network administrator to configure boards and enable parameters from a menu.

information systems network (ISN)   AT&T's combination of local area network and packet-switching network transmission methods; provides connections to a wide variety of devices.

infrared   Electromagnetic radiation with frequencies in the electromagnetic spectrum range just below that of visible red light.

Institute of Electrical and Electronics Engineers   *See* IEEE.

Integrated IS-IS   Open Systems Interconnection (OSI) protocol that extends the Intermediate System-to-Intermediate System (IS-IS) protocol, allowing it to route other protocols in addition to OSI—for example, IP. *See also* IS-IS.

Integrated Services Digital Network   *See* ISDN.

intelligent hub   Unit combining the function of a hub with processing capabilities. *See also* hub.

interchange channel   *See* IXC.

interexchange carrier   *See* IEC.

interface   Point at which a connection is made between two elements so they can work together.

InterLATA   Circuits that cross from one local access and transport area (LATA) into another.

intermediate system   Open Systems Interconnection (OSI) system that may not be an end system but that serves instead to relay communications between end systems. *See also* repeater; bridge; router.

Intermediate System-to-Intermediate System protocol   *See* IS-IS.

internal PAD   Packet assembler/disassembler (PAD) located inside a packet-switching node.

Internet   Collection of networks and gateways that use the TCP/IP suite of protocols. Lowercase, it is an abbreviation for "internetwork."

Internet address   A 32-bit address assigned to hosts using TCP/IP.

Internet Control Message protocol   *See* ICMP.

internetwork   Collection of two or more connected networks that might be dissimilar.

interoperability   Ability to transmit information in a heterogeneous network.

IntraLATA   Circuits that are totally within one local access and transport area (LATA).

IP   Internet protocol. TCP/IP protocol that governs packet forwarding.

IP address   *See* Internet address.

IPX   Internetwork Packet Exchange. NetWare protocol, similar to the Xerox Network Systems (XNS) protocol, that provides datagram delivery of messages.

IS-IS   Intermediate System-to-Intermediate System protocol. Open Systems Interconnection (OSI) protocol by which intermediate systems exchange routing information.

ISA   Industry Standard Architecture. Bus design for IBM PC/XT and PC/AT computers.

ISDN   Integrated Services Digital Network. Evolving set of standards for a digital network carrying both voice and data communication.

ISO   International Organization for Standardization. International organization that establishes global standards for communication and information exchange as well as for many other fields of commercial activity.

ISOCON Novell diagnostic tool that provides information about a NetWare server or router Open Systems Interconnection (OSI) stack and about other OSI networks on the internetwork; uses SNMP.

IXC Interchange channel. Channel or circuit between exchanges (central offices).

jabber State of a network adapter in which a network device continuously transmits.

jitter Type of analog communication-line distortion that results in data transmission errors, usually at high speeds.

Kbit/s Kilobits per second. Data rate equal to 1024bps.

LAN Local area network. Group of computers and other devices connected by a communication link that allows any device to interact with any other device on the network.

LAT Local area transport. Network terminal protocol developed by Digital Equipment Corporation.

LATA Local Access and Transport Area. Telephone subdivisions established in the U.S. as a result of the AT&T divestiture that distinguished local from long-distance service. Circuits with both end points within one LATA (IntraLATA) are generally the sole responsibility of the local telephone company; circuits that cross outside the LATA (InterLATA) are passed on to an interexchange carrier.

leased line Point-to-point circuit rented from a common carrier for a flat monthly fee. Logically, one unbroken data communication channel.

line Circuit, channel, or link that carries data communication signals.

link Channel or line; normally refers to a point-to-point line.

link layer *See* data-link layer.

link-level protocol Set of rules that define methods for communicating over a channel, circuit, or link.

link-state routing algorithm Routing algorithm in which each router broadcasts information on the state of its links (network attachments) to all nodes in the internetwork. Reduces routing loops and traffic but has greater memory requirements than the distance vector algorithm.

load balancing Scheme for distributing network traffic among parallel paths. Load balancing provides redundancy while efficiently using the available bandwidth.

load sharing Ability of two or more remote bridges to share their traffic load in a parallel configuration; if one bridge fails, traffic is routed to the next parallel bridge.

local access and transport area *See* LATA.

local exchange carrier Local telephone company.

local loop The part of a communication circuit that connects subscriber equipment with equipment in a local central office.

LocalTalk A 230.4Kbps baseband network using the CSMA/CA access method; defines the physical and data-link layers of the AppleTalk network protocol.

loopback Diagnostic test in which a signal is transmitted across a medium while the sending device waits for its return.

loopback plug Special connector used to perform echo testing.

LSP Link-state packet. A packet that is generated by a router in a link-state routing protocol and lists that router's neighbors.

MAC Media access control. Data-link layer protocol that governs access to transmission media.

MAN Metropolitan area network. Shared medium that is bigger than a LAN but smaller than a WAN—for example, a network used for a city or campus. *See also* IEEE 802.6.

managed object Device that is connected to a network and that can be managed by network management software or a protocol such as SNMP.

management information base *See* MIB.

MAU Media attachment unit. In IEEE 802.3 networks, it performs the physical layer functions of the Open Systems Interconnection (OSI) model. Also, in IBM Token Ring networks, a multistation access unit.

Mbps Data rate equal to 10 to the sixth power bps; often called megabits per second (1,000,000bps).

media access control *See* MAC.

megabit One million bits.

megabyte One million bytes.

mesh network Network topology in which each device is connected by a cable to every other device in the network. Multiple links to each device provide network link redundancy.

message Logical grouping of information at the application layer.

message switching Routing messages among three or more locations by using store-and-forward techniques.

MIB Management Information Base. Database of network management information used by the Common Management Information protocol (CMIP) and the Simple Network Management protocol (SNMP).

Microcom Networking protocol *See* MNP.

microwave Radio carrier system that uses frequencies with very short wavelengths.

MNP Microcom Networking protocol. Widely used proprietary error-correcting protocol for modems developed by the Microcom Corporation.

modem Device that performs modulation and demodulation, allowing data communication to occur in analog form over telephone circuits.

modem eliminator Device that simulates a modem connection by providing connections, a clock, and automatic crossover of transmit and receive pairs.

MONITOR Novell utility that monitors the operation of a local Novell file server.

multicast Special form of broadcast in which copies of the packet are delivered to multiple stations but only a subset of all possible destinations. *See also* broadcast.

multidrop Line or circuit connecting several stations/nodes along a single logical link; typically used in IBM SNA architecture.

multihome host Computer connected to more than one physical data link; data links might or might not be attached to the same network.

multiplexor *See* MUX.

multivendor network Network comprising components from different vendors.

MUX Multiplexor. Device that allows a single communication circuit to take the place of several parallel ones; often used to allow remote terminals to communicate with front-end processor ports over a single circuit.

name resolution Ability to associate a name that the network administrator has assigned with its network location.

NASI NetWare Asynchronous Services Interface. Memory-resident program that works with IPX/SPX; it is loaded on a workstation before any supported communication application. NASI allows communication applications to use Novell's CPECFG or NACS utility.

NAUN Nearest active upstream neighbor. In a Token Ring network, the NAUN acts as a reference point.

NCP NetWare Core protocol. Provides control for interaction between clients and file servers; defines its own session control and packet-level error checking. Also, in SNA environments, refers to the network control program, which does the routing and addressing of SNA devices.

neighboring routers For the Open Shortest Path First (OSPF) protocol, two routers that share a route to the same network.

NetBIOS Network Basic Input/Output System. Application program interface typically used on local area networks comprising IBM and compatible microcomputers. Separates application programs from the networking subsystem so application program implementers can support multiple network designs and so a network system can support independently developed applications.

NetView IBM network-monitoring software for Systems Network Architecture (SNA) networks.

NetWare Novell's network operating system, which provides the ability to transparently share services across dissimilar platforms. Uses the NetWare Core protocol (NCP) and Internetwork Packet Exchange (IPX) and Sequenced Packet Exchange (SPX) protocols.

NetWare Core protocol *See* NCP.

NetWare Hub Services PC-based software from Novell that supports the management of any hub card that complies with the NetWare Hub Management Interface (HMI) specification.

NetWare Loadable Module *See* NLM.

NetWare MultiProtocol Router PC-based software from Novell that enables network managers to connect LANs using IPX, IP, OSI, or Apple-Talk over a wide range of LAN and WAN types.

NetWare MultiProtocol Router Plus PC-based software from Novell that replaces NetWare Link/64, NetWare Link/T1, and NetWare Link/X.25. It provides wide area connectivity for geographically dispersed multivendor networks over T1/E1, fractional T1, X.25, or low-speed synchronous leased lines.

NetWare for SAA PC-based software from Novell that enables network managers to connect their local area networks to a Systems Network Ar-chitecture (SNA) host.

network Group of computers and associated devices connected by com-munication facilities.

network adapter Hardware installed in workstations and servers that enables them to communicate on a network. *See also* adapter.

network address Network-layer address that refers to a logical network device. Also known as a protocol address.

network analyzer Software- or hardware-based device that analyzes data transmission on a network. Some can troubleshoot network problems by decoding packets; some filter, program test, and transmit packets.

network architecture Framework of principles to facilitate the operation, maintenance, and growth of a communication network by isolating the user and application programs from network details. Protocols and software are packaged together into a usable network architecture system that organizes functions, data formats, and procedures.

network layer Third of seven layers of the Open Systems Interconnection (OSI) model; ensures that information arrives at its intended destination and smooths out the differences between network media so higher layers need not account for the distinctions.

network management Process of ensuring consistent reliability and availability of a network, as well as timely transmission and routing of data. Can be performed by dedicated devices or programmed general-purpose devices.

network monitoring Network management function that constantly checks the network and reports any problems.

network topology Arrangement of nodes on a network; usually a star, ring, tree, or bus organization.

NFS Network File System. Distributed file system developed by Sun Microsystems that allows a set of computers to cooperatively access one another's files in a transparent manner.

NLM NetWare Loadable Module. Application or driver that resides on a NetWare server; provides additional resource management capabilities.

NLSP NetWare Link Services protocol. IPX link-state protocol used by IPX routers to share information about their routes with other devices on the network. Enables network managers to interconnect small or large networks without routing inefficiencies.

NMS NetWare Management System. System responsible for managing a network. The NMS talks, via a network management protocol, to NetWare management agents that reside in the managed nodes. *See also* agent.

node Device connected to a network that is capable of communicating with other network devices. In NetWare, an end system, such as a workstation.

noise Unwanted changes in waveform that occur between two points in a transmission circuit.

non-seed AppleTalk router interface that receives its network address and zone information from the network.

null modem cable Cable or plug that crosses over transmit and receive pairs to provide proper data terminal equipment (DTE) to data communication equipment (DCE) interconnection between closely located communication devices.

octet Group of 8 binary digits operated on as a unit; also called a byte or character.

ODI Open Data-Link Interface. Supports media- and protocol-independent communication by providing a standard interface that allows network-layer protocols to share a single network board without conflict.

off-hook Activation of a telephone set. By extension, a data set automatically answering on a public switched system is said to go off-hook. The off-hook condition indicates a "busy" condition to incoming calls.

office, central (or end) Common carrier switching office closest to the subscriber.

on-hook Deactivation of a telephone set. A telephone not in use is on-hook. *See also* off-hook.

Open Shortest Path First protocol *See* OSPF.

OSI model Open Systems Interconnection model. Seven-layer model for data communication.

OSPF Open Shortest Path First protocol. Hierarchical Interior Gateway protocol (IGP) routing algorithm for IP that is a proposed standard for Internet. Incorporates least-cost routing, equal-cost routing, and load balancing.

out-of-band signaling Method of signaling that uses a frequency within the passband of the transmission facility but outside a carrier channel normally used for data transmission.

packet Unit of information transmitted as a whole from one device to another. In packet-switching networks, a transmission unit of fixed maximum size that consists of binary digits representing both data and a header.

packet assember/dissembler *See* PAD.

packet forwarding Copying a packet from one interface to another through an intermediate system.

packet-switch node *See* PSN.

packet switching Process whereby messages are broken into finite-size packets. The message packets are forwarded to the other party over different circuit paths. At the other end of the circuit, the packets are reassembled into the message, which is then passed on to the receiving terminal or device.

PAD Packet assembler/disassembler. Used by devices to communicate via X.25 networks by building or stripping X.25 information on or from a packet.

passive hub Signal splitter used to propagate a signal to devices on an ARCnet network.

PBX Private branch exchange. Telecommunication switching system owned by the customer; acts as an in-house central office with advanced switching features and capabilities.

PC-based routers Routers that function on a standard Intel-based hardware platform such as the NetWare MultiProtocol Router on an i386 or i486 PC.

PDN Public data network. Network that provides data transmission services to the public; usually a public packet-switched or circuit-switched network.

peer-to-peer Communication between devices that operate on the same communication level on a network without the intervention of any hierarchical devices such as a host or server.

permanent virtual circuit *See* PVC.

physical address Data-link layer address of a network device.

physical layer Layer 1 of the Open Systems Interconnection (OSI) model; it details the protocols that govern transmission media and signals.

physical unit *See* PU.

ping Packet internet grouper. Program used to test the reachability of destinations by sending them an Internet Control Message protocol (ICMP) echo request and waiting for a reply.

platform-specific routers Routers based on vendor-specific proprietary hardware architecture.

point-to-point link Communication link directly joining two stations.

Point-to-Point protocol *See* PPP.

point of presence *See* POP.

polling Any procedure that sequentially and periodically contacts terminals in a network.

POP Point of presence. Usually a central office for telco services or long-distance carriers.

port For hardware, a connecting component that allows a microprocessor to communicate with a compatible peripheral. For software, a memory address that identifies the physical circuit used to transfer information between a microprocessor and a peripheral.

PPP Point-to-Point protocol. Industry-standard protocol used on point-to-point links.

PRI Primary rate interface. Used on Integrated Services Digital Networks (ISDN). In North America and Japan, PRI is 1 64Kbps D channel and 23 B channels. Elsewhere, it is 1 D channel and 30 B channels.

Private Branch Exchange *See* PBX.

private leased circuit Leased communication circuit that connects premises to a remote location; a clear, unbroken communication path available 24 hours per day, seven days per week.

promiscuous mode Mode in which the hardware on a LAN receives and passes to the upper-layer protocols all packets that arrive.

propagation delay Time necessary for a signal to travel from one point on the circuit to another—for example, transmission from a satellite dish to a satellite. Usually denotes a delay caused by signal-processing equipment in the transmission path of data sent over long distances.

protocol Set of rules that allows computers to connect with one another, specifying the format, timing, sequencing, and error checking for data transmission.

protocol dependent Refers to routing based on a network layer or software address. Specific to the type of network-layer protocol, such as IP, IPX, or DDP.

protocol stack Representation of the hierarchical nature of a protocol suite.

protocol suite Hierarchical set of related protocols.

proxy ARP Technique in which one machine, usually a router, answers ARP requests intended for another machine. By faking its identity, the router accepts responsibility for routing packets to the real destination. Allows a site to use a single IP network address for two physical networks.

PSN Packet-switch node. Nodes in the ARPANET and MILNET.

PTT Postal Telephone and Telegraph. Government agency that administers and operates the telecommunication infrastructure within a country.

PU Physical unit. Node in a Systems Network Architecture (SNA) network supporting one or more logical units (LUs) and providing communication and/or data processing.

public data network *See* PDN.

public network Telephone network, also called the direct distance dial network, accessed when a telephone is used.

PVC Permanent virtual circuit. Continually available communication path connecting two fixed end points.

query Process of extracting data from a database and presenting it for use.

RARP Reverse Address Resolution protocol. Internet protocol used by some hosts to find an Internet address at startup; maps a physical address to an Internet address.

RBOC Regional Bell Operating Company. In the U.S., any of seven holding companies, each a collection of local Bell Operating Companies, formed after the divestiture of AT&T to permit the new BOCs to remain efficient and achieve economies of scale.

RCONSOLE Novell utility that allows network supervisors to remotely manage NetWare 3.x-based and future-generation routers and servers.

redirector Software within a computer that redirects a request to the proper resource; most often used for a DOS TSR that redirects requests for disk access to a network server.

redistribution Ability to spread routing information to other areas through a routing protocol update.

redundancy Spare capacity that can be called upon when a failure occurs; having more than one path to a signal point.

Regional Bell Operating Company *See* RBOC.

Regional Holding Company *See* RHC.

remote bridge Bridge that uses wide area links to connect separate LANs.

remote digital loopback test Capability of some modems to be looped back remotely, allowing testing of the entire circuit.

repeater Device used to boost the strength of a signal; spaced at intervals throughout the length of a communication circuit. Also called a repeater/amplifier.

Request for Comment *See* RFC.

Reverse Address Resolution protocol *See* RARP.

RFC Request for Comment. Document series, begun in 1969, that describes the Internet suite of protocols and related documents. Not all RFCs describe Internet standards, but all Internet standards are written as RFCs.

RHC Regional Holding Company. In the U.S., another name for a Regional Bell Operating Company.

RIP Routing Information protocol. Distance vector-based protocol that provides a measure of distance, or hops, from a transmitting workstation to a receiving workstation. *See also* IGP.

RJ-11 Modular four-conductor telephone plug; the plug on standard telephones, called a permissive connection by the telephone company. Although generally used on two-wire circuits, can also be used on four-wire circuits.

RJ-45 Modular eight-conductor telephone plug similar to the RJ-11 plug except that it is called a programmable connection and is used on four-wire circuits.

route discovery Process of determining available routes in a source-route network.

routed protocol Protocol that can be routed by a router. IPX, IP, Apple-Talk, and OSI are examples of routed protocols; LAT is an example of a protocol that cannot be routed.

router Device that connects two networks using the same networking protocol. Operates at the network layer (Layer 3) of the OSI model for forwarding decisions.

Routing Information protocol *See* RIP.

routing protocol Protocol that enables routing through the implementation of a specific routing algorithm. Examples include the Routing

Information protocol (RIP), Open Shortest Path First (OSPF) protocol, and Intermediate System-to-Intermediate System (IS-IS) protocol.

routing table Table stored in a router that keeps track of routes (and in some cases, metrics associated with those routes) to a particular network destination.

routing updates Message sent from a router to indicate network reachability and associated cost information; typically sent at regular intervals and after a change in network topology.

RPC Remote procedure call. Easy and popular paradigm for implementing the client/server model of distributed computing. A request is sent to a remote system to execute a designated procedure using arguments supplied, and the result is returned to the caller.

RS-232C Technical specification published by the Electronic Industries Association that lays out the mechanical and electrical characteristics of the interface for connecting data terminal equipment (DTE) and data communication equipment (DCE). Functionally compatible with the CCITT recommendation V.24.

RS-422 Standard, operating in conjunction with RS-449, that specifies electrical characteristics for balanced circuits.

RS-423 Standard, operating in conjunction with RS-449, that specifies electrical characteristics for unbalanced circuits.

RS-449 Electronic Industries Association standard for data terminal equipment (DTE) and data communication equipment (DCE) connection that specifies interface requirements for expanded transmission speeds (up to 2 million bps), longer cable lengths, and ten additional functions.

RTMP Routing Table Maintenance protocol. Distance vector protocol that updates tables every 10 seconds; routers use RTMP to exchange information.

RTS Request to send. RS-232 control signal between a modem and user digital equipment that initiates the data transmission sequence in a communication line.

SAA   System Application Architecture. Set of IBM-defined standards that provides a consistent environment for programmers and users across a broad range of IBM equipment, including microcomputers, minicomputers, and mainframes.

SAP   Service Advertising protocol. Responsible for disseminating services information to all nodes in an IPX network.

SAS   Single-attached station. Fiber Distributed Data Interface (FDDI) that supports connections to a single fiber ring.

satellite communication   Geostationary satellite orbiting the earth; receives and transmits microwave signals from the earth station.

satellite dish   Special antenna used to transmit signals to or receive signals from a satellite.

SDLC   Synchronous data-link control. Bit-oriented synchronous data-link protocol developed by IBM as a link-access technique for the Systems Network Architecture (SNA).

seed   AppleTalk router interface that has network addressing and zone information configured by a network administrator.

Sequenced Packet Exchange   *See* SPX.

serial transmission   Method of transmission in which bits are sent one after the other on the same wire.

session   Time during which two computers maintain a connection.

session layer   Fifth layer of the Open Systems Interconnection (OSI) stack; allows dialog control between end systems.

shared memory   Portion of memory accessible to multiple processes.

shielded cable   Cable with a layer of insulation to reduce electromagnetic interface.

short-haul modem   Modem that transmits data on twisted-pair wire over a limited distance on a customer's premises, but not through telephone company central offices.

shortest-path routing   Term often used for the Dijkstra algorithm, in which paths to all destinations are computed given complete knowledge of a network; shortest paths are determined by a cost associated with each link.

signal   Something sent over a communication circuit; it might be a control signal used by the system to control itself.

single-mode fiber Fiber-optic cable with a narrow diameter in which only one mode propagates.

SLIP Serial Line IP. Internet protocol used to run IP over serial lines such as telephone circuits or RS-232 cables, interconnecting two systems. SLIP is being replaced by the Point-to-Point protocol (PPP).

smart hub *See* intelligent hub.

SMDS Switched multimegabit data service. MAN technology based on the IEEE 802.6 standard. Has certain LAN-like characteristics while spanning distances of city size.

SMT Station management. The part of the Fiber Distributed Data Interface (FDDI) that manages stations on a ring.

SNA Systems Network Architecture. IBM's proprietary network architecture.

SNMP Simple Network Management protocol. TCP/IP protocol that allows network management.

SONET Synchronous Optical Network. High-speed (up to 2.5Gbps) synchronous network approved as an international standard in 1988. In the U.S., Regional Bell Operating Companies are likely to make SONET the transmission system underlying SMDS.

source address Address of a sending network device.

source-route transparent bridging *See* SRT bridging.

source routing Bridging mechanism to route frames through a multi-LAN network by specifying in each frame the route it will follow. The route is determined by the end stations through a discovery process supported by source-route bridges.

spanning tree Loop-free subset of a network topology connecting all the nodes.

Spanning Tree Algorithm Algorithm used by bridges to dynamically discover and maintain a loop-free subset of a complex network topology; specified in IEEE standard 802.1d.

SPX Sequenced Packet Exchange. Protocol by which two workstations or applications communicate across the network. Uses NetWare IPX to deliver the messages but guarantees delivery of the messages and maintains the order of the messages on the packet stream.

SRB Source-route bridging. *See also* SRT bridging.

SRT bridging Source route-transparent bridging. Bridging scheme proposed by IBM that attempts to merge the two most prevalent bridging strategies (source-route bridging and transparent bridging); employs both technologies in one device. No translation is done between the bridging protocols.

standard Set of rules or procedures that have been agreed upon by industry participants.

star topology Network design in which nodes are connected to a common device such as a hub or concentrator.

start-stop signaling Signaling in which each group of code corresponding to a character is preceded by a start signal that prepares the receiving mechanism for the reception and registration of the character. Also referred to as asynchronous transmission.

static route Route that is manually entered into the routing table.

statistical frequency division multiplexing Multiplexing method that continually changes the allocation of channels to accommodate the demands and needs of the attached devices.

statistical multiplexor Time-division multiplexor (TDM) that dynamically allocates line time to each of the various attached terminals, according to whether a terminal is active or inactive at a particular moment. Buffering and queuing functions are also included. Also called a stat mux.

stub network IP network that uses a subset of an existing IP network address and is serviced by a proxy router.

subnet address mask Bit mask used to select bits from an internet address to create a subnet.

subnetwork Portion of the backbone that is partitioned by repeaters, bridges, or routers.

switch Device that routes calls to different locations such as a PBX or central office.

switched virtual circuits *See* SVC.

synchronization In T1 transmission, the timing function provided by the framing bit.

Synchronous data-link control *See* SDLC.

Synchronous Optical Network *See* SONET.

synchronous transmission   Data transfer in which information is transmitted in blocks (frames) of bits separated by equal time intervals.

System Application Architecture   *See* SAA.

Systems Network Architecture   *See* SNA.

SVC   Switched virtual circuits. Dial-up, end-to-end circuit switching that network managers use on a need-only basis.

T-connector   T-shaped device used with thin Ethernet to connect two segments with one male BNC connector, which is used to attach to the network board.

T1   High-speed leased lines, transmitting at rates up to 1.544Mbps (in the U.S.).

T1 multiplexor   Device that divides the 1.544Mbps of T1 bandwidth into 24 separate channels of digitized voice or data.

T1C   A 3.152Mbps digital transmission standard offering 48 channels; also known as T2.

T3   A 44.736Mbps digital transmission standard offering 672 channels.

tariff   Complete description of a common carrier's service, including the rate charged for that service.

TCP   Transmission Control protocol. Major transport protocol in the Internet suite of protocols, providing reliable, connection-oriented, full-duplex streams; uses IP for delivery.

TCP/IP   Transmission Control protocol/Internet protocol. Protocol suite developed by the Advanced Research Projects Agency (ARPA); includes TCP as the primary transport protocol and IP as the network-layer protocol.

TCPCON   Diagnostic tool from Novell that provides information about a NetWare server or router TCP/IP stack and about other TCP/IP networks on the internetwork.

TDM   Time division multiplexing. Method of allowing lower speed channels to share time on a high-speed communication circuit by allocating separate time slots to each channel. *See also* MUX.

telecommunication   Exchange of information, usually over a significant distance, using electronic equipment for transmission.

telephony   Generic term to describe voice telecommunication.

Telnet   Protocol in the TCP/IP suite that governs character-oriented terminal traffic.

10Base-2   IEEE 802.3 standard for 10Mbps baseband over thin wire (50 ohms and 200 meters).

10Base-5   IEEE standard for 10Mbps baseband over thick wire coaxial cable (50 ohms and 500 meters).

10Base-F   IEEE standard for 10Mbps baseband over fiber-optic cable.

10Base-T   IEEE standard for 10Mbps baseband over unshielded twisted-pair wire.

terminal   Device, usually equipped with a keyboard and display, capable of sending and receiving data over a communication link.

terminator   Used in Ethernet and ARCnet bus topologies for the electrical resistance at the end of the transmission line to absorb the signals and keep them from bouncing back.

Thinnet   IEEE 802.3, 10Base-2 standard for cable; used in Ethernet networks.

throughput   Total amount of useful information that is processed or communicated during a specific time period.

time division multiplexing   See TDM.

time slot   Time reserved for a particular channel's communication in time division multiplexing (TDM).

timeout   Protocol procedure that requires a device to make some response to a command or message block within a certain period of time. If the device doesn't respond, a timeout condition occurs.

token   Special sequence of bits that is passed between token-passing LANs; possession of the token gives the possessor permission to transmit.

token bus   Local area network using a bus topology and token passing, as in the IEEE 802.4 standard for media access control (MAC).

token passing   Using a logical token, typically either a free token or a busy token, to regulate network access.

Token Ring network   Local area network using a ring topology and token passing, as in the IEEE 802.5 standard for media access control (MAC), or the IBM Token Ring network.

topology Physical layout of network components (cables, stations, gateways, and hubs). Three basic interconnection topologies are star, ring, and bus networks.

translation bridging Bridging required on networks that have dissimilar media access control (MAC) sublayer protocols; resolves differences in header formats and protocol specifications.

Transmission Control protocol *See* TCP, TCP/IP.

transmission medium Physical path for carrying information, such as twisted-pair wires, coaxial cable, fiber-optic cable, terrestrial microwave, and satellite transmission methods.

transparent Describes a function that operates without being evident to the user.

transparent bridging Bridging scheme used for Ethernet and IEEE 802.3 LANs in which bridges pass frames along one hop at a time based on tables associating end nodes with bridge ports.

transport layer Layer 4 of the Open Systems Interconnection (OSI) model; provides reliable, end-to-end delivery of data and detects transmission sequential errors.

traps Unsolicited messages sent by a Simple Network Management protocol (SNMP) agent to a network management system that indicate the occurrence of a significant event. The SNMP manager that receives a trap can poll for additional information.

tree topology Connection of links with branches at several levels but containing no loops.

tunneling Process of encapsulating information within another packet format in order to transfer information across a link that services a different protocol type than the source and destination end points.

twisted-pair wire Two wires continuously twisted throughout their entire length; typically used in a local loop.

two-wire circuit Circuit formed by two conductors insulated from each other. It is possible to use the two conductors as a one-way transmission path, a half-duplex path, or a full-duplex path.

Tymnet British Telecom's public packet-switching network in the U.S.

UDP User Datagram protocol. Transport protocol in the Internet suite of protocols. UDP, like TCP, uses IP for delivery; however, unlike TCP, UDP provides for exchange of datagrams without acknowledgments or guaranteed delivery.

UTP Unshielded twisted-pair wiring. Transmission medium for 10Base-T.

V.24 Consultative Committee for International Telegraphy and Telephony (CCITT) equivalent of the signals in the American National Standards Institute (ANSI) RS-232C standard.

virtual circuit In packet-switching networks, a circuit that appears to be a physical point-to-point circuit. It connects two end points, conveying sequenced data packets reliably; in fact, it shares the underlying links and relay systems with other users of the network.

WAN Wide area network. Network that transmits over large geographic areas using lines provided by a common carrier of private telecommunication facilities.

wideband *See* broadband.

word In data communication, a word is generally six characters (five characters plus a space).

workstation Input/output equipment at which an operator works; station from which a user can send data to, or receive from, a computer for the purpose of performing a job.

X-Windows Standard set of display-handling routines developed at MIT for UNIX workstations; they allow the creation of hardware-independent graphical user interfaces.

X.3 International standard for the packet assembler/dissembler (PAD) facility in the public packet networks.

X.21 Consultative Committee for International Telegraphy and Telephony (CCITT) standard that defines the interface between data terminal equipment and data circuit terminating equipment for circuit-switched networks.

X.25 Set of protocols developed by the Consultative Committee for International Telegraphy and Telephony (CCITT) organization to define the interface between an X.25 public data network and a packet-mode user device.

X.28 Consultative Committee for International Telegraphy and Telephony (CCITT) standard for a DTE/DCE interface accessing the packet assembler/dissembler (PAD) in a switch network in the same country.

X.29 Consultative Committee for International Telegraphy and Telephony (CCITT) standard for user data and exchange of control information between the packet assembler/dissembler (PAD) and packet-mode data terminal equipment (DTE) or another PAD.

X.75 International standard for connecting two packet-switched X.25 networks to each other; often referred to as an X.25 gateway.

X.400 Open Systems Interconnection (OSI) standard that defines how messages are to be encoded for the transmission of electronic mail and graphics between dissimilar computers and terminals; defines what is in an electronic address and what the electronic envelope should look like. The X.400 standards are a subset of, and conform to, the X.25 standard approved by the Consultative Committee for International Telegraphy and Telephony (CCITT).

X.500 Open Systems Interconnection (OSI) standard that defines where to find the address to put on the electronic envelope of an X.400 transmission. It becomes an X.500 directory of names and addresses similar to the yellow pages of a telephone directory.

X.nn Series of Consultative Committee for International Telegraphy and Telephony (CCITT) standards relating to transmission over public data networks.

XCONSOLE NetWare utility that allows a UNIX workstation to connect to NetWare 3.x- or 4.x-based router or server consoles.

zone On a local area network such as AppleTalk, a subgroup of users within a larger group of interconnected networks.

Installing and Using the Internetworking Configuration Program

The disk that accompanies this book includes a unique MS-Windows program called the Internetworking Configuration program.

NOTE

The Internetworking Configuration Program is not shareware or freeware. Rights of duplication and distribution must be obtained from the authors. License for use of the Internetworking Configuration Program for private self-instruction and training is granted to the owner of this book (*Novell's Guide to Multiprotocol Internetworking*).

System Requirements

Here are the system requirements for the Internetworking Configuration program:

- ▸ 386- or 486-based personal computer
- ▸ 4Mb RAM
- ▸ MS-Windows 3.x
- ▸ Color VGA display (16-color is acceptable)
- ▸ 3Mb hard drive space
- ▸ High-density 3½-inch disk drive
- ▸ Mouse

Installation Instructions

The Internetworking Configuration Program (ICP) must be run from a hard drive, not a floppy drive. To install the program, follow these steps:

1 · Insert the Internetworking Configuration Program disk in a high-density 3½-inch floppy drive <drive> (for instance, drive B).

2 · From the Windows Program Manager, select File ➤ Run.

3 · Type **<drive>:\INSTALL** and click OK to begin the installation program.

4 · You are prompted for a destination directory. Enter a destination directory if the default is not acceptable. (C:\IPC is the default.) Click OK. The install program decompresses all the files and copies them to the selected directory. It also creates an Internet Configuration program group and an ICP program item. Upon successful completion of the installation, you are prompted to read the README.TXT file. This file contains important information about display incompatibilities. Take a moment to review the information.

5 · To start up ICP, double-click the ICP program item.

Program Contents

The Internetworking Configuration program includes the following applications:

- ▸ Internetwork Designer
- ▸ Configuration Tool
- ▸ Carrier Information
- ▸ Glossary

These applications can be launched from the Options page, as shown in Figure C.1.

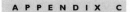

FIGURE C.1

Access the applications from the Options page.

Internetwork Designer Application

The Internetwork Designer application helps you determine whether your internetwork requires a bridge or a router for local connection and suggests WAN link types (such as T1 and X.25) based on network configuration information that you supply.

Configuration Tool

Try your hand at configuring a multiprotocol router! The Configuration Tool program, shown in Figure C.2, is based on Novell's MultiProtocol Router installation program, INETCFG.

306

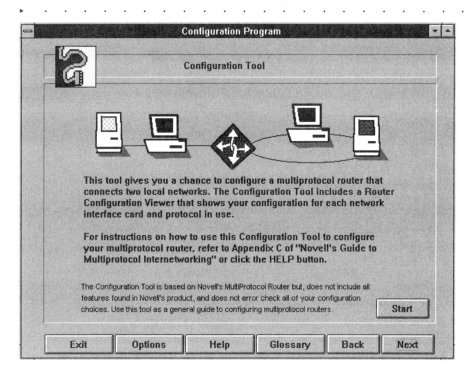

A Configuration Tool for multiprotocol routers.

Use the Configuration Tool to select LAN and WAN Board Parameters and configure the network interface cards and logical boards you want to install in a multiprotocol router. Use the Protocol Parameters option to enable TCP/IP, AppleTalk, and SAP filtering. When you attach a protocol to a board, assign appropriate network addresses for each logical board configured. Finally, view the results of your configuration by selecting View Configuration Graphic.

For step-by-step instructions on configuring your multiprotocol router using the Configuration tool, refer to the section "Step-by-Step: Configuring a Multiprotocol Router" later in this appendix.

Carrier Information

The Carrier Information program contains a listing of U.S. and International carriers, modem and CSU/DSU vendors, and the WAN installation checklist, as shown in Figure C.3.

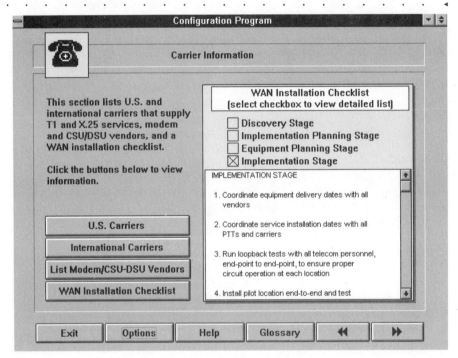

Glossary

Over 500 internetworking terms are available by clicking the desired character and then selecting the term from the alphabetical listing, as shown in Figure C.4.

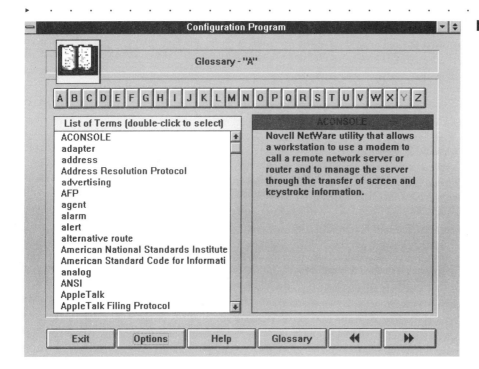

FIGURE C.4

Networking terms are
defined in the Glossary

Navigation Tools

Across the bottom of every page you will find a standard set of navigation buttons. Figure C.5 shows the navigation buttons and provides a description of each button.

Capturing Screens and Printing

The Configuration Viewer and Internetwork Designer recommendation screens have a print button that sends your configurations to the printer. You must supply a configuration title when prompted. For best results,

FIGURE C.5

Navigation buttons

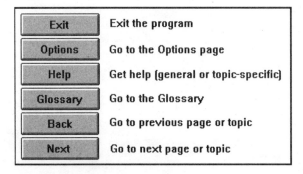

configure your printer (in Windows) to print in landscape mode.

Any screen in the Internetworking Configuration program can be captured to the MS-Windows clipboard by pressing the Print Screen key on your computer's keyboard. The MS-Windows Clipboard Viewer is located in the Main group.

Step-by-Step: Configuring a Multiprotocol Router

The Configuration tool is used to create a multiprotocol router that connects IPX, TCP/IP, or AppleTalk networks using Ethernet or Token Ring cards. After selecting the Configuration Tool and clicking Start, follow the steps outlined below to configure an IPX-TCP/IP multiprotocol router that uses one Ethernet card and one Token Ring card.

STEP 1: CONFIGURE THE NETWORK INTERFACE CARDS

Our sample configuration uses two network interface cards in our multiprotocol router; one is an NE2000 (Ethernet) card and the other is a Madge (Token Ring) card.

From the Internetworking Configuration main menu, select LAN and WAN Board Parameters.

If you've already entered some information into the Configuration tool, press the Reset button to clear all the entries and begin a new configuration.

NOTE

Click the first (Select to configure) line. Click NE2000 to select the NE2000 LAN driver. The Logical LAN Board Configuration screen appears. The top portion of this screen is for the first logical LAN board, which we will configure to support IPX. The bottom portion is for the second logical LAN board, which we will configure to support TCP/IP.

Enter **BOARD 1** for the first logical LAN board and enter **Int=3 Port=300** in the LAN board parameters area. Click the button under the frame type area. A list of available frame types appears. Select Ethernet_802.3.

Click the button at the top of the second logical LAN board section. A board name and the board parameters are automatically put into the second logical LAN board area. Click the button under the frame type area of the second logical LAN board. Select Ethernet_II. Click OK. The board information is placed into the logical LAN board table. Board 1 is configured.

Click the third entry on the board name list; (Select to configure) is the current entry. Follow the same steps to configure board 2, but select MADGEODI as the driver and enter the LAN board information shown in Figure C.6.

When you click OK, you can view the board configuration screen. It should have the same entries as those shown in Figure C.7.

Click OK to return to the main Configuration menu.

STEP 2: ENABLE PROTOCOLS

To create a multiprotocol router that provides. TCP/IP routing services, you must enable the TCP/IP protocol. (IPX is enabled by default.)

Select Protocol Parameters from the main menu. If you started with a new configuration (by clicking the Reset button before you began configuring),

▶ · ◀

F I G U R E   C.6

Configuration parameters
for the Token Ring card

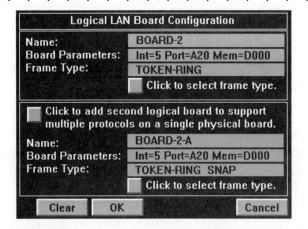

▶ · ◀

F I G U R E   C.7

Logical LAN board
configurations

TCP/IP and AppleTalk are disabled by default. Click the Disabled area next to TCP/IP.

The TCP/IP Configuration screen is displayed. Click Disabled to change the entry to Enabled. Click the (Select for list) area to configure an SNMP manager.

Click Clear to remove any entries from the SNMP manager table. Enter **130.57.8.9** at the left side of the screen. Click Add to add this entry. Click Save.

Click OK in the TCP/IP window and in the Protocol Parameters window to save this information and return to the main menu.

STEP 3: ATTACH THE PROTOCOLS TO THE LOGICAL LAN BOARDS

Now we're ready to attach the protocols, TCP/IP and IPX, to the logical LAN boards. When you attach the protocols to the boards, you'll need to assign a unique network address to each logical LAN board attachment.

Select Protocol Attachment to Board from the main menu. There should be four (Select to configure) entries in the Protocol/Address column. Click the first entry to configure the first logical LAN board. Use the information detailed below to attach each of the logical LAN boards to the protocols.

> BOARD-1
>
> Protocol: IPX
>
> Network Address: DE-AD-BE-EF

> BOARD-1A
>
> Protocol: TCP/IP
>
> IP Address: 140.45.3.2
>
> Use default subnet mask: YES

> BOARD-2
>
> Protocol: IPX
>
> Network Address: DE-AD-BA-BE

> BOARD-2A
>
> Protocol: TCP/IP
>
> IP Address: 130.42.1.2
>
> Use default subnet mask: YES

When you complete the configuration, your configuration screen should look like the one in Figure C.8.

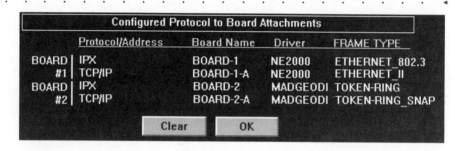

		Protocol/Address	Board Name	Driver	FRAME TYPE
		Configured Protocol to Board Attachments			
BOARD	IPX		BOARD-1	NE2000	ETHERNET_802.3
#1	TCP/IP		BOARD-1-A	NE2000	ETHERNET_II
BOARD	IPX		BOARD-2	MADGEODI	TOKEN-RING
#2	TCP/IP		BOARD-2-A	MADGEODI	TOKEN-RING_SNAP

Clear   OK

Click OK to accept your configuration.

STEP 4: VIEW AND PRINT YOUR CONFIGURATION

Now you are ready to view and print your configuration using the Configuration Viewer.

Select View Configuration Graphic from the main menu. You jump immediately to the viewing screen, as shown in Figure C.9.

Finally, you can print the results of your configuration by simply clicking the Print button. Your Windows print setup is used to define the printing parameters. For best results, print in landscape mode.

NOTE

For additional information on configuration options available for multiprotocol routers, refer to Chapters 4 and 9.

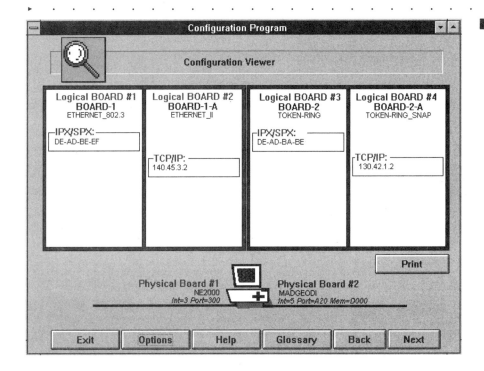

FIGURE C.9

Configuration Viewer

Index

. . . .

G

H

I

N

S

About the Disk

Asymetrix® and ToolBook® are registered trademarks of Asymetrix Corporation, ©1989–1991.

WHAT ABOUT INSTALLATION?

For complete installation instructions, refer to Appendix C and the inside front cover of this book.

A 3½-inch high-density drive is required.

IF YOU HAVE PROBLEMS WITH THE DISK...

For problems other than a defective disk, please fax a description of the problem to

ImagiTech
(408) 729-1580